Leaving Home

LEAVING

John Lawrence Reynolds

HOME

The REMARKABLE LIFE of PETER JACYK

FIGURE 1 PUBLISHING Vancouver

Cataloguing data available from Library and Archives Canada
978-0-9918588-1-1 (cloth)
978-0-9918588-2-8 (ebook)

Jacket and text design by Peter Cocking
Jacket photograph courtesy of Nadia Jacyk
Printed and bound in Canada by Friesens

Figure 1 Publishing Inc.
Vancouver BC Canada
www.figure1pub.com

We are what we consistently do.

Excellence, therefore, is not an act but a habit.

ARISTOTLE

He could boast that he inherited

it brick and left it marble.

AUGUSTUS

Contents

1
—

June 1941

I go the way Providence dictates
with the assurance of a sleepwalker.
ADOLF HITLER

IT HAD BEEN a long, hot day in western Ukraine—a day that was about to dissolve into an evening of horror.

Two weeks earlier, nineteen-year-old Petro (Peter) Jacyk had waited for a train to carry him into the city of Stryi, where he worked as an assistant railroad engineer. Fit and energetic, Peter had earned his elevated position through a six-month training course on railroading. On this morning, he was informed, the trains were not coming from the west, because the German army had bombed the railroad tracks leading to Poland. Finding other means of transportation, he managed to reach the railway yard, where he learned to his astonishment that the Soviet Union was at war with Germany.

Peter and his fellow employees were instructed to remain at the railway yard, eating and sleeping in a large communal hall until further orders were issued. Loudspeakers installed in the hall repeatedly proclaimed that brave Soviet troops were advancing deep into German-occupied territory on their way to a glorious victory of Communism over Fascism.

No one believed it. How could they, when the sound of distant German artillery competed with the loudspeakers, and German Messerschmitt aircraft were attacking the city, unhindered by either anti-aircraft fire or Soviet planes?

For a few days, Peter managed to avoid leaving the railway centre aboard trains travelling east and west. Those sent west toward the front were loaded with troops and supplies. Trains dispatched east toward the Soviet Union conveyed bureaucrats as well as labour leaders and "higher intelligentsia" in comfortable passenger cars in which they would safely escape the expected carnage. Meanwhile, following Stalin's orders to "destroy all that cannot be evacuated," factories and food supplies were either blown up or shipped east, along with almost half of the cattle on Ukrainian farms.[1]

Amid this chaos and destruction, Peter was finally assigned to manoeuvre trains within the rail yard in preparation for their loading and departure. Day after day, the news from the incessantly chattering loudspeakers grew more outrageous and unbelievable. By the end of the month, the Soviet propaganda machine declared that the unvanquished Soviet army was actually approaching Berlin, even while German artillery fire crept closer by the hour.

On this day in late June, the sound of Panzer tank divisions could be heard on the city's outskirts, announcing the advance of the German Sixth Army and the success of Operation Barbarossa, Germany's long-planned invasion of the Soviet Union. Despite the preposterous claims of victory for the Soviet Union forces, more

---

1. Bohdan Krawchenko, in *Ukraine during World War II: History and Its Aftermath*, edited by Yury Boshyk (Edmonton: Canadian Institute of Ukrainian Studies Press, 1986), 16.

than 4.5 million Axis troops and 600,000 motorized vehicles were moving steadily east along a front extending from the Baltic Sea to the Black Sea, almost three thousand kilometres.

The noise of war so near to the city was frightening, though perhaps not as alarming in western Ukraine as elsewhere in Europe. While the Germans were feared, the Soviets, who had occupied eastern Ukraine for almost twenty years and western Ukraine for barely two years, were hated, and almost anything or anyone who would drive off the commissars and soldiers was considered beneficial. It's not that anyone welcomed the Germans—they were invaders, after all—but compared with the Soviets, some might hope they would be the lesser of two evils.

When German artillery began shelling the city at the end of the day, however, choosing sides took a back seat to finding means of survival. The artillery barrage began killing residents indiscriminately, and as the barrage crept closer to the rail yard, Peter and two companions decided it would be safer to spend the night in a passenger railway car rather than the massive communal building. Smaller targets, they assumed, were less likely targets.

This was not the case. Sometime after midnight, German artillery started blasting switches and roundtables in the rail yard. Would the artillery batteries target the trains themselves next, assuming passenger cars were as worthy of destroying as freight cars? Peter didn't know, but convincing the other young men that they would be safer elsewhere, he led them away from the rail yards and toward the centre of the city.

By 3 a.m., what should have been a soft summer's night had become a simulation of hell. The flash of distant guns firing toward the city, the whistle of artillery shells passing overhead, the thunderous explosions when they hit their targets, the rumble of encroaching Panzer tank divisions, and the screams of frightened residents created a nightmare experience that the young men could not imagine becoming more horrifying. But it did.

With dawn beginning to break, the three men reached a jail that had been converted to a prison operated by the NKVD (Narodnyy komissariat vnutrennikh del, or People's Commissariat for Internal Affairs), the dreaded Soviet secret police. They watched as a Soviet guard scurried down from his watchtower and ran off, leaving the prison gate unlocked behind him. Assuming the guard was the last to leave the prison, Peter and the others entered the building.

The prison entrance opened into a large courtyard, empty except for a handful of prisoners left behind who wandered around dazed, asking "Have the Russians gone?" and "How close are the Germans?"

Peter couldn't tell them. Besides, the view through two doors, opening into what appeared to be a communal shower room, had caught his attention. Heaped against the far wall of the larger room were stacks of men's clothing, obviously removed in haste and tossed aside. But it was the oversized drain in the centre of the tiled floor that drew Peter's eye. The drain and much of the floor surrounding it were heavily splattered with blood. A massacre had taken place here just hours ago, Peter realized. But where were the victims? And what of the Soviet guards? Would they return if the Germans failed to enter the city immediately? The risk was too great to linger in such a dangerous place, and turning to his friends, Peter suggested they leave the jail.

The sun was up by now, and walking out of the prison, Peter noticed for the first time a concrete slab bordering the jail, measuring about four metres wide and fifty metres long. Atop the slab were two openings, each about fifty centimetres square. As he passed the slab, he saw that the cover of one of these openings appeared partially open, and curious, he lifted it to look inside. To his surprise and horror, he saw a man's face, covered in blood and excrement, staring back at him. Even more shocking, the man appeared to recognize him. "Peter," the man said in a voice almost too weak to utter the words, "what are you doing here?"

In amazement, Peter almost dropped the cover back into place. He recognized the man as his cousin, Adam Kamianka, from their village of Verkhnie Syniovydne. No one in the family had heard from Adam since his arrest by the Soviets weeks earlier. Calling for help from passersby, Peter began lifting his cousin out of the concrete pit, which he realized, with revulsion, was the prison's septic tank.

Freeing Adam through the small opening was difficult, and his cousin cried out in pain. "Please be careful," he moaned. "I have been shot." Once Adam was out of the tank, Peter could see he was naked except for a thin vest. Lying on the ground, waiting for someone to bring a stretcher, Adam began to describe the horror he had experienced.

He likely had never been formally charged with any offence, let alone tried for a crime. With many other prisoners, he was probably arrested on a tip, on a whim, or just as a means of terrorizing young Ukrainian men suspected of engaging in anti-Soviet activities. It didn't matter. He had been imprisoned, questioned, and threatened with torture.

With the Germans drawing near to the city, the Soviet guards had been ordered to abandon the prison and flee east. Either fearing the prisoners would provide damning information to the Nazis or out of some purely sadistic motive, they decided to kill as many as possible before leaving.

One by one, the men had been taken from their cells, marched into the shower room, ordered to undress and lie on the tiled floor, and shot in the head. Then they were dragged to the septic tank and dumped inside. The number of prisoners in the jail who were brutally executed by the Soviets that day without a trial—or, in most cases, without knowing the charges against them—has never been determined. In other cities, the numbers in each case have been estimated in the hundreds.[2]

In addition to his head wound, Adam Kamianka had been shot in the chest before being tossed into the tank among dozens of corpses and years of accumulated human waste. Somehow he managed to make it to the small opening in the septic tank and lift it high enough to breathe fresh air, which is when Peter found him.

With the help of others, Peter carried his cousin to the nearest hospital. With no professional care or medications to treat him, Adam Kamianka lingered in agony for three days before dying.

The chaos of war and the inhumanity of his cousin's treatment at the hands of the Soviets could not help but affect the young Peter Jacyk. Although he never forgot discovering his cousin in such appalling circumstances—how could he?—his actions from that point forward were aimed at achieving three goals.

The first was simply to survive, and in the short term, this may have been the most challenging. Depending upon the source, between 7.5 and 12 million Ukrainians perished in the period between 1939 and 1945, dying from an almost endless list of causes, including summary execution, military conflicts, government-sanctioned starvation, exposure, and disease.[3]

---

2. An estimated 150 Ukrainian prisoners were brutally executed by retreating NKVD in the Stryi prison, as reported by Taras Hunczak in *Ukraine during World War II: History and Its Aftermath* (Edmonton: Canadian Institute of Ukrainian Studies Press, 1986), 43, quoting Milena Rudnytska, ed., *Zakhidnia Ukraina pid bolshevykamy*, IX. 1939–VI, 1941 (New York, 1958), 441–92. In nearby Berezhany (Brzeżany), between June 22 and July 1, the crew of the local NKVD prison executed without trial approximately three hundred Polish citizens, among them a large number of Ukrainians. Anna Gałkiewicz, *Informacja o śledztwach prowadzonych w OKŚZpNP w Łodzi w sprawach o zbrodnie popełnione przez funkcjonariuszy sowieckiego aparatu terroru*, Biuletyn IPN, Vol. 7 (August 2001).

3. Stalislav Kulchytsky, "Demographic Losses in Ukraine in the Twentieth Century," *Zerkalo Nedeli* (October 2–8, 2004). Also: "Losses of the Ukrainian Nation," 1 (in Ukrainian).

His next goal was to prepare himself for whatever future extended beyond the insanity of war that surrounded him. Someday it must end, he knew, and when it did, he must be prepared to act.

His third path led to the dream of building not only a life free of the horrors and despotism that had dominated his country for decades but one that provided the means to assist his native land and its people in achieving freedom, identity, and security. The fact that Peter Jacyk made this dream a reality is a tribute to the human spirit in general and his own fortitude in particular. It's doubtful that even he, however, could have imagined the degree of success he would achieve and the extent to which he would employ it to support Ukrainian studies and culture.

More than a decade after his death, Peter Jacyk's story continues to resonate on a number of levels. During the fifteen years from 1930 to 1945, the area of the world marked on the west by Berlin, on the east by Moscow, on the north by the Baltic Sea, and on the south by the Black Sea saw the violent deaths of an estimated 14 million people. Peter Jacyk not only survived this age of carnage, he also managed to acquire sufficient assets to aid him in reminding the world of the violence and the people who suffered.

His story recounts one man's ability to seize the advantage and overlook the challenge of arriving in a land that appeared to welcome him on one hand as a refugee from war-torn Europe and dismiss him on the other hand because he lacked British roots. It traces his financial success and the manner in which he applied these resources toward supporting and extending his heritage. And it explains the deep-seated love he felt for his adopted country of Canada.

Half a century after that June night of horror in Stryi, Peter Jacyk reflected on the resources he had accumulated that enabled him to assist Ukraine in so many ways. He took his first steps toward realizing that goal, he noted, when he set off for Canada in

1949 with $7 in his pocket, arriving alone in a land where he knew little of the language and even less of the culture.

He landed in Canada, in his words, a "poor-penny immigrant." At the end of an eventful life filled with accomplishments, he was recognized as one of the more successful businessmen in Canada and a generous philanthropist. His generosity, much of it directed toward improving the culture and wider appreciation of his beloved Ukraine and its people, continues to yield benefits to millions.

His business achievements generated thousands of jobs in construction and in residential and industrial real estate. In the academic arena, perhaps a similar number of lecturers, researchers, and scholars were able to pursue their studies thanks to the largesse of Peter Jacyk.

How did he achieve so much against such high odds? His simplest explanation was to claim he had been "rich in spirit," meaning he had the willpower and ambition to keep moving forward. It is an inspiring phrase but perhaps inadequate in depicting all the challenges and barriers he overcame and the number of lives he enriched in so many ways.

2

Ukraine, 1920–1939:
A Beleaguered Nation

*Stalin was sincere when, during the war, he said he was
having more trouble with the peasants in the collectivization
program than he was having with Hitler. The casualties
of the man-made famine in Ukraine are grim testimony of
the deadly nature of the struggle between Russian communist
imperialism and the independent Ukrainian farmer.*

CHARLES J. KERSTEN

PETER JACYK'S achievements cannot be appreciated without
understanding the role his Ukrainian heritage played in his life.
That role, in turn, cannot be grasped without knowing the events,
tragic and horrendous, that his native land endured during much
of the twentieth century. It's safe to say that few nations on earth,
over the decades from 1920 to 1950, faced a more determined
effort by other countries to dominate their existence and subju-
gate their citizens than Ukraine.

Growing up amid this constant upheaval and foreign domination forged Peter Jacyk's personality—and undoubtedly fuelled his
ambition. "Until the age of 22," he wrote while in his mid-sixties, "I
lived and worked under Polish, Russian and German governments

in Ukraine. Having been one of the slaves, I am a little more familiar with that mentality than a person who was raised in a Western
culture."[1]

The area of the world occupied by Ukraine was first blessed
by its climate and geography, then cursed by its neighbours and
their avarice. The second-largest country in Europe, Ukraine's
more than 600,000 square kilometres encompasses wide plains
and plateaus irrigated by major rivers such as the Dnieper, Dnies-
ter, and the delta of the Danube. With a predominantly temperate
climate—the southern region is more Mediterranean than central
European—most of Ukraine is ideal for producing cereal crops.
Over many generations, its farmers became adept at raising bum-
per harvests of wheat, rye, oats, barley, and corn, which should
have guaranteed both a strong economy and a well-fed populace.
Unfortunately, the bounty of grain also targeted Ukraine as an area
to be coveted, dominated, and exploited by Lithuania, Turkey, Aus-
tria-Hungary, Germany, and, most significantly, Poland and Russia.
All sought to influence the region from the Middle Ages through
the twentieth century.

Although Peter Jacyk viewed all of Ukraine as his homeland, he
identified most closely with western Ukraine, known as Galicia/
Halychyna, and the mountainous region surrounding his ancestral
village of Verkhnie Syniovydne. "Galicia/Halychyna" is derived
from the medieval principality of Halych, conquered by the Polish state in the fourteenth century and annexed by the Austrian
Habsburgs in 1772. The ancient Ukrainian name of Halychyna was
transformed into Galicia/Halychyna, representing a Crown land
that also included Polish territories, with Lviv, the ancient Ukrainian "city of lions," designated as the capital. It is more familiarly
known today simply as Galicia.

---

1. These and other direct quotations not otherwise attributed are from an uncom-
   pleted memoir drafted by Peter Jacyk in the year before his death.

Under the Poles, Habsburgs, and others, Ukrainians yearned to establish their own political, cultural, and linguistic identity and enjoy sovereignty over their own land. The nineteenth century witnessed a growing sense of national identity among Ukrainians, aimed at ultimately producing unification and independence. Beginning in the 1870s, a host of movements sprang up, strengthening and clarifying Ukrainian identity on a number of levels. Much of the activity was driven by a sudden burgeoning of populist clubs and societies that inspired theatrical productions, adult education classes, village reading rooms, and textbooks and novels dealing with Ukrainian literature and history.

On a commercial level, the movement generated a spurt of cooperative associations, extending from the 1890s to the outbreak of WWI, when more than five hundred co-ops and credit unions flourished throughout the region. Their success provided peasants and tradespeople with the financial resources to build and manage their farms and businesses in a manner previously unavailable, and their influence extended beyond commerce to the building of a strong national identity. As one reputable historian put it, "The cooperative movement made possible a process of organic social growth in which an improvement in economic standards developed hand in hand with an increase in Ukrainian national consciousness."[2]

Unlike eastern Ukraine, Galicia had not been part of a Russian state before the twentieth century. Its inhabitants saw themselves as central Europeans rather than eastern Europeans and demonstrated this allegiance in various ways. Habsburg rule had brought contact with the West, the freeing of serfs, and a constitutional order permitting elections and political activity. Ukrainians in Galicia overwhelmingly belonged to the Greek Catholic

2. Paul Robert Magocsi, *A History of Ukraine: The Land and Its Peoples* (Toronto: University of Toronto Press, 2010), 473.

Church, united with Rome rather than with the Russian Orthodox Church.

Unifying Ukraine through much of the twentieth century
was a daunting task, given the fractious nature of the country's
development. With the nearing end of WWI, Poles sought to
incorporate all of Galicia into a restored Polish Republic. After
Ukrainians successfully moved out from under the authority
of the Austro-Hungarian Empire and declared eastern Galicia
as the West Ukrainian National Republic on November 1, 1918,
they found themselves at war with a newly constituted Polish
state. Meanwhile, when eastern Ukraine attempted to escape
the long-term influence of Russia, it was attacked by both Russian Reds (Communist supporters) and Whites (loosely allied
anti-Communists).

Attempts by Russia, and later the Soviet Union, to replace
the Ukrainian language with the Russian language represented
an effective means of destroying the identity of an entire nation.
Genocide, by definition, ends lives; eradicating a language, and all
the cultural spinoffs associated with language, eliminates character and spirit.

Ukrainians were compelled to abandon their mother tongue
and speak, write, and read Russian. To Anglo-Saxon and other non-
Slavic eyes, the language differences may appear minimal, if only
because the Cyrillic characters employed in the two languages
look similar. In fact, the languages, though related, are not alike.
This distinction is crucial to understanding the impact of Russia
on Ukraine's national identity, the desperation of Ukrainians to
retain and honour their own heritage, and, ultimately, the goals
and character of Peter Jacyk.

Supporters of Ukrainian independence found a sympathetic
home in Galicia. Under Austrian dominance, Ukrainian books
could be published and the Ukrainian language could be used in
schools. Under Poland, the situation worsened. The dominant

Poles tried to enforce Polish as the main language, limit the number of high schools in Ukraine, and "Polonize" the universities. But a movement had begun, and it gained momentum. The opportunity to organize and demand political rights, granted by the Habsburgs, influenced growing numbers of Galician Ukrainians and drew the peasantry into the national movement. A cadre of Galician Ukrainians began to view all Ukrainian territories as their homeland, regardless of who ruled them and what religion their residents professed, especially in the years immediately following World War I.

That war had seen Russia and Austria on opposite sides of the conflict, a battlefield rivalry that brought large-scale destruction to Galicia and short-term occupation by Russian troops. As a tactic to counter the Russians, Austria permitted the formation of a Ukrainian military unit. Its existence, following the collapse of first the Russian Empire and later the Austrian Empire, gave Ukrainians their chance to form independent states. The downfall of Austria in October 1918 gave the Galician Ukrainians a hope for national self-determination, and inspired Galicians to pronounce the eastern part of the Austrian Crown land a western Ukrainian National Republic, on the basis that they represented the majority of the population. On January 22, 1919, they declared their unity with the Ukrainian National Republic, which had been established in eastern Ukraine after the fall of the tsar in 1917.

The reaction was swift. Galician Poles opposed to the declaration rose in revolt, supported by the new Polish state, which attacked the West Ukrainian National Republic with troops armed by the Entente. The conflict effectively ended in July, when the Polish army, heavily supported by France,[3] succeeded in driving the Ukrainian forces out of Galicia. Things were formalized a

---

3. Among the French advisors assisting the Poles in defeating the Ukrainians was a young captain named Charles de Gaulle.

few weeks later with a declaration by members of the Paris Peace Conference, influenced by the U.K. and the U.S., who feared encroachment from Bolshevist Russia. The declaration declared Poland administrator of Galicia. Meanwhile, the new Communist regime in Moscow seized control of eastern Ukraine, obliterating the Ukrainian National Republic.

But things had changed in the minds of Galician Ukrainians. The massive support by the Ukrainian population during Galicia's struggle for independence, and the declaration of unity between Galicians in the west and Ukrainians to the east, marked a crossing of a Rubicon in nation building.

Many Ukrainians refused to accept the legitimacy of Polish rule and tried to continue their active resistance. Others resisted passively, attempting to employ educational and economic rights to contend that the territory was Ukrainian, not Polish. In response, the Polish state asserted that the land would always be Polish, renaming Galicia "Eastern Little Poland" and replacing many Ukrainian schools from the Austrian era with predominantly Polish schools. It refused to permit a Ukrainian university and discriminated against Ukrainians in university admittance and employment. To seal the action, Polish colonists were encouraged to emigrate to Galicia and change the region's national composition.

To be sure, Poland was not a totalitarian nation like the Soviet Union. It was, however, an aggressively nationalist state that was growing increasingly authoritarian, especially where the treatment of minorities was concerned. International pressure limited Polish responses to Ukraine's national movements, but the tension periodically exploded in violence, including incidents during the Pacification of 1930, when the army attacked villages harbouring Ukrainian activists. Ukrainian reprisals produced assaults on Polish estates and assassination attempts, prompting a retaliatory cycle on both sides.

Both Poland and Russia (including Soviet Russia) pursued domination of Ukraine, but the difference in attitude of the two nations was quite distinct. The Poles, as noted by Mykola Ryabchuk of the Ukrainian Centre for Cultural Studies in Kyiv, were unfriendly toward Ukrainians, whereas the Russians "loved" them as family members. Paradoxically, the latter have been more destructive to Ukraine than the former. "The Poles," Ryabchuk explains, "even if they disliked Ukrainians, regarded them as a separate nation." Russians, he suggests, "typically treated Ukrainians as a subgroup of their nation... The Polish view of Ukrainians, however biased and distorted, usually does not question the existence of a separate Ukrainian identity and nationality. The Russian view of Ukrainians, however friendly and sympathetic, typically denies this very essence."[4] Ukrainians, he concludes, were able to have a meaningful dialogue with Poles as equal sovereigns—but not with Russians.

INTO THIS CATACLYSMIC post-WWI environment, Peter Jacyk was born on July 7, 1921, in the village of Verkhnie Syniovydne in Galicia, near the old Hungarian border, a region known as the Boyko land. The Boykos lived in the central and western areas of the Carpathians, and by the early twentieth century, they strongly identified themselves as Ukrainians—an important factor in a region that various ethnic and national groups have claimed as their home over several centuries.

The landscape of the Carpathians may have been wondrously beautiful, but it was not a land of agricultural abundance. Rural life was more difficult there than in more productive regions of Ukraine, a situation that had motivated almost an entire gen-

---

4. Mykola Ryabchuk, "The Ukrainian 'Friday' and the Russian 'Robinson': The Uneasy Advent of Postcoloniality," *Canadian-American Slavic Studies* 44 (2010), 6–23.

eration of residents to depart for the New World. What the mountaineers lacked in material wealth, however, they compensated for with their industrious nature.

The mountains also represented the roots of resistance against medieval serfdom, an attitude that engendered many Robin Hood–like figures. Among them was Oleksa Dovbush, whose legend of robbing from the rich to give to the poor remains alive today in Ukrainian folklore as well as in the names of streets and parklands.

All of these Galician and Boyko qualities—a tradition of seeking freedom from outside influences, an attachment to their own traditions and civic culture, a powerful work ethic, and a perceived tradition of both acquiring and spreading wealth—influenced Peter Jacyk's values and, in many ways, guided his future career.

PETER WAS THE ELDEST of seven children of farmers Mariana Melenczuk and Dmytro Jacyk. Dmytro had served in World War I, along with two brothers. Only Dmytro survived, though his health was weakened, perhaps as a result of gas attacks. Dmytro Jacyk, a widower with two small children, met Mariana upon returning home to Verkhnie Syniovydne. Unlike Dmytro, Mariana could read and write, and she valued education and culture. "My mother was very much in favour of learning," her son Peter wrote many years later, a value that he supported throughout his life. Both Mariana and Dmytro were the children of farming families, and they led the rural life that had maintained their ancestors over several generations.

Rural life in 1920s Galicia was productive but not easy, and Peter and his siblings were called upon to help work the family farm. Around them, political upheaval was either boiling in sudden explosions of nationalist fervour or simmering just beneath the surface. Like most rural peasants, the Jacyk family avoided politics, preferring to be left alone to tend their crops and animals.

We know few details of Peter's early life, though one incident he related as an adult demonstrates his compassion and perception. "I remember my father ploughing the land with our one horse," he recalled during a film interview in the 1990s. "The horse was exhausted, I could see that, but my father kept beating the animal over and over, trying to get it to work harder and longer than the poor animal was capable of working."

The young Peter suggested that his father stop beating the horse and help it work, a concept that his father apparently had not considered. The senior Jacyk was following a peasant tradition where work animals were concerned. Each spring, his father would buy a horse to work the fields in the coming season. Each fall, with the harvest complete, his father dispensed with the animal by one means or another, having exhausted its energy and use. Perhaps, Peter argued, if they cared for the horse instead of working it literally to death, the horse would be worth keeping year after year, instead of spending money searching for another suitable animal each spring. The idea made economic sense and revealed an admirable humanitarian view in the young man. His persuasiveness failed to match his compassion, however; Peter didn't convince his father, though the memory of the animal's unnecessary suffering remained with him throughout his life.

Peter was probably not surprised that his suggestion was ignored. He was, after all, a young boy who, in addition to learning the Ten Commandments and the Catholic catechisms, had been taught that respect for one's elders represented a moral standard that he and his brothers and sisters were expected to follow. Unable to convince his father to treat the horse more humanely, he apparently refused to abide by the common edict of the time that "children should be seen and not heard." If his concern for the animal's suffering had made little impact on his father, his ability to argue a point was widely acknowledged. Many years later, as a successful and acclaimed businessman, he recalled, "I liked to listen and talk to older people. Many of them suggested that I become a lawyer. Not a lawyer for money's sake, but a lawyer as a defender of justice."

Through grade school, little seems to have disturbed Peter's childhood. Time spent helping his family tend their crops was balanced with studies in the village schoolhouse. There was little time for play, though Peter, like all children, joined in games with friends whenever school and farm work could be set aside for a while.

During the 1920s, an enforced calm settled over western Ukraine. In some ways, the country and its people were exhausted by the events of previous decades. A series of uprisings on behalf of Ukraine and its people, all failing to provide the independence they sought, had proved fruitless. Towns and cities were centres of active political resistance, and villages were at times centres of agrarian strike and suffered greatly from the Pacification. By the mid-1920s, most Ukrainians began to focus on raising their crops and maintaining their lifestyle in peace. Concepts of freedom and democracy remained only dreams for most Ukrainians, and unrealistic dreams at that, as they had for centuries.

Ukrainians in Galicia looked east toward the "Great Ukraine" for help. In the 1920s, when the Soviet authorities supported the development of Ukrainian language to win Ukrainian acceptance of Soviet rule, many Galicians even hoped this would lead to some form of solace.

Unlike Polish-dominated Galicia, the Soviet Union at first permitted the use of Ukrainian, but after the 1920s, the Ukrainian language was downplayed, and Russian-language textbooks were favoured for use in classrooms. The lessons in these textbooks inevitably delivered a pro-Russian bias to the students. The influence extended beyond secondary school to universities, where Russian-speaking professors earned substantially larger salaries than those who employed the common language spoken off campus.

In tsarist Russia, children read their lessons in Russian, received their instructions in Russian, and were encouraged to converse in the classroom and the schoolyard in Russian. The situation was not much better in Soviet Ukraine following World War I. That Ukrainian language and culture endured as it has in the face of such pressure and tactics is a tribute to the strength of its people and their fierce rejection of enforced Russian values and influence. With the inhumane tactics applied in east Ukraine by Stalin and his regime in Moscow, mere survival became a goal that an unknown number of millions of Ukrainians could not achieve.

FOR HUNDREDS OF years, farmers in eastern Ukraine produced substantial crops free of any political philosophy or government manipulation. Ukrainian farmers knew when and how to sow their crops in spring, nurture them in summer, and harvest them in autumn—and how to do it as well as farmers elsewhere in Europe.

Stalin knew better, or so his brand of Communism suggested. Instead of individual farms, Stalin decreed that combining the land into collective farms, or *kolkhozy* (in Ukrainian, *kolhospy*), operating under orders from a centralized authority, would optimize production and efficiency. Moscow-based government apparatchiks, supposedly more capable of making key decisions than peasants and workers, would direct the farmers' actions, creating greater efficiencies and benefits for everyone.

But they did not. Warm and well fed in Moscow, Stalin and his team set quotas of grain and other crops for the *kolkhozy* that were so high, the farmers could not possibly meet them, even with ideal weather conditions. When the *kolkhozy* failed to deliver their quotas, Moscow blamed the farmers. Stalin raised the quotas even higher, and representatives of his regime often seized every bushel of grain the farmers produced. Farmers who had invested an entire year's labour in the harvest found themselves with no food for themselves and their families. When those who managed to survive the famine lacked both the energy and incentive to meet their quotas the following year, many without seed grain to plant the new season's crops, the grand experiment became like a colossal mechanized monster in which various parts ceased to function even as the machine operator—Stalin, at the controls—kept pressing the throttle in pursuit of more speed.

A native Georgian but with Russian chauvinist attitudes, Stalin especially distrusted Ukrainian peasants because he and other Bolsheviks had been driven out of Ukraine twice while trying to impose their ideas. Along with apparent retribution for this insult, Stalin's attitude toward the peasants may have been driven by a sense of desperate need. If Stalin's regime failed to achieve its industrialization goal, Communism risked being declared an abject failure, and Stalin and his team would be seen as fools for believing it would succeed. This could not be allowed to happen.

The result was a famine that was at once horrific in the extreme yet still controversial among Ukrainians regarding the motives and the extent of its impact. Although the events remain complex in their origins and scope, the results on the population of east Ukraine—the region under Soviet domination through the 1930s—remain nightmarish and without doubt influenced Peter Jacyk and the attitude toward both Ukraine and Russia he held throughout his life.

The impetus behind Moscow's laws regarding the collective farms continued to be viewed from different perspectives more than eighty years after the event. Did Stalin, for example, impose the famine as a means of starving the Ukrainian peasants into submission, as a form of deliberate genocide—a belief shared by many

Ukrainians? Or was it a by-product of his single-minded effort to impose collectivization on Ukrainian farm operations?

Motive aside, the results remain mind-numbing, and the tales of suffering by Ukrainians who felt the impact of the policy remain both disturbing and incomprehensible, as was the reaction of the world beyond Ukraine. In 1933, Malcolm Muggeridge, one of the few outsiders who attempted to alert the world to the situation as it unfolded, wrote of his experience encountering the famine situation:

> On a recent visit to the Northern Caucasus and Ukraine, I saw something of the battle that is going on between the government and the peasants. The battlefield is as desolate as in any war and stretches wider; over a large part of Russia. On the one side, millions of starving peasants, their bodies often swollen from lack of food; on the other, soldier members of the GPU [Communist state political administration] carrying out the instructions of the dictatorship of the proletariat. They had gone over the country like a swarm of locusts and taken away everything edible; they had shot or exiled thousands of peasants, sometimes whole villages; they had reduced some of the most fertile land in the world to a melancholy desert.[5]

IN RESPONSE TO the stubbornness of the peasantry, who he believed refused to play their role in his plan, Stalin called upon urban industrial workers to enforce his edicts. Labelling the workers "the best sons of the fatherland," Stalin dispatched several thousand urban-based enforcers throughout the Ukrainian countryside to ensure that the collective farms fulfilled the demands

---

5. Malcolm Muggeridge, "The Soviets' War on the Peasants," *Fortnightly Review* (May 1, 1933), 564.

of Moscow. With the backing of the Soviet army and the dreaded NKVD secret police, the enforcers began expropriating property, insisting that the collective farms meet the quota levels. Entering farm properties without notice, they would seize every measure of harvested grain they could locate and ship it off for whatever destination was determined by Moscow.

The enforcers were especially aggressive against kurkuls (in Russian, kulaks), farmers who appeared to possess more material wealth than their neighbours. The supposedly prosperous kurkuls, Stalin believed, refused to accept the promised glories of Communism and, in their own self-interests, urged other peasants to resist Stalin's orders. What qualified a peasant for kurkul status? The measures were minimal. Through the collectivization process, any peasant who owned more than one cow, who farmed more than an acre of land, whose family appeared less emaciated than their neighbours, or whose home seemed less decrepit than others was branded a kurkul.

Kurkuls were declared "class enemies," and those who weren't executed on the spot were deported to Siberian work camps. Peasants permitted to remain on their farms were warned that any transgressions would lead to similar treatment and reminded that they were expected to maintain the quotas set for them. Protest or refusal to cooperate identified the complainer as a kurkul or a kurkul supporter, and thus an enemy of the revolution, resulting in banishment to Siberia, imprisonment, or execution.

If Stalin believed his actions would act as an incentive, he was grossly mistaken. Under these insane conditions, many peasants chose to abandon farming and escape to the cities, further reducing agricultural production capacity. Instead of grasping the true reason for the failure of his policies, Stalin continued to blame the peasants. The fault, he raged, lay not with himself or with Marxism. The disaster was due entirely to rebellious and subversive peasants, who insisted on retaining their language and customs and who, if not already labelled as kurkuls, strove to emulate them.

Faced with crop failures due to weather, insects, and disease, the collective farms fell short of quotas over and over, eliciting paroxysms of fury from Stalin. The result was the Great Famine, or Holodomor (Death by Hunger), a conscious decision by the Stalinist regime to control and punish Soviet Ukraine and its peasant farmers through a policy of intentional starvation.

Statistics measure the size of the impact, but they cannot begin to describe the extent of the human tragedy. Nevertheless, the figures reveal their own measure of heartbreak. During the Holodomor, Ukrainian life expectancy at birth dropped from about forty-three years for men and forty-six years for women to barely seven years and fewer than eleven years respectively.[6] The only explanation for such dramatically shortened expected lifespans is enormously high levels of infant mortality. Stories abound of starving families forced to choose who among their children would be permitted to starve to death, so that food could be directed toward others in the family with a stronger constitution and thus a more likely prospect of survival.

Peasants who tried to avoid starvation by consuming grain set aside for the following year's crop (assuming any remained after authorities seized it as part of the collective farms' quota) risked being charged with "the theft of Socialist property," a crime punishable by death. Administrators dispatched into the country were more than ruthless in their treatment of the peasants; they were incompetent. Quantities of grain seized from farmers were left to rot in the open air or be consumed by rats and other pests. And when large numbers of peasants attempted to leave their villages

---

6. France Meslé, Gilles Pison, and Jacques Vallin, "France-Ukraine: Demographic Twins Separated by History," *Population & Societies*, No. 413 (May 2005), 2.

in search of food elsewhere, authorities issued internal passports to confine them to their immediate area, ensuring death by starvation for many.

The wickedness of the crisis, as seen (and recorded) through the eyes of those who survived the famine, screams from the pages of books such as *The Black Deeds of the Kremlin*, published in two volumes.[7] One witness recalls visiting the ironically named October Revolution Hospital with a surgeon friend:

> When I arrived he took me to a large garage in the yard. A guard unlocked the door and we entered. [My friend] switched on the light and I beheld an unforgettable picture of horror.
>
> Piled like cord-wood against the walls, layer on layer, were the frozen corpses of the victims picked off the streets that morning. Some of the bodies, I later learned, were used for dissection and experiments in the laboratories. The rest were simply buried in pits, at midnight, in nearby ravines out of the sight of the people.
>
> "This," my friend whispered softly, "is the fate of our villages."[8]

Those too weak to work in the fields were branded as idlers and anti-social or anti-government elements, subject to imprisonment. Even farmers who managed to both survive and continue their labours were severely punished for the smallest indiscretion. According to one source, they "were sentenced to ten years of Siberian slave labour if they so much as picked a pocketful of wheat heads, to chew the half-ripened grains for nourishment. This crime was known as 'theft of socialist property.'"[9]

---

7. *The Black Deeds of the Kremlin, A White Book, Volume I (Book of Testimonies)* (Toronto: Ukrainian Association of Victims of Russian Communist Terror, 1953). *The Black Deeds of the Kremlin, A White Book, Volume II, The Great Famine in Ukraine 1932–33* (Detroit: The Democratic Organization of Ukrainians Formerly Persecuted by the Soviet Regime, 1955).

8. *The Black Deeds of the Kremlin*, Vol. I, 236.

9. Ibid., 238.

In the midst of this terrorism, some not only survived but prospered. They included the higher ranks of party officials and government workers, NKVD officers and staff, and rural authorities such as the heads of village soviets, party secretaries, accountants, warehousemen, and brigade workers. For them, "secret stores of food were maintained and available at fixed government prices."[10]

The famine resulted in more than human suffering on a scale difficult to imagine so many years later; it physically altered the lifestyle of Ukraine, a nation that had functioned for some time on community life built around villages. When village life grew untenable, those who survived the impact of collectivization and were able to travel moved to cities, abandoning rural villages and the community identity they provided.

Officially, the famine did not exist. Within the Soviet Union, writers were forbidden to publish accounts of mass starvation. Those who even hinted at it were threatened by the NKVD with execution or exile to slave labour camps in Siberia. On the occasion when massive numbers of deaths could not conveniently be hidden, statistical bureaus were ordered to register them as a result of "digestive ailments" and not starvation.[11] Only in the 1960s under Khrushchev was the famine permitted to be discussed, and then in severely restricted terms. It was not until the late 1980s that the famine finally entered open discourse under glasnost.

According to trustworthy figures, the Ukrainians who succumbed to the inhuman policies of the Soviets in their collectivization efforts likely numbered between 4 and 5 million, with perhaps another 2 million victims in surrounding areas such as Kuban. These would include not only those who starved to death but others executed for refusing to follow Moscow's policies. It's unlikely that Stalin and other Soviet leaders saw these deaths as

---

10. *The Black Deeds of the Kremlin*, Vol. II, 85.

11. *The Black Deeds of the Kremlin*, Vol. I, 235.

human tragedies, if they considered them at all. As one commentator observed, "Enemy number one for Stalin and his circle was not the Ukrainian peasant nor the Ukrainian intelligentsia. The enemy was Ukraine itself."[12] Between the Great Famine and the political purges that followed, as many as 80 percent[13] of Ukrainian politicians, lecturers, labour leaders, and dissidents were executed, died of starvation, or were shipped to gulags,[14] never to be seen again.

Broad public recognition and acknowledgement of the Holodomor has been slow in arriving. Canada, for example, officially noted the disaster only in 2008 with the passage of a federal government bill recognizing the famine of 1932–33 as an act of genocide and establishing Ukrainian Famine and Genocide Memorial Day.[15]

IN GALICIA, THE Jacyks escaped the genocide but were aware of its extent and impact—and of Soviet Russia's complicity. As news of the famine spread among Ukrainians in the 1930s, Galicians viewed the Soviet Union as their major enemy, while chafing under the control of Poland.

Things could have been worse. Despite administrative harassment, censorship, and discrimination, the Poles permitted Ukrai-

---

12. James Mace, as reported in *The Ukrainians—Unexpected Nation*, third edition, by Andrew Wilson (New Haven and London: Yale University Press, 2009), 145.

13. "Interwar Soviet Ukraine," *Encyclopedia Britannica*, fifteenth edition.

14. The term "gulag" is derived from *Glavnoe upravlenie ispravitel'no-trudovykh lagerei*, or Main Administration of Corrective Labour Camps.

15. Text of the bill included this passage:

   Between 1932 and 1933 a massive famine struck the Ukraine as well as parts of the northern Caucasus and the lower Volga River areas of the then Soviet Union. Food shortages were so severe that it is estimated that between six and seven million people died in the Ukraine alone.

   The famine resulted from the forced collectivization of farms under programs initiated by Joseph Stalin. Under forced collectivization small-hold farms were eliminated in favour of large collective farms. The farmers were not allowed to retain any of the produce for their own use until the required quotas had been given to the state. In 1932 and 1933 the quotas were set so high that there was insufficient produce remaining to feed the Ukrainian population.

nian-based political parties to recruit adherents and tolerated the presence of the Ukrainian Catholic Church, an active press, and a vibrant business community. Life under Polish rule was hardly the choice that increasingly national-minded Ukrainians craved, but at least their peasant farmers were permitted to tend their crops free of Stalin's collectivization madness. What's more, Galician residents remained connected to European culture. "Poland was a small and poor country with a weak government administration," Peter Jacyk commented, "but it was exposed to influences of Western thought and culture, primarily French and German."

Galicia avoided the iron heel of the Stalinist Communists, including the disastrous move toward collective farms, the insane enforcement of unattainable farm quotas, and the famine. Although life could not have been easy for Peter and his parents and siblings, their knowledge of the disaster occurring among Ukrainians to the east made them aware of what might await them from that quarter were they to fall under the thumb of Soviet Russia.

In 1939, these fears were realized in a violent and unspeakably bloody manner, when the misery of the Great Famine was replaced by the horror of war.

3

Surviving the Horrors, 1939–1945

*A Russian knows only one of two extremes
and the middle between them doesn't interest him,
which is why he knows nothing or very little.*

ANTON CHEKHOV

AWARE OF THE tragic events unfolding in east Ukraine, Peter Jacyk managed to graduate from his village's seven-grade primary school at age fourteen, before enrolling for evening classes in agriculture, with the assumed ambition of pursuing a life's career in farming. His career decision was likely not entirely his to make. When his father died suddenly that year, Peter was expected to assume at least part of the duties on the farm as quickly as he could complete his education.

His life, along with those of millions of others, changed completely when Nazi Germany invaded Poland on September 1, 1939, triggering a declaration of war by Britain and its allies. The invasion was made possible by the terms of the Molotov-Ribbentrop non-aggression pact signed by Nazi Germany and the Soviet Union barely a month earlier. According to the treaty, Poland lost control of Galicia, and its governed territories were to be divided between Germany and Soviet Russia.

With the fall of Poland, the country's border guards stationed in Galicia withdrew from their posts, many heading for Romania. The Border Protection Corps (Korpus ochrony pogranicza, or KOP), had been created in 1924 to defend the country's eastern borders against Soviet incursions and local bandits. Many KOP troops were of German nationality and although the three regiments consisted of volunteers, all had received intensive training in Polish military units before their posting. Their role as border guards was expanded to include activities normally associated with policing and militia groups, such as pursuing suspected intruders through reconnaissance, ambushes, provocation, and intelligence, and they were regarded with muted hostility by most Galicians.[1]

The mutual hostility exploded in 1939 when KOP troops, seeking to escape the Soviets, began killing Ukrainian villagers as the Poles abandoned their posts. In response, partisan groups were formed to defend the villagers. When a cousin of Peter announced that he was joining the partisans, Peter agreed to accompany him.

They quickly located a nearby camp of partisans, about two hundred men armed with weapons ranging from revolvers and shotguns to farm implements such as rakes and sickles. "The partisan reconnaissance leader informed us that four trucks of artillery were approaching," Peter Jacyk recalled many years later, "and about twenty of the men aboard the trucks were members of KOP."[2] When the partisans approached the small KOP convoy, the Poles halted their trucks, took shelter behind the vehicles, and began

---

1. Tomasz Piesakowski, *The Fate of Poles in the USSR, 1939–1989* (London: Gryf Publications, 1990), 36.

2. The description of this encounter was related during a speech to the graduating class of generals at the Ukrainian military academy, Kyiv, in 2000. See page 265 for details.

spraying the Galicians with machine gun fire. Perhaps through sheer numbers, the untrained partisans managed to overwhelm the Poles. According to Jacyk's description, they left four KOP dead and seven wounded before the Poles fled. That night, he was given a rifle and assigned to guard the partisan camp. He forever remembered "how scared I was at the rustle of every leaf in the woods."

Within a few days, Galicia was free of the KOP and Poles generally, leaving the border open for the arrival of the Soviet army. With their immediate enemy gone, the partisans faced three choices: flee to Krakow to avoid the hated Soviets; identify themselves as partisans to the Soviets, hoping that their actions against the Poles would win them some measure of reward from the new invaders; or simply return home and await the next development.

"Maybe eighteen men from my village marched in threes to welcome the 'liberators,'" Peter said. "Some thought if the Red Army overpowered the Polish elite and we, as partisans, helped them do this, [they] would honour us for our participation." At first, Peter believed this represented the best choice. But as he marched with the others, he began asking himself if there was really any difference in occupiers. The Poles were gone, replaced by the Soviets. And if the non-aggression pact between Germany and the Soviet Union was as cynical as most Ukrainians believed, would the Germans follow the Soviets as the next occupiers?

Occupiers, he believed, were not to be welcomed under any circumstances. They were to be resisted, not by ragtag partisans prepared for the most part to become martyrs for their cause but by a strong army and government responsible for the needs of its people. With that in mind, he walked away from the other young men and returned to his village. "All those who went to welcome the Red Army," he recounted sixty years later, "were photographed, arrested and…were never seen again."

Soon the Soviets were in total control of all of Ukraine, including Galicia.

THE MOLOTOV-RIBBENTROP PACT stands as one of the most cynical agreements between two powers in recorded history, with Germany assessing it as an opportunity to wage war on the western front free of concerns about the Soviet Union, and the Soviet Union seeking an opportunity to widen its holdings over its neighbours. The moves of both Germany and the Soviet Union regarding Ukraine under the terms of the Molotov-Ribbentrop pact were conducted smoothly and swiftly, like two old friends dividing found treasure in a previously agreed manner.

At the outset, the Soviets painted an appealing picture of their occupation of Galicia. Ukrainian, they declared, would be the language used in administration matters, jobs would be created, and citizens would enjoy more social justice. Not surprisingly, these promises held a good deal of appeal to those who were not politically engaged.

Almost no one believed the German-Soviet non-aggression pact would hold, and it did not. When the accord ended in the summer of 1941, broken by Germany's assault on Soviet Russia, it unleashed the most devastating conflict in human history, a war whose impact, many have argued, was more ruinous to Ukraine, by every measure, than to any other nation caught up in the war. One contemporary observer suggested World War II was "in many costly ways...a Ukrainian war," adding that "no single European country suffered deeper wounds to its cities, its industries, its farmlands and its humanity."[3]

Peter Jacyk surveyed the practices and attitudes of Ukraine's occupiers, especially the Soviets, and formed opinions that would colour and direct his actions through much of his adult life. But first he had to survive almost four years of war.

---

3. Edgar Snow, "The Ukraine Pays the Bill," *Saturday Evening Post* (January 27, 1945), 18.

WITHIN A FEW weeks of the Soviet Union assuming control of western Ukraine, Peter Jacyk enrolled in a six-month training course for railroad workers. The move represented an abandonment of agricultural life, and his motivations remain unclear. They were likely rooted in the death of his father in 1936, an event that propelled Peter into the role of the family's eldest male at just fourteen years of age. He had been expected to assume the leadership role in managing the family farm, and he accepted the responsibility with some success, learning at that early age the skills he employed so effectively many years later as a businessman in Canada. It lasted only until the arrival of the Soviets, however.

A possible reason for exploring a career off the farm may have been the expectation that the Soviets would impose the system of collective farming that had led to such widespread disaster over the previous decade in eastern Ukraine. While farmers suffered terribly under the catastrophic collective farming experiment, urban industrial workers fared much better, a realization that may have drawn the young man off the farm.

Whatever Peter's motive, his first month's railroad training involved modifying existing railroad tracks to accommodate the wider-gauge Russian trains and permit direct rail linkage with the Soviet railroad system. The decision, which underlined the presumed permanency of Soviet dominance, must have been disheartening to Peter and his countrymen. Nevertheless, his ambition and intelligence impressed the authorities so much that they awarded him the title of *Stakhanovets*, an honour named after a vaunted Soviet miner awarded for exceptional diligence in increasing production. The recognition brought Jacyk a raise in pay and, upon completion of his training, an appointment as assistant to a qualified railroad engineer.

His railroad career lasted barely two years—basically the life of the cynical Germany-Soviet non-aggression pact. During this period, he had the opportunity to watch the Soviet system and its administrators at work, and the experience repelled him not only through the short period while he laboured on the railroad but through the balance of his life.

"The first shock to Ukrainians came with their view of the occupying Soviet troops," notes Professor Frank Sysyn, director of the Petro Jacyk Centre for Ukrainian Historical Research at the Canadian Institute of Ukrainian Studies at the University of Alberta and an acquaintance of Peter Jacyk. "The Soviets looked like badly dressed rabble, poorly equipped and poorly led."

It was neither an impressive nor a reassuring debut, especially to people who were anticipating the Soviets would keep their promises about delivering widespread social justice. Early actions by the Soviets generated concerns among Ukrainians that would soon prove prophetic. The installation of collective farms in Galicia, which had avoided that aspect of Communism under the Poles, was not welcomed. Nor was the Soviets' launch of widespread anti-religious propaganda, creating an immediate negative reaction within the deeply religious Ukrainian society. These moves were soon followed by even more alarming actions, including the arrest and deportation of prominent citizens.

"At first the Soviets arrested and frequently deported Polish administrators, Jewish entrepreneurs, wealthy landowners, and Ukrainian political leaders," Sysyn explains. "They turned their attention initially to the intelligentsia of all the peoples of Galicia, and then to an ever-wider group of the populace. By 1941, the Soviets were quite generally hated. They were by then arresting more and deporting ever more people. Even those locals who were pro-Communist did not believe in this brand of Communism, so it can be said that when the Germans invaded in June of 1941, a very large percentage of the Ukrainian population assumed the new regime could not be worse."

Peter Jacyk was aware of the Soviet actions and despised them as much as other western Ukrainians did. He soon found another reason to scorn the new occupiers: Soviet Russia was not a creative society, he realized, but a destructive one. The country's embrace of Communism barely two decades earlier provided it with new means and a new justification for actions benefiting the Soviet Union at the expense of whatever nation it chose to pillage. All actions, the Communists could claim, were taken for the ultimate benefit of the working class, as Marx had decreed. Peter determined that Soviet actions reflected not the values of Communists specifically but the needs of Soviet Russia generally. He, like many western Ukrainians of his generation, saw something intrinsically Russian in the Soviet system, echoes of Russia's historical dominance of the region. What's more, the Soviet actions he witnessed were not successful in providing the Soviet Union with any benefits. They were simply destructive.

His opinions were shaped after witnessing some of the more outrageous (and foolish) actions of the Soviet occupiers, such as the seizing of washroom fixtures from locations throughout the region where Peter was employed. Porcelain sinks and toilets were rare in the Soviet Union, and the sight of them in railway stations and other public facilities was too much for the Russians to resist. They seized and dismantled sinks, mirrors, and porcelain toilet bowls in the railway depots and elsewhere, with plans to ship them to the Soviet Union. Unfortunately, the Soviets either did not know how to prepare the porcelain and glass for the long, rough journey or simply didn't care.

"I watched how the porcelain sinks and toilet bowls were loaded on the train to be sent to Soviet Russia," Peter Jacyk wrote many years later. "I imagined that at the first stop of the train, when the buffers of one car hit the buffers of the next, all the porcelain sinks and bowls would come crashing down and nothing would be left of them except for bits and pieces." He mused about the waste of energy and resources to achieve only destruction: "One must build the locomotive [and] the freight car, burn lots of coal and use water to move the train… then one has to ruin another country and waste a lot of human labour, money and energy to deliver to Russia a trainload of ceramic scrap!" The Russians' actions were worse than theft, Peter suggested. "This is robbing and destroying others without reaping any benefit to oneself or anyone else."

He had other opportunities to watch the Soviets and their thieving policies at work. The Soviets appeared to base their actions on the assumption that every country they entered represented a treasury to be cleaned out. In this case, the "treasury" consisted of sinks and toilets, perhaps, but they were treated like gold and jewels nevertheless. "The attitude of the Soviet Russian authorities was destructive and imperialistic," Peter noted in his unfinished memoirs. "Based on limited abilities and poor world views, it was arrogant and superior for no other reason [except] that it was Russian."

Soviet management personnel, brought in from the east, assumed control of the railway system and employees. While young employees like Peter wore tattered work clothes, Soviet Russian managers dressed in special dark uniforms marking them as a privileged caste. "If there were any lineups for food or other goods, the Soviet railway employees in their dark uniforms never waited in line," he recalled. "They pushed themselves right into the store and were served first because they were part of the ruling elite."

Meanwhile, he noted with open disgust, Soviet Russian professors in local universities delivered lectures extolling the constitution and praising the Soviet Union's respect for human rights and equality, even while the claims were contradicted by the reality of the students' everyday life. "From that time on," he declared, "I have viewed Russians as representatives of a destructive and parasitic political culture that, instead of sowing the fields and harvesting them, wanted to appropriate the fruits of labour of other people, or simply destroy other peoples' goods so that there would be a shortage, as in Russia."

The Soviets' attitude toward its neighbours, Peter pointed out, was not new, nor was it a by-product of Communism. "Their attitude was to organize power and hold on to it," he wrote, "expand [their borders by] taking over neighbouring countries who were smaller but had better standards of living, rob them, [and] enslave their people as a non-compensated workforce."

It is a sobering assessment. In Jacyk's view, the horrors and disasters suffered by the Russian nation and its people through much of the twentieth century should not be directly attributed to Communism exclusively but must be seen as the manifestation of the Russian tradition. The imposition of Communism, he believed, simply changed the methods of terror and fear employed by Russians. "Russian communists would occupy other countries," he continued, "create laws under which they branded leaders and managers of those countries as bourgeois nationalists, and condemn them to a slow death through inhuman conditions in jails and in Siberian gulags."

The mention of bourgeois nationalists is telling. Being labelled in that manner was the accusation under which many Ukrainians were executed or deported to the gulag in the 1930s through the 1950s. The strange contradiction that Ukrainians would be punished for respecting their native language and culture and Russians would be praised for the same treatment of their own language and culture offended Peter Jacyk's sense of justice.

He had even more reason to despise the Soviets. Knowing the fate and suffering of the sector of society that he had been born into generated an intense revulsion toward Communist leaders throughout the Soviet Union. "The generals and commissars exploited the lower masses," he wrote, "with complete disregard for any human rights. By enjoying all the privileges of a higher class of superpower, they degenerated to the point where they were unable to realize that brute force, guns, tanks and Siberian gulags do not motivate people to think, work, create and produce."

Peter Jacyk, who built a lifelong reputation for fairness and generosity, firmly believed in his scathing opinion of Soviet Russia and of Communism and did not waver in his opinion. "After sixty years," he wrote toward the end of his life, "I am still convinced that my conclusion was correct."

Events justified his view of the Soviet Union as a destructive force. Within months of the arrival of its soldiers and commissars in west Ukraine, Soviet Russia dropped the smiling face it had worn on earlier occasions and replaced it with a dark and inhumane policy toward any Ukrainian who dared to express the slightest support for Ukrainian independence or even a distinctive Ukrainian identity. Once identified as "enemies of the people" by whatever source the Russians chose to believe, thousands of Ukrainians were arrested, often in the dead of night, and packed into railway cars destined for Siberia or Kazakhstan, where they faced years of hard labour under appalling conditions. No warning was issued, no trials were held —indeed, no formal accusations were provided. In many cases, entire families were secretly dispatched to the labour camps. Many did not survive.

The first wave of arrests and deportations, launched soon after the arrival of the Soviets in 1939, targeted former leaders and members of the local elite. Concern may have been raised about their fate by other citizens, but based on the privileges enjoyed by the upper class, it engendered little sympathy. In the spring of 1940, however, a second wave spread the policy more widely. No longer could any Ukrainian group shrug its collective shoulders at the seizure and deportations. "From then on," one survivor put it, "no one, literally no one, was sure whether his turn would not come the next night."[4]

Germany's breaking of the non-aggression pact with its June 1941 invasion of the Soviet Union unleashed a third merciless wave of deportations and murders. The Soviets panicked, knowing they had no way of stopping the forces of Nazi Germany, thanks to Stalin's incompetence in recognizing and preparing for Hitler's deceit. Their only response was to destroy as much property and as many lives as possible before fleeing.

No one will know for certain how many Ukrainians and other nationals perished at the hands of the Soviets during their two-year occupation of the country under the terms of the Molotov-Ribbentrop pact. In a letter to the Vatican dated November 1941, a Ukrainian Catholic priest estimated that 400,000 residents of Galicia had been deported or executed during the period. In London, representatives of the Polish government in exile suggested that total population losses among Poles, Ukrainians, Belarusians, Jews, Lithuanians, Germans, Czechs, Armenians, and others in Soviet-occupied areas of Poland numbered as many as 1.5 million victims.

During the two-year life of the Nazi-Soviet non-aggression pact, the NKVD arrested thousands of Ukrainians and others on suspicion of "anti-Soviet activities." Most NKVD prisoners were suspected of engaging in political activity considered threatening to the ruling Soviets, though such activity may have been as "menacing" as organizing soup kitchens for the poor and homeless. Many remained in Ukraine, housed in local jails and prisons, where they were interrogated and tortured.

---

4. *The Black Deeds of the Kremlin, A White Book*, Volume 1 (*Book of Testimonies*) (Toronto: Ukrainian Association of Victims of Russian Communist Terror, 1953), 241.

It's at least a passing criticism of the NKVD's efficiency to note that no one in the secret organization, whose primary goal supposedly was to protect the Soviet Union and its territories from threats to their security, appears to have had any forewarning of Germany's unilateral rejection of the pact and the launch of its invasion plans. When in the early summer of 1941 the first Panzer units crossed the long north-south line established by the non-aggression pact, NKVD operatives were as surprised as anyone—perhaps more so.

Lacking both the time and the facilities to evacuate their prisoners to another location where, supposedly, they might provide badly needed intelligence about German moves, the NKVD simply shot them on their way out the door. Generations after the fact, details of the events remain gruesome. In the prison at Sambir, the NKVD crammed two large cells with women, locked the doors, and dynamited the inhabitants. In at least one prison, the rooms were stacked to the ceiling with putrefying corpses, a sight so horrifying that the townspeople chose to fill the space with cement instead of attempting a decent burial, let alone conduct identification. Others located torture chambers containing body parts—eyes, ears, noses, tongues—removed as part of the NKVD "interrogation" process. Again, the actual number of victims is not known, nor is it likely to be. Reliable estimates suggest that ten thousand perished, many through horrifying means, in Galicia alone.[5]

The facts remain troubling seventy years later, but they are essential in understanding, to a degree, the attitude of Ukrainians to the arrival of the German forces in the summer of 1941. After two years of Soviet brutality and Communist incompetence, any change offered hope for those not fully aware of Nazi race theories.

5. Yuri Boshyk, ed., *Ukraine during World War II: History and Its Aftermath* (Edmonton: Canadian Institute of Ukrainian Studies Press, 1986), 12.

THE NAZI GERMAN army of summer 1941 was the dominant fighting force in the world. Nothing in that year could hope to challenge it successfully. Its aircraft and ground weapons remained superior to any technology available to the Allies, and its soldiers had been battle-hardened by victories over the previous two years of fighting.

The Soviet Union, meanwhile, was hopelessly weak in armament, training, and leadership. Stalin's purges of the 1930s had eliminated many of the army's best officers, and Stalin himself proved an incompetent commander. His orders issued from the Kremlin, to be followed without the slightest modification by battlefield leaders, proved slapdash and inept, leading to the encirclement and capture of entire army divisions by the Germans. Although it was clear that nothing could prevent the juggernaut of German forces from advancing through the Soviet lines toward Moscow, a more effective defence and withdrawal would have saved the lives of perhaps millions of Soviet soldiers lost on the battlefield or in the appalling conditions of German POW camps.[6]

For Peter Jacyk and others in western Ukraine, the easy success of the invading Germans initially proved a blessing, if only because they displaced the hated Soviets. The front moved quickly through western Ukraine, limiting the initial devastation. In time, Galicia and all of Ukraine suffered as much destruction as any region in Europe. By every measure imaginable—physical, economic, social, and human—Ukraine was devastated. Through capture and deportation, or by their own initiative, Ukrainian political leaders and much of the intelligentsia had vanished, leaving a vacuum of power and managing skills. Beyond the cities, the Soviets hastily

---

6. The fate of POWs bothered Stalin not at all. A Soviet soldier who permitted himself to be captured, in the Soviet dictator's mind, was a traitor and deserved any fate he suffered.

shipped thousands of cattle out of Ukraine, leaving the collective farms even more bereft, and the behaviour of the Soviets in the face of the advancing German army deepened the already bitter feelings of Ukrainians toward the Communists.

After discovering his cousin Adam Kamianka at the abandoned prison, and Adam's death three days later, Peter had little choice but to return to his village. With skirmishes continuing to rage around him and many bridges destroyed, the journey took him two days. Shortly after he arrived home, the German army entered the village on motorcycles. "They brought their secret service with them to intimidate the people," he recalled, "but they also brought their civil administration to establish order and peace behind the front lines."

Initially, Peter Jacyk and his family and neighbours responded to the German forces with some disorientation. On the one hand, they had no reason to celebrate the arrival of the Nazi fighters, based on their actions in other countries and the awareness that Germany's presence and actions were designed primarily for the benefit of Germans, not Ukrainians. On the other hand, Germans, in sharp contrast with the brutish Soviets, were considered to be cultured and more interested in the creation of things rather than their devastation. Where the Soviets had ripped out toilets and sinks from the railway stations and other public facilities, the Germans restored them, adding fresh paint to walls and fences and even planting flowers in parks and boulevards. Peter Jacyk and other Ukrainians could never conceive of Germans acting so foolish as the Soviets. Germans might in fact "liberate" other peoples' belongings, but they would be expected to treat them as objects of value. And even though no one expected Nazi Germany to install true democratic changes, the Germans were considered, at the outset at least, more competent in their decision-making and administrative dealings. Soon residents of Galicia and others would discover how illusory that image was.

The initial displacement of the Soviet Russians led some Ukrainians to greet the arrival of the Germans with broad smiles and tossed flower petals while dressed in traditional Ukrainian national costume. It remains uncertain whether this occurred as a spontaneous response to the withdrawal of the hated Russians or was a widely dispersed tool created by Joseph Goebbels's Nazi propaganda machine. More than seventy years later, the images were used to promote the concept of Ukrainians embracing Nazi Germany's goals and values, a severe distortion of the truth. "The German forces also expropriated Ukrainian property," Peter Jacyk wrote, adding: "At the same time, they introduced many positive, constructive changes in administration and industry."

All of this perceived welcoming of German forces in Ukraine must be viewed against the background of the horror of the Holocaust. The grisly legacy of Auschwitz, Treblinka, and other death camps and the executions of Jews throughout Ukraine, as well as the barbaric Nazi race policies toward Slavs, may make any less than reproachful comment curious and confusing. It should be remembered, however, that any admirable traits described by Jacyk and others belonged to German society and not Nazi policies. Many positive qualities had been attributed to Germans in pre-Nazi years and remain appropriate today; think of the auto manufacturers who boast of "German engineering" and the aura built around German consumer marques such as Daimler-Benz, BMW, and Bosch. It is not the engineering and administrative aspects of Germany that are questioned and condemned; it is the demonic and ghastly Nazi actions and philosophy that continue to generate moral outrage.

Images of Ukrainians welcoming the Germans in place of the Soviets may resurrect an oft-held view that Ukrainians were involved in at least facilitating the Holocaust, a claim that Ukrainians vehemently deny. Yes, Nazi collaborators existed during the occupation years, they agree, but to no greater extent than those found in countries such as Norway, France, the Netherlands, and elsewhere during the same period. Similar evidence exists to confirm that individual Ukrainians risked—and gave—their lives to harbour Jews during the Nazi occupation.

Ukraine had already suffered enormously during the Holodomor as a direct result of Stalin's policies. The precise number of deaths in Ukraine between 1930 and 1945 as a result of actions by the Soviet Union and Nazi Germany will never be known; we must rely on fact-based estimates. Among the most recent are those submitted by historian Timothy Snyder, who proposed that 3.5 million Ukrainians perished as a result of Stalin's actions between 1933 and 1938, another 3.5 million succumbed during the Nazi occupation from 1941 to 1944, and perhaps another 3 million inhabitants of Ukraine died as a direct consequence of military actions.[7]

Comparing the number of Ukrainian deaths from Stalinist and Nazi policies with those of Jews as a result of the Holocaust is an odious practice, a macabre contest proving nothing except the degree of man's inhumanity. Both groups endured tragedy and terror on a scale that we can only hope is never seen again.

The only comparison that appears reasonable in this context is that of Nazi versus Soviet occupation of Ukraine. When your life is constantly threatened by both sides, any subtle difference in attitude or policy grows magnified, and this appears to have been the case with Peter Jacyk and his colleagues.

Frank Sysyn suggests that the view of occupying Germans depended to some extent on the community's response to their presence. "In Western Ukrainian rural areas, you were expected to give a certain amount of food to the Germans," he explains.

7. Timothy Snyder, *Bloodlands: Europe Between Hitler and Stalin* (New York: Basic Books, 2010), 404.

"Initially if you delivered to the Germans they left you alone, and as a result many communities began administering themselves. In effect, you bought them off." If a town or village failed to provide food and other assistance, the German troops made things very uncomfortable and even lethal for the Ukrainian residents.

In the vortex of occupation and war, Peter decided on a major career change. "I did not want to go back to the oily and dirty overalls of the railway job," he wrote. "So I entered a one-year dairy school training program to work with milk and butter in a clean, healthy environment." It was an insightful decision. Dairy cooperatives had been one of the most successful forms of Ukrainian commercial activity before the Soviet occupation.

With his farming background and the managerial talents he had demonstrated during his short tenure on the railway, Peter Jacyk quickly grasped the program studies. He also absorbed wisdom along the way that would guide him in his behaviour as an adult, including an observation by one of his lecturers, a man named Khronoviat. "Remember that you are going to work with farmers and will inspect dairy products produced mostly by women," Khronoviat instructed the students. "Be respectful to them and never forget that, if you do so, somebody will do the same for your mother."

AS HE HAD with his railway studies, Peter impressed the school administrators with his abilities and, upon graduation, was appointed an inspector of dairies covering the districts of Berezhany, Rohatyn, and Pidhaitsi. The districts included 7 regional dairies and 257 dairy product collection centres.

Amid all the upheaval, tension, and misery during this period, it's revealing that he fell easily into filling a supervisory position at such a young age and that he learned an early lesson in humility recalled many years later. "People sensed that I thought I was knowledgeable," he wrote in his memoirs, "and they behaved accordingly," meaning they deferred to his supposedly greater knowledge. This might have stroked his ego, but it hindered his effectiveness as a manager. Cooperation was low, and he found it difficult to secure all the information he needed from various groups. "It took me about six months," he said, "to realize that these people might not have my theoretical knowledge, but they had practical experience in how to do their job on a day to day basis. Once I realized my problem, my work with people became much easier."

Carrying out his job responsibilities involved a good deal of travel through the area, and German authorities provided the necessary documentation to enable him to move freely from place to place, an unusual privilege. It may also have provided cover for Jacyk to take part in underground activities directed, it is assumed, at furthering Ukrainian national interests. The travel papers, he wrote, "allowed me to be an inspector of dairies in daytime and an active member of the Ukrainian underground movement at night." He did not provide details of his work on behalf of the Ukrainian underground movement. One explanation suggests he may have served as a courier of intelligence data.

Whatever role he performed, he risked suffering the wrath of the Germans, who, with the passage of time and the declining state of their assault on the Soviet Union, changed from planters of flowers and painters of fences into a brutal occupying force. Their early actions appeared benign, even helpful. Where the Soviets had rounded up perceived dissidents and shipped them east and north to Siberia as gulag prisoners, in late 1941 Germans sought Ukrainian volunteers to travel to Germany, where they would find work, shelter, and plenty of food. Some Ukrainians accepted the offer on their own. Others were assigned the role under direct orders from the Nazis. Community leaders were ordered to select citizens to be dispatched as immigrant workers, whether they agreed or not. As time went on, the means of recruiting workers became more brutal.

Whether as volunteers or "draftees," those who made the journey discovered upon their arrival in Germany that they were to be treated like third-class citizens, forced to wear humiliating badges identifying them as *Ostarbeiter* (Workers from the East), fed subsistence rations, and subjected to harsh labour discipline.[8] When word of their treatment reached Ukraine, potential volunteers quickly withdrew their offers to assist the Germans. In response, the Nazi occupiers began arbitrarily herding Ukrainians into churches, cinemas, and other public places for transportation to Germany, and in the summer of 1942, they decreed that all Ukrainians between the ages of eighteen and thirty were required to provide a mandatory two years of labour service in Germany.

The Nazis' attitude toward Ukraine extended broadly and deeply. Historians, most recently Timothy Snyder, point out that Hitler and the Nazi regime valued Ukraine as a dependable source of agricultural products every bit as much as Stalin. To Germany, Ukraine was clearly "the most valuable part of the Soviet Union," and occupying the country would free Germany from economic worries.[9] The prize could only be considered won, however, not by merely occupying Ukraine but by eliminating all but the minimum number of peasants it might take to effectively work the land and produce crops for shipment to Germany.

By 1942, Ukrainian schools in the Reichskommissariat, or civilian occupation regime, above the fourth grade were ordered closed, a move that Hitler, on a visit to Ukraine that year, revealed

---

8. Paul Robert Magocsi, *A History of Ukraine: The Land and Its Peoples* (Toronto: University of Toronto Press, 2010), 679.

9. Snyder, 161.

was taken because Ukrainians "should be given only the crudest kind of education necessary between them and their German masters."[10] Textbooks were not to be printed, most cultural organizations were ordered disbanded, the publishing of all books and magazines was prohibited, and by mid-1942 barely a third of the newspapers available for Ukrainians to read the previous year were still available. Even these were heavily censored, their news reports skewed to praise German achievements.

The Germans' behaviour in Ukraine was more brutal and inhumane than in western Europe. Once they had consolidated their power in the region, every edict from Hitler and his Nazi regime was carried out with dispatch, and the early image of efficient administrators and gardeners was exchanged for marching jackboots and bayonets. Any difference in the treatment of the inhabitants of Ukraine was based on identity. Where the Soviets had deported selected Ukrainian intelligentsia to gulags, the Nazis rounded up Jews and Gypsies and shot them on the spot or, as in the case of Babyn Yar, herded them into massive killing grounds and executed them by the thousands.

Nazi German leaders expressed primary revulsion for Jews and Gypsies, but Slavs fared little better. The actions of the German occupiers ranged from the petty to the outrageous, such as designating latrines, washrooms, and even retail stores "For Germans Only." Other actions exposed the basic inhumanity and astonishing racism of individual Nazi leaders. Goering suggested that "the best thing would be to kill all men in Ukraine over fifteen years of age," and Himmler preached, "The entire Ukrainian intelligentsia must be destroyed—do away with it, and the leaderless mass would become obedient." And German Reichskommissar Erich

---

10 Ihor Kamenetsky, *Secret Nazi Plans for Eastern Europe: A Study of Lebensraum Policies* (New York: Bookman Associates, 1961), 106–07.

Koch famously boasted, "If I find a Ukrainian who is worthy of sitting at the same table with me, I must have him shot."[11]

The result of these actions was to provoke a small but vibrant underground movement among younger Ukrainians, a form of "counter-chauvinism," as one observer put it. The movement proved strongest and most resilient in western Ukraine, where, in 1942, the Ukrainian Insurgent Army (Ukrainska povstanska armiia, or UPA) reportedly could boast fifteen thousand armed combatants within an area of fifty thousand square kilometres housing 2 million people. By 1944, the UPA claimed forty thousand participants.[12]

Was this the underground group that Peter Jacyk supported during his travels as a dairy inspector? It is certain that the UPA or a spinoff of some kind would attract his support and efforts, clearly at risk of his life, rather than the Soviet-backed partisan forces elsewhere in the country. The latter group, estimated by some sources at 250,000 members, claimed that 60 percent of those members were Ukrainian.

Yet the Nazi approach to Galicia in the early stages of the German occupation differed to a measurable degree compared with the rest of Ukraine. "German rule became increasingly harsh toward Ukrainians in Galicia, and many were arrested and sent to concentration camps while others were killed on the spot. Many others were sent as forced labourers to Germany," notes Sysyn.

---

11. Koch, who declared himself a faithful Christian, fled Germany at the end of the war but was captured in 1949 and tried for war crimes that included responsibility for the deaths of 400,000 Poles. He was never tried for the deaths of untold numbers of Ukrainians. Koch was sentenced to be executed, but the sentence was commuted to life imprisonment. Koch died, still a prisoner, in 1986, at ninety years of age. It is revealing to compare his treatment with that of John Demjanjuk (see Chapter 13).

12. Bohdan Krawchenko, *Ukraine during World War II: History and Its Aftermath*, edited by Yury Boshyk (Edmonton: Canadian Institute of Ukrainian Studies Press, 1986), 29.

"But the absolute reign of terror, massive executions and starvation that occurred in the Reichskommissariat Ukraine did not occur in Galicia among the Ukrainian population." In fact, during the early stages of Nazi occupation, many Ukrainians in Galicia hoped that the Germans would permit Galicia to function as a satellite state similar to the arrangement with Slovakia. When this failed to happen, the Ukrainian nationalist movement swung toward a decidedly anti-German posture.

Others continued to view the Soviets as an even worse enemy than the Germans. Which side to choose? Ultimately, the choice became one of simple survival.

DESPITE THE APPALLING actions of the occupying German forces, Peter Jacyk managed to avoid much of their impact. He also made a choice between the two forces. When word of the Soviets' success in the defence of Stalingrad (at the cost of as many as 2 million lives) was soon followed by news of a German retreat in the face of advancing Soviet forces, he approached a local office of the German occupation forces and volunteered to serve in a Ukrainian division to turn back the Soviet army.

The existence of the division illustrates the complex relationship that developed in Ukraine under the German occupation. In March 1943, around the time the defenders of Stalingrad achieved victory, the governor of Galicia succeeded in persuading Heinrich Himmler, head of the SS, to create a separate Ukrainian division whose role would be to assist in repelling the now advancing Soviets.

Himmler agreed, although he expressly forbade the division to be identified as a Ukrainian force. Ultimately, it was designated 14. *Freiwilligen-Grenadier-Division der SS (galizische Nr. 1)*, or 14th Volunteer Grenadier Division of the SS, 1st Galician. By mid-1943, 82,000 men had volunteered, 90 percent of them between the ages of eighteen and thirty; these were pared down to 13,000 trained and equipped soldiers.[13]

Why would so many young Ukrainians choose to join a German force? The reasons were perhaps more closely related to achieving Ukrainian identity than to any relatively short-term goal. One explanation is the possibility of exacting at least a minimum level of leverage by appearing proactive. Most believed that the occupying German forces would forcefully recruit combatants if necessary; by volunteering to participate in the unit's formation, the Ukrainians could influence its character and defend the interests of the soldiers. In addition, the Germans would provide key training and equipment opportunities, producing a battle force that, should Germany collapse, could form the nucleus of a national army capable of defending Ukraine's interests and supporting moves toward sovereignty.

In view of other aspects of behaviour by the Nazi Germans, the Ukrainians actually managed to acquire some control. They demanded, and apparently won, a guarantee that the new force would be used against Soviet forces only, the assignment of Ukrainian and German chaplains, and the creation of a Military Executive Committee to oversee recruitment and represent the interests of the soldiers. Not every request was successful. The division was not incorporated into the Wehrmacht, all senior officer posts were assigned to Germans, and the Galicia/Halychyna lion, not the trident of Ukraine, was chosen as the force's insignia.[14]

---

13. Myroslav Yurkevich, "Galicia/Halychyna Ukrainians in German Military Formations and in the German Administration," *Ukraine during World War II: History and Its Aftermath*, edited by Yury Boshyk (Edmonton: Canadian Institute of Ukrainian Studies Press, 1986), 76–77.

14. According to Myroslav Yurkevich in *Ukraine during World War II*, the initial fate of the division was tragic. In July 1944, it was dispatched to reinforce the 13th Panzer Division near Brody, in western Ukraine. Historical documents indicate that the

The German officer who greeted Peter Jacyk when the young Ukrainian offered to volunteer was, according to Jacyk's description, about forty years old and apparently possessed an inclination to shrug off the German War Office's directives. The officer may have represented a growing proportion of Germans who were disenchanted with Hitler's mad schemes, or perhaps he felt a pang of protective instinct for the intense young dairy inspector. Whatever his motive, the officer's response to Peter's request was to simply smile and shake his head. "Your plans are courteous," he said, "but they are not wise. Nobody is going to stop the Russians," and he suggested that Peter return to his work as a dairy inspector.

Over the next several months, the German officer's judgement proved well founded. By the summer of 1944, the Soviets were clearly poised for victory, whereas the Germans, their sense of military supremacy vanished, prepared to pull out of Ukraine for their return to Germany, where they would defend the homeland.

Whatever Peter Jacyk's plans had been to this point, news of the Soviets' return crystallized his decision. He could not remain in Galicia/Halychyna under Soviet rule. The decision was not based on his deep-seated disgust with Soviet Russian values and actions, though this clearly played a role. The dominant influence was simple and predictable: the Soviets would likely execute him.

It can be difficult for Westerners to appreciate the impact of first Soviet, then German, and once again Soviet domination and occupation of Ukraine. As Timothy Snyder explains: "The departure of one foreign ruler meant nothing more than the arrival of

---

Galicia/Halychyna volunteers were directed to the heaviest areas of fighting "to close gaps." In reality, they became cannon fodder; of eleven thousand soldiers engaged in the battle, only three thousand managed to escape death, wounding, or capture. A year later, the replenished division was sent to Slovakia, where most of its soldiers managed to survive and be captured by Allied forces, who refused to turn them over to the Soviets.

another. When foreign troops left, people had to deal with the consequences of their own previous commitments under one occupier when the next one came; or make choices under one occupation when anticipating another." [15]

The consequences of decisions made under one occupier were not as trivial as cheering for a side that ultimately loses a sporting match; they could lead to immediate summary execution, regardless of the original motivation, need, or even command, under threat of death, to cooperate with the previous occupier. With each encroachment by the Soviets, Peter Jacyk realized the risks he faced. His travel documents, permitting him to move about the region unhindered while inspecting dairy operations, had been granted by the Germans. As unmilitary and non-subversive as his actions had been, they might well have identified Peter Jacyk to the invading Soviets as a collaborator, and in the insanity of war that gripped both sides, he would be shot.

Among his choices at this point was to join the resistance, and he headed for a group operating in the Carpathian Mountains. Arriving at the partisan camp, he was dismayed at the sight of what he believed to be amateurs dedicated to fighting a professional army. It had been four years since his experience fighting the KOP, and although the Carpathian fighters were undoubtedly better organized, Peter perceived that the ultimate destiny for most was likely to die for their cause. Dying for one's cause may be heroic, he believed, but it was not a notable achievement in itself. "I did not know what awaited me across the border," he explained, "but I was convinced that if I were able to survive I would do something for Ukraine. So I took my knapsack and headed into the unknown." [16]

In later writings, Peter Jacyk noted that he fled west out of Ukraine and into Austria and Germany because "I did not want

15. Snyder, 190.

16. Speech at the National Defence Academy of Ukraine, Kyiv, June 2000.

to help the destructive force [i.e., Russian Communists] in the future, but left my native country with a hope that I would find a productive force in the West." He could, he added on another occasion, have chosen to join resistance and guerrilla groups, "living and fighting in the forests," as he put it, but for what purpose? Later, he added: "My philosophy was that, if I survived, I would do something for an ideal [that] I could only die for here, in Ukraine." The ideal he had in mind was to search for truth and excellence, an opportunity that would have been impossible under the rule of either Nazi Germany or Soviet Russia.

Whatever his motive, his fate had he remained in Ukraine was as clear to him in 1944 as it is to us today: he almost certainly would not have seen his twenty-third birthday.

4

Escape to Canada

*The state is an instrument in the hands
of the ruling class, used to break the
resistance of the adversaries of that class.*

JOSEPH STALIN

UNLIKE OTHER retreating armies, German forces departing
Ukraine generally rejected a scorched-earth policy or even
a rear-guard action to slow the advancing Soviet Russian army, a
choice that made it relatively easy for Peter Jacyk to follow them as
far as Austria.

Even so, it was a daunting journey. Setting out from Stryi,
he faced almost one thousand kilometres of travel to Austria.
Although we do not know his means of travel, he enjoyed a good
deal of company over at least the first hundred kilometres or so.
One source estimates that in 1944, 120,000 Ukrainians fled out of
Galicia, behind the Germans and ahead of the advancing Soviets.
Of these, perhaps 30,000 crossed into Slovakia and 90,000 into
Hungary.[1] Many paused after crossing the border, anticipating that

---

1. Orest Subtelny, "Ukrainian Political Refugees: An Historical Overview," *The Refu-*
   gee Experience: Ukrainian Displaced Persons after World War II, edited by Yury Boshyk,
   Wsevolod Isajiw, and Roman Senkus (Edmonton: Canadian Institute of Ukrainian
   Studies Press, 1992), 13.

the Germans might counterattack or that some other nation would displace Soviet Russia from Ukraine, enabling them to return.

Most refugees walked or rode aboard horse-drawn wagons. Those who worked for the Germans had access to rail transportation, though some were fortunate enough to drive their own vehicles, assuming they could obtain gasoline. Much depended on timing; many abandoned the region following the disastrous battle at Brody, when the 14th Ukrainian Grenadier Division was essentially annihilated.

The journey, assuming a good deal of it was made on foot, may have been even more difficult for Peter Jacyk. In his unpublished memoirs he makes reference to his damaged lungs. No explanation for the cause of this damage is provided. Was it the result of a childhood disease, a farming accident, or the industrial atmosphere in the railroad facility?

By whatever means, he reached a transit camp in Strasshof, Austria, where he stayed with other refugees for a few days. Remaining in the crowded camp was out of the question for an ambitious young man, so after resting for a week, he set off for Vienna in search of work. At a Viennese employment office, his qualifications won him work in the nearby town of St. Pölten, about seventy kilometres farther west, where the retired Austrian army officer who hired him owned three dairies. The officer set one condition: the job opening would not be available for two weeks, so during that time Peter Jacyk was told to remain in Vienna while accommodations near the dairies were arranged.

Even in the horrors of war, humanity can shine through, and it did for Peter Jacyk at this point. An employee of the dairy, overhearing his boss's instructions to Peter, expressed concern for the new worker's safety. "This man has no place to stay in Vienna," the employee pointed out, "and Vienna is being bombed every night. I live near the dairy with my family, so I will find room for him where he can sleep for the next two weeks. At the same time, we'll have a much-needed employee." Many years later, Peter recalled the Austrian's actions with gratitude. "I was pleasantly impressed by the man's unselfish act," he wrote. "[It] showed… his compassion and understanding of my situation, and also his interest for the needs of the business that employed him."

The Austrian's generosity was balanced by another aspect of human nature when Peter, anxious to leave the dangers of Vienna and travel to his new home in St. Pölten, returned to the refugee camp in Strasshof to claim his belongings, only to discover they were gone. All of his possessions were in the knapsack, stolen by the family he had entrusted it to, and he arrived in St. Pölten owning literally the clothes on his back—and nothing more.

Still, he may have thanked his good fortune. St. Pölten was a comfortable town that remained relatively unscathed by the war, thanks to an absence of military and industrial targets. He had work that he enjoyed and knew how to perform well, he stayed in comfortable quarters first with the employee's family and later in a building adjacent to the dairy, and he apparently earned a good salary—within less than a year he had accumulated substantial savings.

He shared his room with four other workers—two Ukrainians and two Russians. "All of us were in the same boat," he recalled, "having to work as labourers in a foreign land." He had little to say about the Ukrainians, beyond their hometowns and their support for Ukrainian sovereignty, but he made several observations about the two Russians, based as much on their ethics as on their nationality.

Both were former professors. This quality on its own probably intrigued him as much as any; Peter was conscious of his lack of formal education, and residing with two former professors likely encouraged him to listen closely to their words and assess their wisdom. It also inspired what appears to have been a lively exchange of ideas and opinions. One of the Russians, named Petka, had been a professor before the overthrow of the tsar. Petka was a devoted Orthodox Christian, which generated verbal fireworks with Mishka, the other Russian and a militant atheist. "There was no end to discussions and sharing stories during our free time," Peter wrote.

They often were joined by others, young men and women perhaps attracted as much by the anticipation of sharing the dairy's milk and cheese as by the opportunity to debate. Whatever the appeal, the group apparently enjoyed intellectual discussions and social gatherings. Otherwise, the months in Austria were surely less than idyllic. War continued to rage around them, shortages of food and supplies offered a daily challenge, and Peter was far from his homeland with no assurance that he would ever return.

It all came to an end in April 1945, with the last paroxysms of the Third Reich and looming victory by the Allies, a good news/ bad news situation: the imminent fall of the Nazis was good news; the rumour that the Soviets were approaching Austria and preparing to occupy it was not. In May 1945, Peter gathered his possessions into a knapsack, along with his savings from his work at the dairy, and headed for Bavaria, where the U.S. was establishing control.

This time he was accompanied by Mykola, a friend from Peter's village who had studied with Peter at the dairy school, worked with him in Stryi, and also found a job at an Austrian dairy after fleeing western Ukraine. The railway tracks out of St. Pölten had been damaged, forcing the two young men to follow the useless tracks to another railway depot, where they hoped to board a train to Munich.

The next morning, as they were crossing some fields, a U.S. warplane suddenly banked, turned, and flew toward them, its guns blazing. Diving into a nearby ditch, Peter and Mykola managed to escape the strafing attack, and they lay cowering until the sound of the plane faded away. When Peter finally climbed out of the ditch, he began to laugh loudly and uncontrollably, causing Mykola to explode in anger. "What are you laughing at, you fool?" Mykola shouted. "We could have been killed!"

Peter couldn't explain his reaction at the time, nor could he many years later when he recalled it. It was probably a common nervous response to escaping danger, though Peter also speculated that he could have been scornful about the American pilot's poor aim and his waste of bullets. Whatever the cause of his laughter, it marked the last time the war would threaten his life. From this point forward, he would face other risks and challenges, but none as deadly as those encountered from the barrel of a gun.

They finally boarded a train bound for Munich but travelled only as far as Regensburg, where the bridges over the Danube had been destroyed by Allied bombing. Munich may have offered more work opportunities, but Regensburg, a medieval town whose historic buildings had managed, for the most part, to escape serious damage, appealed to Peter, and he decided to stay there for a period. In fact, he remained in Regensburg for more than three years.

Those years marked a major change in many of his perceptions of people and of life. How could they not? He was a young man, uprooted from life in a farm village, disconnected from family, dealing with the aftermath of war in a foreign culture. Nothing he had experienced as a child remained, and the degree of change he underwent may have surprised Peter Jacyk, especially when he looked back on it from the perspective of his adult years.

His opinion of Germans changed—but in a somewhat surprising manner. Europe, still staggering from the impact of the war with Germany, now understood the full extent of the policies carried out by the Nazis, and with every liberation of concentration camp survivors, the disgust with Nazi Germany's actions grew. It was easy to view all Germans as at least partially responsible for the destruction of Europe and the loss of millions of innocent lives.

Peter Jacyk was as familiar with this view as anyone, but he was also aware that the Nazis were not the only threat to peace and harmony. He had first-hand experience with the excesses of the Poles and Soviet Russians when it came to dealing with other nations. This did not absolve Germany of its guilt and responsibility—far from it. It suggested, however, that all factions are capable of performing both good and evil acts. It also led him to make a clear and critical distinction between two cultures he identified in his unpublished manuscript simply as "Eastern" and "Western."

With no clearer description than this, it's impossible to precisely identify and distinguish them. It is apparent, however, reflecting his open and oft-expressed animosity to pre- and post-Communist Russia, that he identifies Eastern culture as that dominated (at the time) by the Soviets, and Western culture as that influenced by Britain, France, Germany, and the rest of western Europe, along with the U.S. and Canada.

"The Eastern culture was never democratic in its thinking," he wrote of his refugee years, almost fifty years later. "Historically it was a dictatorship—order from the top down, and passive opposition from the bottom up." He would, of course, have to discount the contemporary German experience at the time, twelve years after the ascent of the Nazis in Germany, which he associated with the West. Still, the Nazis had seized power through ruthless manipulation of a basically democratic system, which lent some substantiation to his argument.

This recognition, while he was still in Europe as the war wound down around him and with no certainty of his future, inevitably influenced his attitude toward Ukraine, which he clearly categorized under Eastern culture. By embracing so-called Western culture at this early stage of his life, he surely realized the dichotomy he faced; his choice could not help but appear as a repudiation of some aspect of his beloved homeland.[2]

Earlier, he had recognized that the Germans who occupied Ukraine demonstrated administrative and organizational skills that the Russians appeared to lack. In Regensburg, thanks to the influence of a family with whom he boarded for six months (he paid for his accommodation with his savings from the Austrian dairy), he learned something else about Germans. "My landlord was a postal worker," Peter explained. "His wife was referred to as Mutti.[3] They had a 21-year-old daughter who was married, and a son Rudi. Every day, Mutti took her bicycle and visited local farmers to purchase things they could no longer find in the stores. Every evening, the family sat down to supper, and they never forgot about me. Soon we grew close, and I felt like a member of their family."

Peter's recollection of the family's acceptance of him—"they never forgot about me"—has a poignancy about it, considering the circumstances. In his memoirs, he never revealed the surname of his German hosts, but he is forthright in crediting them for helping establish many of the values he supported throughout his life.

One touching lesson was delivered by Mutti. "One day I asked Mutti why, when cleaning her family's shoes, she also cleaned my shoes, the dirtiest of all," Peter wrote. "With tears in her eyes she replied, 'You know, Peter, my son-in-law is a prisoner of war in the east,' meaning he was probably held in a Soviet Russian POW camp. 'You have heard nothing from your mother. Perhaps she

---

2. He expressed this view, which appears to have originated during his time in Germany prior to emigrating to Canada, in an extended rejection of the wisdom of investing in Ukraine following the fall of the Soviet Union. In Jacyk's eyes, as long as Ukraine continued to reflect the "Eastern" culture, it represented a serious risk to Western business people seeking to launch businesses there.

3. "Mother" in German—the parents in the family were likely referring to each other as "Mother" and "Father."

cleans his shoes.'" Do a good deed for someone else, Peter mused, and you never know when, where, and how this good deed will come back to you.

"Mutti's sincere good-heartedness remained engraved on my memory," he wrote years later, "and I see it as one of the basic differences between Western and Eastern cultures. For me, the Western culture was simple, straightforward, and based on goodwill, like the Austrian man who had offered me a place to stay in St. Pölten, and Mutti's willingness to clean my shoes so that God would intervene and send aid to her son-in-law."

What are we to make of this sentimental view of a family whose nation was continuing to conduct some of the most ghastly actions in human history? The question can be answered in a variety of ways. The most obvious is to recognize that individuals do not reflect all aspects of the state. Setting aside the legitimate but ultimately impossible-to-answer question regarding how many Germans supported the Nazi Party and its actions, it is extremely foolish to assume that every German citizen was a clone of Hitler, Goebbels, Goering, and the rest. Jacyk was fortunate to be welcomed among an apparently warm and caring German family.

He had scorned Soviet Russia as a destructive force, a role the country had played throughout history; the advent of Stalinist Communism simply added to the nation's destructive potential. Now he saw things on a broader scale. His six months with Mutti and her family shifted his values sharply toward a Western tradition that emphasized freedom and opportunity over centralized power and restrictions. The benefits of Western values were evident even in the post-war devastation surrounding him.

His time with the postal worker's family bridged the final days of World War II and the first few months of post-war recovery. With the eye of a social scientist, he watched a nation struggle to cast off its role as a global villain and begin to rebuild itself physically, emotionally, and morally. The experience was nothing less than life-altering.

He had lived under three regimes before Germany, he noted—Poland, Soviet Russia, and Nazi Germany, all occupying forces. Each represented a foreign nation, and each had exploited the citizens of the country it was dominating. Clearly, none had demonstrated any admirable qualities. "I had to find answers to the many questions beginning with 'Why?'" Peter noted, adding, "I had good examples for comparison."

One of the answers was literally right before his eyes, there in the staggering German social structure. "At the beginning, I criticized everything that was different [from] what I was used to. After half a year, I started to question my assumptions and examine my observations." As proud as he might have been about his culture and heritage, Peter Jacyk had to admit that Germany's overall living standards were much higher than those he had witnessed in Ukraine. "I thought, if we were so much better, as our culture tells us, why are German people better fed? Roads are in better condition, rivers are better regulated, electricity is available everywhere, housing is better and cleaner. During war time, when all resources were directed to support the war efforts, all articles of necessity were rationed to citizens but everyone had enough to live. Even at the time when German cities were bombarded day and night, every woman each morning received her ration of milk, cream, butter and bread in the store." Peter himself did not lack for essentials, even as a foreigner visiting during a time of crisis and need. "If I needed some clothes," he wrote, "I received an appropriate ration permit and bought it at an affordable price."

How could he fail to compare the situation in war-ravaged Germany with his experience living in Ukraine under Russian control? "I considered the horrors and disasters of war in my country under the Russian Soviet system," he wrote, decrying "the complete lack of order, administration or transportation—an environment in which any army officer could place all kinds of demands on a helpless and impoverished population. If [the officer's] demands were not met, he could sadistically punish innocent people, with any reason." As could the Nazis, of course, but to Peter and to a gradually growing number of others, the Nazis were seen as an anomaly in Western civilization, something that could occur in any society if the people permitted it to happen. They were not the rule; they were the exception that proved the rule.

Meanwhile, he had to cope with a changed world. As an outsider, he drew lessons from the things he observed and the actions of others in dealing with near-total devastation. "Germany lay in ruins. All highways, railroads, bridges and major city buildings were turned into piles of rubble. Yet everyday life went on, according to routine based on German customs and traditions, and on established laws and order. Every German family lost at least one member in the war, and many returned home crippled." The situation, Peter Jacyk appears to speculate, might have led to an almost complete breakdown of society in an every-man-for-himself scramble. It didn't happen. "I do not remember one individual or organization left without attention," he wrote with some surprise. "There were shortages of everything, but all institutions managed to distribute their rations as honestly as they could under the circumstances." Then he added, "Of course, we know that people are people, not saints."

His comment regarding the absence of saints was punctuated by his discovery of the fate of the two former professors with whom he had lived and worked in St. Pölten. During his stay in Regensburg, he learned that the Soviet Russians had indeed entered and occupied Austria, including St. Pölten, where they dealt harshly with Ukrainians and other Eastern bloc residents.

Petka, the devout Orthodox Christian, behaved in Peter's words as "a complete scoundrel," suggesting the professor said or did whatever he felt would ingratiate himself with the Soviets.

It was not unusual for refugees caught up in the Russian web to report on others as a means of saving their own skins; Petka may have tossed aside his religious morals under these conditions and discarded any concepts of brotherly love. The dedicated atheist Mishka, however, acted in an entirely different manner. Mishka, in Peter's view, "caused no harm to any person. He simply took some dried bread in a bag and, having remained true to himself, returned to the East." Mishka's behaviour was, to Peter Jacyk, "an example that even a Russian communist can be an honest man."

For now, Peter Jacyk was one among an estimated 2 million Ukrainians in Germany faced with the decision to either return to their homeland or abandon it. Most of them were *Ostarbeiter*, the young men and women forcibly transported to Germany to serve as labourers. Many chose to return home, longing to see their families and hoping the Soviet Union would change after the war.

But not Peter Jacyk. As a pre-war Polish citizen, he was not forced to return. Nor would he return of his own volition. He had witnessed the brutality of the Soviets first-hand, and it was a lesson he would never forget. For the moment at least, he would remain in Germany, among more than 200,000 Ukrainian war refugees who preferred to abandon their homeland, as painful as that may have been, rather than subject themselves and their future to Soviet rule, and who managed to avoid forced repatriation.

DURING HIS three-plus years spent in Germany, Peter Jacyk never ceased observing, considering, and assessing people and their actions and values. In every case that he recalled as an adult, his views shifted, sometimes a full 180 degrees, from those of the repressive culture in which he had been raised.

For example, there was his recollection of meeting a young German girl and chatting with her for two hours. "I like you," the German girl said to Peter, words that to his ear were initially scandalous. "I found this statement very immoral," he said, "because in the culture in which I grew up, it was a no-no for a girl to admit her true feelings." Whether it was the girl's charms or Peter's inner reflection, he eventually re-evaluated his views and his opinion of her. "It took me some time to convince myself that the behaviour of this German girl represented grounds for honest and open human relations," he recalled, "and that her expression of her feelings was not negative but, on the contrary, represented a positive view of communicating and co-operating."

On a broader scale, he found himself defining and evaluating aspects of life in a civilized society, or as he put it, "I started to question an average Ukrainian person's understanding of culture." It is a mark of Peter Jacyk's qualities that he gave any thought to questions of culture at all, given his background and the state of affairs. He was raised in a rural village, and his education beyond the seventh grade was limited to operating a railroad locomotive and managing a dairy operation, both conducted within the daily chaos and anxiety of war raging nearby. Neither his upbringing nor his circumstances would seem to lead him to give serious thought to the role of culture in society. But he did, revealing an apparent egalitarian attitude toward the subject.

To average Ukrainians, he suggested, "culture is limited to music, theatre, literature, and in some cases education. But this is culture to a limited cast of people." Culture, in his view, was more accurately measured in the living standards of every member of a tribe, a community, or a nation, not just an elite few. His musings may not have been overly sophisticated, but they were clearly expressed in an earthy manner: "If ordinary people lack the most basic necessities of life, such as toilet paper, what kind of culture is it?"

As he would in other instances during his life, he found a suitable negative example in Soviet Russia. "Even if they have the Bolshoi Ballet and a multitude of poets and musicians," he pointed out, "these people represent one percent of the entire population. Isn't it wrong to use propaganda to represent the culture of a fraction of one percent as the real culture, and the culture of the remaining 99 percent as something of secondary importance?"

Such an imbalance was at best "a self-deception and a misrepresentation of the actual state of things." His insight on the true definition of culture marked another turn in Peter Jacyk's view of the world and his place in it. "Slowly but surely I started to compare various elements of Western and Eastern cultures, and decide for myself what is good and what is bad."

PETER RECALLED WITH obvious fondness the six months he spent with the German postal worker's family. Their hospitality and values helped ground him while he watched the war officially end and the long, painful process of forgiveness and renewal begin. He was far too motivated to drift along as a boarder, however, especially after he learned that a camp for displaced persons (DPs) was being established by the United Nations Relief Agency in Regensburg on the far shore of the Danube. Most of the UNRA residents were Ukrainians, along with a few hundred Poles and other refugees from various Baltic states, none of whom wanted to return to the Soviet Union or any country under its jurisdiction. With his savings from working in the Austrian dairy depleted and few job opportunities available, he moved from the German postal worker's home to the Regensburg DP camp.

Leaving the warm refuge of the boarding house would be a difficult emotional break, but the camp offered amenities and opportunities not available elsewhere. Originally built to house the families of German soldiers, it consisted of one-and-a-half- or two-storey bungalows suitable for up to four families per building. Although they were hardly models of outstanding architectural design, they were competently constructed and boasted running water, electricity, and heat. In addition to shelter, the UNRA camp provided food and clothing to residents and funded a health clinic on site.

The six thousand or so residents of the camp divided management responsibilities according to sharply defined nationalities: the majority of the administrative staff were Ukrainians, whereas hospital operations and finances were handled by Poles, Lithuanians, Latvians, and Estonians. The Regensburg DP camp evolved into a small Ukrainian town, with a church, school, choir, and cultural and sport facilities, a cosy enclave for those whose roots extended back to Galicia/Halychyna and beyond. Professors from a Ukrainian college, the Ukrainian Technical and Husbandry Institute in the Czech town of Poděbrady, arrived soon after the camp's inauguration to organize classes at the high school level and beyond.

The news elated Peter Jacyk as much, perhaps, as the ending of the war a few months earlier. He had grown "painfully aware" of his lack of education and general knowledge. Now he could live in a Ukrainian environment while filling the void in his education, and he seized the opportunity with the determination and single-mindedness he would display later in his business dealings. "First, I enrolled as a special student in the program," he explained. "The professors had created a secondary school course for people like me. Having graduated from these courses, we became normal students." He demonstrated more than ambition in obtaining the education he had lacked up to this point; he was hungry to learn. "I understood my lack of education and did not wait for the teachers to teach me; I studied hard on my own."

The next three years were not easy, despite the relative comforts of the UNRA facility. As a healthy and vibrant young man, he apparently did not qualify for maximum perks within the camp. Or, as he put it: "For a young man like me, the supplies provided by the camp administration were definitely not plentiful." It hardly mattered. "I had a roof over my head and limited food rations… and most of my basic needs were met at no cost."

He also enjoyed other interests available at the camp, including playing sports and singing in the camp choir, a pastime he continued to relish for most of his life. Beyond these activities, however, it appears that all of his available time was spent on studies and on absorbing philosophies of life that formed the foundation of his success in later years.

The first of these philosophies, Peter Jacyk believed, came from a German writer who penned, according to Jacyk's recollection, "One who bases his life on the outcome of his head and hands will never be disappointed." To this Peter Jacyk added a basic tenet of economics and added a capitalist flourish: "If one produces something that people need, and produces it better and in bigger quantity than people around him, money will come." Then he tacked on his own cogent directive: "If something is no good, make it good." The latter guideline, under the guidance of Peter Jacyk, applied not only in an economic sense that helped ensure his business success but in a cultural sense that eventually benefited the land of his birth in a number of ways.

PETER JACYK'S educational achievements generated a good deal of pride. In recalling his achievements at the school many years later, he indulged in a little uncharacteristic boasting, for which he can be forgiven because it is richly deserved: "I completed my secondary school education with honours. Then, I completed four semesters of the political economy program as well as two years of foreign languages (German, French, and English)." He achieved all of these goals within three years.

He also saw his views on many aspects of life change, or as he put it, "My association with the professors and the camp administration, as well as some contact with local Germans... forced me to question some of my basic assumptions and prejudices." He had already begun to speculate on the vast difference between the standards of living in Ukraine and Germany. The latter, despite the extensive destruction suffered as a result of war, enjoyed comforts well beyond those of Ukraine, Russia, and the Slavic nations. What was the explanation?

"I began questioning and making assumptions about our own Ukrainians," he wrote later in his life. "I thought that we were so good, that we were so hard-working, and that our culture was highly-developed." He started to understand the full impact of his land being exploited by its neighbours for generations. He also, in a manner that was remarkable for a young man in an environment of such upheaval and uncertainty, began to assess wider issues of life, politics, and culture.

Although each of us is an individual, he reflected, we cannot help but base our view of the world on the environment in which we develop as human beings. The environment thus influences us in various ways, some predictably, others haphazardly. In his case, his psyche and system of values had been pulled in various directions, and each pull added a new facet to his identity. "In my own life," he explained, "my process of psychological growth was strongly affected by a direct experience of radical changes... My quiet life in a small farm village, first with my father, then without him, was completely disrupted by the outbreak of World War II. This was followed by several changes of the ruling government: first Polish, then Soviet, then German, and changes of administrative structures and ruling political principles."

These upheavals, he noted, preceded his escape to western Europe, resulting in a hefty blow of culture shock. The five years of constant upheaval and danger were followed by three years of intense accumulation of theoretical knowledge, which is when, as Peter Jacyk put it, "I started to search for my own individual place under the sun."

His search for his place "under the sun" began with an assessment of the manner in which cultural mores differ and the effects these differences have on nations and their destinies. "It would be fair to say that, in order not to feel inferior," he recalled in his memoirs, "every country, nation, or civilization finds means to justify the way they are and see themselves as superior. I had similar feelings at the time. I had believed that we Ukrainians were the best and our culture [was] the best. However, as I matured and increased my level of education and practical experience, my understanding of human relations changed. I reflected on the situations I had witnessed, [the] three different governments that exploited the political situations, foreign relations, and their own people, and I had to find answers to the many questions that began with 'Why?'"

Why could one nation and culture seek to exploit another so successfully? Why did this attitude extend down through generations, long after the initial goal of domination had been achieved?

One answer could be found, he determined, in tradition. Older generations, political and community leaders, teachers and religious authorities, and customs on both a local and national level extend their influence and shape a nation's ethos. This was understandable. "It is...normal that people grow to revere their culture to such a degree that they are ready to die in order to defend it," he observed. "I entertained the same feelings."

He was thinking beyond mere patriotic pride, however. It was those maddening differences in living standards that continued to needle him. At first, the higher standards of Germany appeared decadent and corrupt, though he chose to use neither word. Simply put, he had difficulty embracing the concept that people could live so well, that they could enjoy many aspects of life considered unattainable luxuries in his homeland. He realized that the difference in living standards between two countries occupying the same land mass could not be accounted for by moral behaviour alone. There had to be a better explanation for the living conditions in Germany, amid the ravages of war, and those in Ukraine, even in peacetime and beyond the impact of Stalin's madness. What was the reason? Values? Ethnicity? Even though Peter Jacyk had given some thought to the true difference, it took an economics professor's classroom challenge to fix the reason in his mind.

"One day, during a lecture on statistics," Peter wrote, "the professor stated that the Germans produced more wheat per hectare on their poor sandy soils than Ukrainians produced from their rich black soils." On the surface, it sounded like an outrageous statement. The soil of Ukraine, the celebrated *chornozem*, was acknowledged to be the finest agricultural medium in the world, ideal for nurturing any crop to maximum growth and return. How could this professor, this arrogant old man, make such a statement? Obviously, in the opinion of the students, he was mistaken. "We young students and hot heads were offended," Peter remembered. "We knew that Ukraine was the breadbasket of Europe. How dare this professor falsify information and devalue our achievements?"

The students' outrage caused a serious disturbance. Telling the class to calm down, the professor announced that he would renew the subject in two weeks. "If you think I am mistaken," he suggested, "go to the libraries and find proof that I am wrong." Descending en masse on the books available to them, the class searched for evidence that the professor was incorrect, that the bountiful soil and extensive skills of Ukraine and its farmers could not possibly be outpaced by German farmers tilling their country's weak, sandy farmland. Two weeks later, when the subject was resumed, the students had nothing and the professor waved even more evidence in their faces. The proof was in the statistics. German farms out-produced Ukrainian farms by every measure.

How could this be? Better farming equipment in the hands of the Germans would account for part of the answer. Knowledge of newer farming techniques could add to the difference as well.

Underlying it all, however, was a difference in systems, values, and cultures, as well as politics and economics.

Peter Jacyk had demonstrated his intelligence and insight years earlier, when he scored well in his studies on railroad management and dairy administration. The professor's dramatic illustration of the benefits of Western methods, at least as measured by farm production, crystallized his view of the future, a view assisted by developments in the two countries, Germany and Russia, that had dominated his environment for almost a decade.

Stalinist Russia, swaggering in the Allies' triumph over Nazi Germany and its restored military power, was insisting on the return of all refugees from the countries under its domination prior to the official outbreak of war. This included all Soviet citizens as well as Soviet POWs. In the eyes of Stalin and his cronies, anyone who escaped death or serious injury during the five years of conflict and continued to reside beyond the Soviet borders was a deserter, not a refugee. Even those who managed to survive the German occupation were suspect; presumably, they should have perished in resisting the Nazis.

The Soviets feared that those who remained abroad, especially survivors of the Great Famine, the purges, and the gulags, would inform the outside world of the reality of the Soviet atrocities and dictatorship, and their insistence on repatriation of survivors often led to ruthless treatment of those who avoided returning to Soviet territory. Refugees from Soviet-dominated nations traded stories of the Soviets' brutal efforts to repatriate them. One witness described an incident in a church in Kempten, Germany, in the months immediately following the collapse of Nazism and Germany's surrender:

> The [Russian] soldiers entered and began to drag people out forcibly. They dragged the women by their hair and twisted the men's

arms up their backs, beating them with the butts of their rifles. One soldier took the cross from the priest and hit him with the butt of his rifle. Pandemonium broke loose. The people in a panic threw themselves from the second floor... and they fell to their deaths or were crippled for life. In the church were also suicide attempts.[4]

Early in the post-war period, Allied troops assisted the Soviets in rounding up refugees for deportation. When the Allies realized the brutality of Soviet efforts to forcibly return Ukrainians and others to Soviet control, they took action to minimize the impact, ruling that any refugee who had been living outside the Soviet Union in September 1939 was not subject to forced repatriation. It was a Band-Aid effort that failed to protect the vast majority of refugees, most of them forced labourers and many from Ukraine. Allied military commanders took some steps to protect them from the worst excesses of the Soviets, even while their civilian leaders expressed little understanding and less sympathy for the plight of the refugees. A former mayor of New York City claimed not to understand why displaced persons refused to return home because they disagreed with their government, in this case the Soviet Russian government of Ukraine. "I often disagree with my government's policies," he claimed, "but that would be no reason for me not to return to my country!"[5]

The punishment meted out to most former Soviet citizens— Russians, Ukrainians, and others—who either chose to return to their homeland immediately after the war or were forced to do so, ranged from being branded as traitors, meaning they were to

---

4. Olexa Woropay, *On the Road to the West: Diary of a Ukrainian Refugee* (London: O. Woropay, 1982), 33.

5. Vera M. Dean, "Tug of War Over the DPs," *The Nation*, November 1946.

be watched and discriminated against for decades, to deportation to a gulag or summary execution. If they managed to avoid any of the more serious punishments, they discovered they were denied decent jobs and grew resigned to living their lives under a shadow.

In the beginning, the Allies cooperated with the USSR's repatriation demands as a simple means of solving the problem of what to do with the displaced persons. Countries such as the U.K., the Netherlands, Germany, and others had enough problems of their own; why be concerned about a few Russians or Ukrainians who would probably be happier in their homelands anyway? When the extent of Soviet Russia's butchering of refugees, including their own people, became known, the U.K. and U.S. refused to cooperate with the Soviets. In response, Soviet intelligence began identifying and arresting those who they demanded must travel east to face their fate. When suspects were located, Soviet army troops descended upon them, often at night, and forced them to travel by train or truck into the Soviet Union. None returned.

The Soviets targeted the Ukrainian DP camp, and only foreknowledge of their plans saved Peter and his classmates. "On a number of occasions at night," he said, "we had to abandon our living quarters and run into the fields. When the trucks arrived to pick us up, there was no one to pick up."

After three years at the camp and with his education at least partially completed, Peter began searching for a new home in another country. Germany was out of the question, even though he had admired certain aspects of German society. "Very often, I had a feeling that Germany was only for Germans, and there was nothing for me," he explained. Others in the camp shared his feelings. "Everyone, including myself, was trying to find out what was the best country to emigrate to."

A wide range of options appeared available, including Tunisia, Argentina, Brazil, Australia, Belgium, England, and the U.S.

Australia provided the first opportunity for Peter Jacyk to emigrate, but he was concerned about the country's distance from Europe, and he declined. Next came a chance to emigrate to the United States, which might appear to represent the most appealing destination for an ambitious young man. Curiously, Peter Jacyk turned down the opportunity. "Because of its high level of commercial development, I felt that I would never feel at home there," he explained.

It's a strong admission from a man whose extraordinary future business success was based to a large extent on meeting the needs of expanding industrial and commercial enterprises. Did he feel, in 1948, that the U.S.'s commercial development had reached its apex? Likely not—even at this young age, Peter Jacyk was too attuned to future prospects to make that error. His comment that "I would never feel at home there" is revealing. Was it perhaps a perceived cutthroat approach to business in the U.S. that concerned him, or some other expectation whose prospect made him uncomfortable?

Canada appeared to be the ideal choice, praised in letters sent to Peter by a classmate in his economics studies at the DP camp. The friend's name was Steve Roshko, and his correspondence was persuasive enough for Peter to apply for an immigrant visa to Canada in 1947, answering a need for loggers in the West. The work may have held a romantic appeal for the young man—labouring among massive trees in the shadow of the Rockies and all of that. In any case, it was not to be; his application was denied because of his defective lungs.

Farm work in Canada placed fewer demands on a worker's lung power than logging, and in February 1949, when four friends in the DP camp applied for employment on a farm near Edmonton, he joined them in their application.

His diligence in learning to speak English, German, and Russian, along with Ukrainian, won him an assignment as interpreter with the immigration guide accompanying the group to Canada, and he took advantage of it. By the time he reached Canada, the prospect of farm work in northern Alberta did not appeal to him. Given his agricultural background and training, this was another curious decision, in line with his choosing not to emigrate to the United States.

"It was winter, and the farmer in Edmonton had no immediate need for me," he explained. "I told the guide that I had a friend who lived in Montreal and I would join him." The guide telephoned Peter's friend, whose landlady confirmed that Peter's arrival was expected and they were ready to receive him; obviously Peter's decision to remain in Montreal had not been an impulsive decision. "The guide gave me permission to stay in Montreal on one condition," Peter wrote later. The guide's condition: he must never catch Peter collecting unemployment insurance.

It was an easy demand for Peter to meet. "I assured him that he would not find me unemployed because I had two healthy hands and a head on my shoulders," Peter recalled. The guide believed him. With his signature on a form releasing him from his obligation to work on the Alberta farm, he walked out of the immigration office and caught a taxi to his friend's rooming house. Peter had arrived in Canada with $7 in his pocket. The taxi ride cost $2. A week's rent at his friend's rooming house cost him $5. "I was penniless," he wrote, "and I began the exciting process of surviving in a capitalistic society."

5

A Sometimes Hostile Land

The Ukraine is the proper place for Ukrainians. If there is such a place as Canada-Ukraine, we do not know of it. Hyphens should be left at the port of embarkation to be applied for when the immigrant returns for good to the land of his fathers.

JOHN W. DAFOE, EDITOR, WINNIPEG FREE PRESS, 1913

JACYK JOINED ALMOST 32,000 other Ukrainian immigrants who landed in Canada as displaced persons between 1947 and 1951. They arrived in a country that, were it to articulate its attitude directly, might have greeted them with: "Welcome to Canada. Too bad you're not British."

Like its principal allies, Britain and the U.S., Canada shared both the glory of defeating Nazi Germany (and, to a lesser extent, Japan) and the cost. In Canada, the cost was measured in dollars and lives, but not in the kind of physical destruction suffered by most European countries. Still, its attitude toward the flood of immigration out of Europe in the immediate post-war years was of two minds. On one hand, Canadians sympathized with the plight of displaced persons and acknowledged the need for Canada to share in the effort to assist their relocation. On the other hand, memories of the Great Depression that preceded the war, and the high unemployment rate it generated, remained fresh, as did years of severe rationing of food, clothing, and other essentials while Canada supported the war effort. Would the new immigrants play their role in helping the country return to the prosperity that most Canadians believed they deserved? Or would they create a drag on the economy, serving as another reason for Canadians to pay high taxes and make various sacrifices?

This latter concern was bolstered by an attitude not exactly xenophobic but clearly anglophile in nature. Eighty years after Confederation, the country's apron strings remained fastened to Britain, a connection that linked the Mother Country to the former colony through language, culture, heritage, cuisine, and virtually every other measure.[1] In defence of the country's attitude, the federal government was focused on a range of other concerns during the immediate post-war years. More than sixty thousand Canadian troops and their dependents needed to be returned to Canada, discharged, and melded into the civilian work force. Wartime policies, including rationing and extensive government spending, were to be wound down and the economy adjusted to a peacetime basis.

In truth, Canada's record for treating immigrants in times of crisis was spotty at best. Many Ukrainian Canadians recalled, with a good deal of justified rancour, the Canadian government's treatment of them and their parents following the outbreak of World War I. The country's 1914 declaration of war with Germany and its allies, in lock-step with the U.K.'s actions, launched the War

---

1. Quebec, of course, retained its own identity during this period—but only to a degree. Until the 1960s, many Quebecois families insisted that their children learn English and adopt anglophone habits and style if they harboured any ambitions for a career above sales clerk or labourer. This was not a matter of choice but of necessity, dictated by the dominance of a society that retained the Union Jack as its flag and "God Save the King" as its national anthem.

Measures Act. The result was the internment of more than eight thousand immigrants who were designated "enemy aliens." Of these, more than five thousand were Ukrainians.[2] Another eighty thousand were instructed to register as such and report their location and activities to local authorities on a regular basis. The "enemy aliens" label was based exclusively on the fact that the residents were former citizens of the Austro-Hungarian Empire; the government of the day conveniently overlooked the fact that the vast majority of them had been actively recruited by Canada during the two decades between 1890 and 1910, when their strong backs were needed to settle the Prairies and transform the land into a productive agricultural area.

The detained "enemy aliens" of 1914 became in effect forced labourers, employed at low cost to develop Banff National Park and build logging sites in northern Ontario and Quebec and mines in British Columbia, Ontario, and Nova Scotia. Disregarding the fact that not one of the "aliens" was proven to demonstrate any animosity toward their adopted country (though they were handed substantial motives for doing so via the War Measures Act), many of the restrictions against them continued to be applied up to two years after the armistice of 1918.

At least some vestiges of this attitude remained following World War II, and the status of the DPs generated intense debate on both official and unofficial levels. When discussing the admission of displaced persons in Parliament in early 1947, Prime Minister Mackenzie King declared, "It is not a 'fundamental human right' of

---

2. Bohdan S. Kordan, *Enemy Aliens, Prisoners of War: Internment in Canada during the Great War* (Montreal: McGill-Queen's University Press, 2002), 130. Fred Langdon Davis, MP for Neepawa, Manitoba, and one of the few politicians to defend the interned men, noted in a speech to Parliament: "If we treat such men as men and brothers, we will make Canadians of them; if we treat them in any other fashion, we will make of them an alien element in Canada."

any alien to enter Canada. It is a privilege. It is a matter of domestic policy. Immigration is subject to the control of the Parliament of Canada." King immediately softened the position by adding, "This does not mean, however, that we should not seek to remove from our legislation discrimination that appears to be objectionable," closing his speech with the observation that "the people of Canada do not wish, as a result of mass immigration, to make a fundamental alteration in the character of our population."[3]

Precisely. Which explains why, to a large segment of the existing Canadian populace, the term "DP" was as much a racial/ethnic distinction as a citizenship identification. Immigrants driven out of Europe by the war were, for the most part, welcomed—as long as they acknowledged that, whatever their origin and education, they were not British. "Nor would they ever be, in the minds of some Canadians during that time," adds Professor Frank Sysyn. The second-rate status associated with the term "DP" extended to the perceived employment of the immigrants within the Canadian economy. Astonishing as it may appear to us in the technology-driven twenty-first century, higher education among immigrants from eastern Europe was viewed not as an asset but as a hindrance.

"Many immigrants had to hide any evidence of higher education, because Canada wouldn't take them if their educational achievements were too high," Sysyn notes. "Canada wanted workers, not thinkers. Thinkers were expected to be British, and workers were expected to be recent immigrants who needed fewer language and social skills. As an immigrant, it was a detriment to be educated." Thus many Ukrainian DP immigrants were drawn to farms, especially in western Canada, where the geography, if not the climate, was reminiscent of Galicia/Halychyna. Most of the rest were welcomed as workers in mines and mills, especially in industrial centres such as Hamilton, Ontario.

---

3. House of Commons Debates, May 1, 1947, 2644–47.

Although the word "prejudice" is not widely applied to Canada's attitude toward DPs, it is clear that Ukrainians, at least, encountered barriers to fulfilling the dreams they may have harboured in choosing Canada as their new home. Official government records confirm that Poles, for example, were favoured as DP immigrants. Their role, in part, was to provide labour that during the war years had been performed by German POWs, who had been returned to their homeland. In time, the dam burst; the quota of five thousand DP labourers to be admitted to Canada in 1947 swelled to forty thousand just a year later, including several thousand Ukrainians.

The quota was not universally applied. Although Ukrainians fared better than Jews, who were effectively barred from some programs, they encountered various obstacles when seeking employment in their new land. An official External Affairs memo, dated October 1946, noted it was difficult to determine who qualified as a Ukrainian, since Poles, Russians, and others might claim the designation if it promised favourable treatment. The author of the memo, a senior officer among Canadian military forces stationed in Germany, felt somehow impelled to make statements that appear outrageous today, considering their blanket assessment of ethnic characteristics. Ukrainians, the Canadian military officer wrote, were "unimaginative, industrious, conscientious peasants, very religious and without initiative, suitable for work that required strong backs and weak minds." To their credit, the memo noted, they were less temperamental than Poles and not as aggressively self-assertive as Jews, suggesting that Ukrainians would serve as compliant citizens, industriously following the orders of their Anglo-Saxon superiors.[4]

In Quebec, where Peter Jacyk chose to launch his new life as a Canadian citizen, he faced a variation on the national attitude

---

4. National Archives of Canada, External Affairs Papers, A12, Volume 2113, Memorandum of Colonel S.M. Scott, November 4, 1946.

toward DPs. French-Canadian opinion, on religious, political, and cultural levels, opposed immigration generally. Fearful of being inundated by anglophones, French Canadians saw massive immigration into their domain as simply another version of the same threat. Immigrants would choose to learn English over French, the Quebecois believed; expanding the number of DPs in La Belle Province represented a back-door means of diluting francophone presence and power.

IF PETER JACYK was aware of the turmoil swirling around the issue of DPs generally and Ukrainian immigrants in particular, he chose not to express his reaction in later years. Nor did he permit it to dissuade him from satisfying his ambition.

The unnamed friend who promised to assist Peter in Montreal greeted him warmly the same day Peter handed over his last $5 to the landlady. The friend was already settling comfortably into Canada; he was earning enough money to hand Peter $50—a good week's wages in 1949—as "a starting deposit," and to boast of a girlfriend whose parents owned a grocery store and whose father possessed a taxi licence.

"I found myself in a free country," Peter recalled, "free to live or free to die. I did not understand the rules or the structure of this society, but there was nothing to be afraid of because I had nothing to lose." His response to this new-found freedom made a major impact on Peter Jacyk's life. It provided him with the opportunity to speak out freely about events, ideas, and actions with which he disagreed, without fear of official reprisal. It offered the opportunity to take business risks and reap the rewards of those risks in a free enterprise culture. Even more deeply, perhaps, it generated love for his adopted country. For the rest of his life, Peter Jacyk's affection for and loyalty to Canada were unchallenged—and perhaps unexcelled. He would forever be Ukrainian-born, and he invested substantial time and money into assisting Ukrainian culture and language to thrive in locations around the world, and it took an initial period of time for him to fully accept the differences between the land of his birth and Canada. But from those first few weeks in Montreal, he began to nurture a love for Canada that he expressed openly and often. "I live in the greatest country in the world!" he would declare on numerous appropriate occasions, and no one who heard him doubted his sincerity.

ALONG WITH SEEKING employment, his first goal was to make contact with other Ukrainians in Montreal. He was searching for two necessary elements to his new life: advice and companionship. "Every immigrant first and foremost looks for some connection with people of his ethnic and cultural background," Peter said later, "people who understand him more easily, accept him, and give him advice as to what comes next. This is especially so because every immigrant confronts the customs and traditions of his new country with a greater or smaller degree of prejudice."

Noting that he came from a region that for centuries had been dominated by foreign powers and whose people were for the most part peasant farmers working small plots of land, he was now in a country that was solidly part of the post-industrialized world, with a commercialized democratic system of economics and politics.

He soon discovered that a number of Ukrainian immigrants had trickled into Quebec, settling in Montreal, between 1890 and 1920. At first they had accepted the lowest-paying jobs but, thanks to a frugal lifestyle and steady ambition, were well established in the city's working-class areas in the late 1940s. "They had built their own churches, established their own organizations, formed their own entertainment groups and even established some schools," Peter marvelled. Gravitating to the Ukrainian social groups, he quickly made friends who offered guidance and advice.

Among them was a man whom he identifies only as "Mr. Senkus," the wealthiest Ukrainian he met in the city. The meeting made a lasting impression on Jacyk. "I asked [Senkus] how he managed to become so successful," Peter wrote. Senkus showed Peter his two hands; both thumbs were missing. "He told me that, at the age of 17, he had worked at a woodworking shop [and] he lost both of his thumbs in a work-related accident." Unable to perform manual labour with his crippled hands, the man learned to speak English and French from his fiancée. With these language skills he obtained a position as a salesman with the Prudential Life Insurance Company, which led to his financial success. "After 30 years on the job," Peter wrote with wonder and admiration, "he sold so many insurance policies that his income far exceeded the income of a healthy manual worker."

Had Peter Jacyk needed it—and there is no evidence that he did—the story of the man who built a career by not letting his debilitating injury defeat him provided inspiration to achieve a similar level of success. The friend who had loaned him $50 on Peter's first day in Canada helped secure him a job washing dishes at a restaurant on Sainte-Catherine Street in downtown Montreal. Earning just $21 per week, plus food, Peter accepted it while keeping his eyes open for more challenging and better-paying work.[5] He found it within a few weeks: cleaning machinery all night long in the meat butchering operation of Pesner Bros., a large grocery retailer on Notre-Dame Street, for $40 per week, with overtime plus food. He also found better accommodation with the assistance of a Ukrainian religious group, enrolled in classes to learn French, and began absorbing the nuances of life in Canada.

---

5. He also acquired a valued skill. Many years later, when his success as a businessman and philanthropist was well established, he recalled this first job, saying: "Every experience in life can be of benefit; the reward for the four weeks of dishwashing is that, for forty years, washing any amount of dishes at home is easy and brings a smile, remembering the beginning of my career in Canada."

Pesner Bros. occupied a large three-storey building on a busy corner. Retail operations occupied the first floor; the upper two floors were dedicated to the store's extensive meat preparation and processing operations. Store management was generous and trusting to Peter and the other machinery cleaner, a Ukrainian named Bill; both men were permitted to go downstairs and help themselves to food for their evening meal, without paying for it.

Peter was doing reasonably well. After rent, food, and other expenses, he was managing to set aside $20 or $25 each week. He wanted to save at least $100 to cover medical emergencies or as a financial cushion in case he found himself unemployed. When he reached his target, he aimed to raise his bank account balance to $1,000.

It is difficult to overestimate the various temptations that might have diverted him from his savings regimen. He was a single young man in a city that, especially in the immediate post-wartime period, was renowned for its nightlife. Bars, dance halls, cinemas, and other distractions were in abundance, but he apparently managed to shun them all. "One has to practice self-discipline and find a proper balance between one's needs and capabilities as well as one's wishes," he wrote much later. "I told myself that one has to overpower misery when one is young and strong. Otherwise the misery would prevail, and an old and weak man would never get out of its clutches. This example of self-discipline in saving money worked for me."

Despite his success in finding steady, albeit unchallenging, employment and a welcoming social network, he was at best ambivalent about his new identity. His memories of those first several months in Canada indicate he was becoming a Canadian more by necessity than by choice. "Reading the newspapers and meeting with people who had news from Ukraine," he wrote years later, "we knew that we could not go home because the Soviets sent all people who came from abroad to the concentration camps in Siberia. Thus, whether we liked our new circumstances or not, we had no alternative but to stay in Canada." Hardly the attitude of an enthusiastic new Canadian. As Peter acknowledged later, his view of Canada was coloured by the system of values and expectations he acquired in Ukraine. "I admit that, even six months after my arrival in Canada, I still approached local people and the social system with prejudice," he acknowledged.

It took an encounter with Steve Roshko, the former classmate at the school in the German DP camp whose letter had enticed Peter to Canada, to begin changing his perception of his new country and perhaps reignite his ambition. Roshko had emigrated to Canada more than a year before Peter, and the two young men spent two days together, trading memories of their wartime experiences and views of Canada and its opportunities. "I expressed my ideas about life in Canada, [which were] mostly negative because I still viewed everything through the prism of my traditional conditioning," Peter wrote. His major complaint was the amount of work he was doing at an unfulfilling job. "A life of working like a horse," he said, "is not a life at all." Instead of spending an entire night, from dusk to dawn, cleaning meat processing machinery, Peter wanted to attend law school.

Peter's friend listened, apparently with a good deal of sympathy and understanding. Then he reviewed his own situation. Thanks to his two years in Canada and the assistance of a brother who had emigrated to Canada thirty years earlier, Roshko told Peter, he had a position as an insurance salesman, and had already travelled twice across Canada, from north to south and from east to west. He had seen far more of the country than Peter and met many more Canadians than Peter had encountered. The experience provided him with a very different view from his friend's. Peter needed time and experience "to get to know and understand the Canadian people and their ability to constructively cooperate with others," Steve suggested. It would take "at least two years to begin to understand local customs and traditions without immediately judging them from the point of view of one's own cultural background."

Then Steve Roshko added an astute observation that Peter Jacyk appears to have taken to heart. "The most ambitious [immigrants]," he noted, "try the hardest to change the reality of their new country to fit their own needs." He went on to suggest that Peter should save every penny he could afford to set aside and purchase a small corner grocery store. Roshko and Walter Klish, a friend from Winnipeg, would invest in the operation, with Peter managing it. He estimated it would require $1,000 capital to launch the business.

It was good advice and represented a promising opportunity. In 1950, almost no large supermarkets existed; the Pesner Bros. store was a rarity in its time. Most families shopped at small locally owned and operated neighbourhood grocery stores. The influx of immigrants and the promise of a recovering economy suggested that well-run retail stores would thrive. Roshko added another attraction to the idea: if the store proved as successful as he believed, Peter could take his profits from the operation, using them to pay for his law studies.

The idea of operating a corner grocery store in Montreal was never acted upon by Peter Jacyk, but his friend's visit restored Peter's optimism and banished at least some of his doubts about choosing Canada as a home. "After two days and nights Steve left for Toronto," Peter recalled, "and I got my hopes up for a better future."

The better future was some months and more than five hundred kilometres away. Meanwhile, his duties of cleaning machinery in the Pesner Bros. butcher operation through the long, dark winter nights remained. The Pesner Bros. butcher shop was vast, covering about 10,000 square feet, or almost 930 square metres. Both men worked in solitude. "Sometimes I saw Bill only at meal time, which was at two a.m.," Peter said, "or while taking a shower before going home. Sometimes we met more often in the night, and talked about many things."

Bill, seven years older than Peter, lacked Peter's English-language skills, but he was well read—he had studied engineering in university but lacked a degree—and he possessed an enquiring mind. Their conversations involved comparing their experience under the capitalist system with life under Communism in the Soviet Union. They recalled their experiences as refugees in Germany and how that country was recovering from the wartime destruction it endured. For the most part, however, they discussed their prospects for the future.

Bill's ambitions mirrored those of Peter's friend Steve Roshko— to operate a small corner grocery or cigar store—and he was saving as much money as he could afford to launch the business. But he saw bigger things for Peter. "Because of my younger age and my knowledge of English, he saw better opportunities for me," Jacyk said. "I would say, to a certain degree, that Bill contributed to the fact that I became more confident in myself."

The confidence appears to have provoked another shift in Peter Jacyk's assessment of the world around him and the people within it. He had arrived first in Germany and later in Canada with seemingly fixed opinions about Ukrainians. For his first few months in Canada, he questioned some aspects of Canadian life and values, perhaps having second thoughts about the wisdom of his decision. With the passage of time, his opinions shifted in a rather dramatic manner. "Based on my practical experience, my theoretical knowledge of political economy, and my nightly conversations with Bill, I differed considerably from other members of the Ukrainian community in Montreal," he noted. "I viewed them as immature children who liked to play, sing, dance, drink, eat and recall the good times, talking endlessly about a free Ukrainian state. How they [would] make Ukraine free or who will give them this freedom, they did not question … [they] wished and desired that, if our enemies died out, we would have a free state."

The latter lines paraphrase the opening lines of the Ukrainian national anthem:

> Ukraine has not yet perished, nor her glory, nor her freedom,
> Upon us, fellow Ukrainians, fate shall smile once more.
> Our enemies will vanish like dew in the sun,
> And we too shall rule, brothers, in a free land of our own.

His observations on some aspects of Ukrainian-Canadian society remained valid, in his opinion, fifty years later, when he observed: "I sometimes think … this lack of a practical approach to politics is a genetic characteristic of Ukrainians because … during the tenth anniversary of Ukraine's independence, these same people opposed Ukraine's democratically elected representatives with the same passion [with which] they had opposed the Soviet-Russian dictatorship."

It is tempting to view Peter Jacyk, through the prism of these statements, as a man rejecting many qualities of his homeland. Such a comment suggests an opinionated man prepared to criticize those whose actions and values conflict with his own.

In reality, neither is true. His opinion of fellow Ukrainians was focused not on their goals but on their attitude. He was a man of action, not of wishes. He continued to hold firm opinions on many matters, especially those related to politics and economics, and enjoyed bantering about them with friends in later years. Without exception, however, those who exchanged ideas and opinions with Peter Jacyk praised his tolerance and respect for opposing views. Should Peter defend his own views with what perhaps could be deemed excess passion, he would telephone his debating opponent the following day and apologize.

His attitude could be summed up: talk is cheap. He shared the same hopes for Ukraine that other immigrants from that land expressed, but he refused to expend his energy simply through talking about them. "Not wanting to waste my time and energy on such fruitless activities," he wrote, "I wanted to follow my own (path) and, if successful, show these people… whose actions are for the general good, and give those who are willing to open their minds the inspiration to act in a similar way."

Then he added, in a declaration that could qualify as a theme of Peter Jacyk's life and career: "I still believe that a living example is the best teacher."

In an interview published several years later, he explained his attitude regarding the efforts of Ukrainian Canadians to maintain and promote their heritage while citizens of their adopted country: "I wanted to build a Ukraine in Canada like many compatriots. Then I realized that all this running around would produce nothing. So I slowly cut myself away from all this unproductive talk and devoted more time to my business."[6]

Others have seen his comments in an entirely different light, portraying him as a stern parent who considered Ukrainians who clung too tightly to their inherited culture as children. The portrayal becomes clearer as Jacyk achieves maturity and success, but it is clearly inadequate. He had high expectations for both himself and those who shared his heritage, and when others failed to take full advantage of all the benefits Canada provided, he grew disappointed. "He felt it was his responsibility," Peter Jacyk's daughter Nadia suggests, "not merely to criticize but also to show by example. And this he did with great success."

ALL OF THIS came to fruition much later. Meanwhile, he continued his dusk-to-dawn shift cleaning blood and offal from vicious

---

6. "Formula for Success," *New Perspectives* (May 1992), 3.

butchering machines at Pesner Bros., accepting every opportunity to work overtime and salting away each penny he could afford into a savings account. Then, in January 1950, he received a letter followed by a telegram from Toronto-based Rogers Dairy, inviting him to come in for a job interview leading to the position of foreman.

It is not known whether Peter applied directly to the dairy, perhaps in response to a newspaper advertisement, or someone with knowledge of his work experience in Ukraine and Austria alerted Rogers. In any case, Peter travelled to Toronto for the interview and was offered the job. Along with much better working conditions and the opportunity to apply the education and experience of dairy management he had acquired in Europe, the position brought a substantial rise in income.

He returned to Montreal, gave Pesner Bros. two weeks' notice, packed his few belongings, and moved to Toronto.

As he soon discovered, he was entering not only a new city but a new environment that would challenge his assessment of life in Canada yet again.

6

Books and Beginnings

There are two things they understand in Toronto:
The British Empire and a good horse.
GOVERNOR GENERAL
LORD BESSBOROUGH, 1931

THE CITY THAT Peter Jacyk travelled to in 1950 was a far cry from today's metropolis, which is acknowledged as a multicultural community on the forefront of various technological and artistic advances. In the middle of the twentieth century, Toronto could have made a legitimate claim for the title of Dullest City in the Western Hemisphere, a grey edifice with a colonial mindset and a dedicated middle-class WASP system of values.

Whatever its failings, Montreal revelled in a decidedly Gallic attitude where food, wine, music, dance, art, and architecture were concerned—in other words, all the measures of delight in life. It balanced these diversions with a vibrant business community; major corporations providing financial, investment, and insurance services were headquartered in Montreal. Toronto's primary identity when Peter Jacyk arrived was its large slaughterhouse operations, qualifying it for the sobriquet "Hogtown."

Toronto's puritanical attitude marked the major distinction between the two cities. Although restrictions on activities such as the consumption of alcohol were province-wide—liquor purchases in Ontario were recorded in a book; men and women were segregated in licensed establishments where no entertainment was permitted—Toronto crystallized them in a manner that was almost medieval in approach. No Sunday activities of any impact were permitted—no sports events, no shopping, no open movie theatres, no purchase or open consumption of alcohol. The city's major department stores even drew drapes across their display windows lest Torontonians attempted to window-shop on the Sabbath. Montreal's permissive approach included selling beer and wine in grocery stores, marking it in the minds of Toronto residents as a French-speaking Sodom and Gomorrah.

Racial prejudice in Ontario's capital, though decried publicly, was practised privately. Restrictions on memberships in various organizations were imposed upon Jews, Irish, and Chinese; two people chatting in a foreign language on a busy Toronto street risked hearing "Speak English or go home!" from passersby. And John Yaremko, Canada's most prominent politician with a Ukrainian heritage, was informed shortly after graduating from law school that he must anglicize his name if he expected to be hired by a prominent Bay Street law firm.

Within the city were a substantial number of Ukrainian Canadians that Frank Sysyn identifies as "secondary immigrants," who had been initially settled in the Prairies but rejected rural life in favour of urban opportunities. "These settled Ukrainians represented a base for a community in Toronto," Sysyn explains, "ready for the big influx of Ukrainians who arrived in the city in the late 1940s and early 1950s." The new immigrants were distinguished in one critical measure from other European immigrants by their higher level of education, despite Canada's acknowledged preference for industrial and farm workers.

The new Ukrainian immigrants were essentially political refugees. "Italians, for example," Sysyn continues, "emigrated to Canada in search of work. This is especially true of those who arrived here from southern Italy. Those were economic immigrations, but the Ukrainians arrived here for a different reason." Italians, in this instance, came to Canada in pursuit of a better life. This was not the initial incentive for Ukrainians, most of whom would have preferred to return, after World War II, to a free and independent Ukraine. "That's what made the Ukrainian community so active through the 1950s and 1960s," Sysyn adds. They were not in Canada because they chose to be as much as because they *had* to be. Assimilation into Canadian society held little interest for many, who preferred to harbour the dream of returning to a free and independent Ukraine.

Ukrainians in Toronto formed a number of émigré organizations, ranging from the Shevchenko Scientific Society to groups dedicated to art and cultural activities. Frank Sysyn sees this process, which greatly outpaced similar developments by other immigrant groups, as a natural reaction to their situation. "This was their way of, after having lost status, seeking to regain it," he explains. "You may be working at some inconsequential night janitor job during the week, but on Saturday and Sunday you're teaching in a Ukrainian school or organizing a cultural or theatre group."

They built upon earlier efforts from older Ukrainian communities in the city, assisted by a relatively high degree of visibility in the media. Newspapers such as the *Toronto Telegram* provided considerable coverage for the ethnic group during the 1930s, '40s, and '50s, raising their profile among themselves as well as among Canadians generally. Other ethnic groups who outnumbered

Ukrainians by a substantial factor could only begin to match them when it came to general awareness. This activity, in the opinion of more than one observer, supplemented the Ukrainians' loss of their European world. In essence, they were creating a New World in the New World.

NONE OF THIS occupied a substantial part of Peter Jacyk's consciousness when he arrived at the dairy on Rogers Road and began to experience the differences between the joie de vivre of Montreal and the "God Save the King" posture of Toronto. His life had improved in various ways. Dairy management was familiar to him and immensely more appealing than washing down butchering machinery, and he began his work with enthusiasm and more than a little success.

"I worked in the dairy in my rubber boots and coveralls from seven in the morning to five in the afternoon," he wrote, "coordinating the process of transforming many litres of raw milk into homogenized milk, pasteurized milk and cottage cheese." Along with his technical abilities, he brought initiative and resourcefulness to the job. "After two months, I managed to streamline the process in such a way that I was able to finish my day's work at two-thirty or three o'clock instead of five." These achievements suggest that he was as pleased to be working at the dairy facility as, presumably, the dairy management was about employing him. This may be true, although in a newspaper interview some years later he suggested that he experienced anti-DP prejudice at the dairy.

The dairy work may have been fulfilling and well paying, but it failed to satisfy Peter's entrepreneurial ambitions, and soon he and Steve Roshko began discussing the idea of launching a bookstore catering to Ukrainians. In Winnipeg, Walter Klish, with whom Peter had begun corresponding, thought the idea had merit and encouraged the two Toronto friends to pursue it.

Toronto Ukrainians, however, were not nearly as supportive. Two existing bookstores dealing in Ukrainian literature were already struggling. How could a third store succeed where they hadn't? If Peter and his friend insisted on opening a retail store, why not sell something more practical than books? "They insisted that a store selling food or clothes would always be more in need for the general public," he wrote, "but a bookstore was not such a great idea. After all, who had time to read?"

Undaunted, Peter and Steve Roshko kept developing their idea, encouraged by Walter Klish, who offered to contribute money to the start-up costs. Finding a suitable location on Bathurst Street, they signed a five-year lease on the six-hundred-square-foot space and set to work transforming it into a bookstore. Their start-up capital was limited to $1,200 in cash. Peter's next move was to visit a hardware store and purchase a saw, hammer, nails, and lumber. "From seven in the morning to three in the afternoon, I worked at the dairy," he recalled. "And from four in the afternoon to ten at night I built shelves at our new store." From time to time, he took a break from building shelves to attend auction sales and purchase glassed showcases, a cash register, and a desk. Three months after signing the five-year lease, the Arka Book Store was ready to be stocked with merchandise.

The enterprise proved successful almost from the start, thanks to local immigrants who provided books they no longer needed and merchandise suppliers who chose to support the young entrepreneurs. "Many people who had come from Europe brought books with them," Peter pointed out, "but they had no place to store them. They gladly gave us books to sell on consignment, and we agreed to pay them after the books were sold." To broaden the range of merchandise, Peter and Steve approached wholesalers of tobacco goods and school supplies. Drawing from their quickly dwindling capital, they paid for the merchandise in advance only to discover that it filled barely a quarter of the space they had assigned to it.

"To our surprise," Peter wrote, "we soon received an offer from the school supplies wholesaler who believed in our project, believed we were good people, and offered us double the amount of credit." The supplier, a company called True Canada Wholesalers, echoed the consignment agreement of local residents, stocking the store's shelves with goods and agreeing that the two store proprietors needn't pay for them until they were sold. Soon afterward, Arka Book Store was fully stocked and opened for business, impressing its potential clientele.

Peter Jacyk's recollection of this period reflects pride and perhaps nostalgia for a period that appeared in hindsight simpler and more rewarding in various ways. "Ukrainian people, who lived in the area, wondered how rich we were, due to the fact that our store was so full of goods to sell. We knew that we had spent every penny of our $1200 capital." They needn't have worried. Almost from its first day of operation, the store was popular with Ukrainians, many of whom had settled in the busy Queen-Bathurst area. Peter and his partners paid their bills in full and on time, encouraging suppliers to offer more merchandise and better credit terms, thus increasing their sales and profits. "After one week we knew we could pay our rent for two months," Peter said.

Sometime after launching the bookstore, Peter broke his finger and was unable to perform his work at the dairy. For three months, he helped at the bookstore while his finger healed, and his helper assumed his duties at the dairy. When Peter returned to work, he realized his helper would be downgraded to his previous status, so instead of snatching back his job and destroying the opportunity for his helper to advance, Peter left the dairy and successfully applied for a position servicing and maintaining steam locomotives with the Canadian National Railway. This time, his work shift stretched from four in the afternoon to midnight, leaving him time to work in the bookstore from ten in the morning until three in the afternoon.

Another critical event was taking place around the same time: in 1951 he married Yvonne (Evanna) Balysky and purchased his first house with $300 down. "It was not much of a house," he described it, "but it was a roof over my head, and I had a chance to work and improve it."

The marriage produced three daughters: Sonia, Vera, and Nadia. Unfortunately, the union did not last, and Peter avoided discussing the circumstances. A private man engaged in major business ventures, he preferred not to permit his personal situation to become an issue beyond his own immediate family, and it did not. As he built his business over the ensuing years, he grew to rely on the support and wisdom of his daughter Nadia.

ARKA BECAME MORE than a book and merchandise retailer. It evolved into a popular meeting place for established Ukrainian Canadians and new immigrants still flowing into Canada from other countries in Europe. On many days, the store was almost too crowded to admit new customers, and in 1952, when Walter, their friend and investor in Winnipeg, announced he was moving to Toronto to work in the store, expansion became a necessity. "Our little store was too small for three big men to work behind the counter," Peter commented, ignoring the fact that it was also too small, in all likelihood, to generate enough profit to make it worthwhile for three partners.

Whether Peter was elected by the other partners to locate and assess a new site or he simply volunteered for the task has not been recorded. In any case, he located and inspected a nearby dilapidated building on Queen Street near Bathurst with 2,200 square feet on each of its three floors. His examination and perception marked the first solid evidence of a talent he would develop and exploit in later years, creating a reputation as a shrewd judge of real estate development and opportunity. "I examined the building and figured we could renovate, after taking a mortgage," he said. "Then we could use the first floor for the store while renting the upper two floors as commercial or residential space."

Peter had the vision and ambition, but he also had two partners to convince. Revealing his ideas to Steve first, and walking him through the building, he calmed his partner's concerns before even discussing the idea with the third man in the picture. "Walter was the smartest of the three of us," Peter suggested later. "He was too conservative to risk the financial obligations associated with the transaction." Somehow, however, Peter won him over and the three men took a major step that involved risking everything they had achieved to that point.

While many skills may be acquired by individuals with ambition, some apparently are bred within the psyche—and none more so than the ability to successfully launch and manage a business. How, where, and when Peter Jacyk acquired his entrepreneurial spirit is unknown but, blended with his enthusiasm and determination, it generated success. Or as Peter himself put it when referring to their venture: "If a person makes things happen, many people start to take interest in what is going on."

The three men submitted an offer to purchase the old structure. When the offer was accepted, they obtained permission to begin renovations prior to the arrival of the closing date, ninety days away. With sufficient capital to buy the materials but not enough to hire contractors, they began investing sweat equity into their business, installing and staining the walls and bookshelves on their own.

In the midst of this activity, while Walter and Peter were working diligently to prepare the store facilities, a man entered the premises, admired their work, and asked how much they were being paid. "No one pays us," Peter answered. "We're working for ourselves." The stranger watched for a few minutes more, then quietly departed.

The following day, Peter received a telephone call from the real estate agent who had handled the sale of the new property. The inquisitive visitor from the previous day had been the vendor of the building they were renovating, and he was obviously impressed by the two entrepreneurs. "These men will make it," the building's vendor told the real estate agent. "If they need a bigger loan, tell them they've got it. I'll put up the money." On the projected date, Arka Book Store opened at its new site with almost four times as much floor space, a much wider range and selection of books and merchandise, and the anticipation of even greater success. As with its predecessor, the new Arka proved an immediate winner.

It is difficult not to be impressed by the achievement. Within two years of arriving in a strange city that treated them and their colleagues with indifference, if not outright hostility, the three men had built a thriving retail business, established a sterling reputation with creditors and suppliers, and now owned a building in a busy commercial area of the city. Each brought a special talent to the business: Walter proved an excellent administrator, Steve enjoyed the one-on-one aspect of customer service, and Peter provided the vision and guidance.

Even after the three partners drew their salaries from the business, Arka was able to generate $20,000 in annual profits, a substantial sum in 1953. The salaries were admittedly low, but in Peter's case his income from the bookstore supplemented the $3,500 in annual wages he continued to earn from his work on CNR steam locomotives. "To anyone on the street," Peter recalled, "we looked like rich people. But few people knew that we were only rich in spirit."

They were also ambitious, with different goals and expectations, and in 1954 the inevitable occurred. Steve began making the obvious observation that if the store had just two partners instead of three his share of the profits would grow. And both he and Walter began hiring outside staff when needed, while reducing Peter's hours in the store.

No evidence suggests animosity between the three partners— just a difference in how each perceived his role. Peter Jacyk took the initiative, proposing to sell his share of Arka to the other two partners. Negotiations and bargaining established a price that each declared fair, 10 percent was added for the business's goodwill, a payment schedule stretching over three years was set, and Peter walked away from the first of a string of business successes.

It appears as though he had already resigned from his job in the locomotive shop at CNR; from this point forward, he makes no reference to it. The funds generated from selling his shares in Arka to the other partners likely yielded sufficient income for his needs. Besides, he was not in need of employment for long.

Within a few months of liquidating his investment in the bookstore, Peter encountered a Ukrainian who had recently arrived from Argentina. Like Peter Jacyk, the Argentinian Ukrainian visualized a business career in retail, selling not books but furniture. The idea intrigued Peter but, establishing a policy he maintained throughout his business career, he tempered his enthusiasm with caution and spent a week discussing and negotiating every aspect of the venture before agreeing to the partnership.

"Again, the cycle repeated itself," he commented. "Renting space, finding a name for our business (this time it was Alfa Furniture), making signs and notifying the public of our grand opening." The store's location would be on Queen Street, in the heart of the area where most Ukrainian Canadians had settled and shopped. At the news of the store's impending opening, the same doubters who had warned against the launch of Arka returned, as sceptical as ever. The most frequent negative comment noted that fifty-three furniture stores were already operating on Queen Street. How could Peter and his partner hope to succeed against such large and established competition? "If there is room for fifty-three stores," Peter responded, "there will be room for one more."

He was correct again. The reaction from customers was immediately positive, and a few months after its launch, Alfa Furniture's inventory turnover exceeded the average of the fifty-three established outlets. What was behind its success? The usual quotient of hard work and customer satisfaction, aided by the fact that, between Peter and the Argentinian, they spoke six languages— English, Spanish, German, Polish, Russian, and Ukrainian. In a city being rapidly flooded by immigrants, this represented a valuable advantage.

In his memoirs, Peter Jacyk provides no details about the basis of the success he and his partner achieved with Alfa. Almost certainly it proved more challenging at various levels than the bookstore. Books, tobacco items, and associated products are relatively easy to merchandise compared with furniture, which involves much higher prices and is susceptible to sudden swings in fashion. Did the Argentinian bring special knowledge of furniture buying and merchandising with him, or did he and Peter possess some innate talent for success in this field? Peter doesn't say.

He does, however, quote a Jewish proverb that suggests the partnership with the man from Argentina was not always smooth sailing: "To know a man, you must first do business with him." Over seven months, as the store's sales grew, so did the portion of rent withdrawn from Peter's share of the profits. When his partner announced he wanted to bring his wife's sister into the business and move to a larger store in the neighbourhood, Peter prudently decided to dissolve the arrangement. The two sides negotiated the value of Peter's share and parted company, but not before yet another prospective partner approached with a proposition.

"The same day I decided to part ways with my partner at the furniture store," Peter explained, "a man belonging to a woodworking partnership came into our store and, in confidence, told me about... his company that was a joint venture owned by eighteen shareholders." The company, Accurate Builders Ltd., had proven profitable over its three-year history, producing quality cabinets and other furniture. It was, the man confided to Peter, an exciting investment opportunity.

Whatever the details, it was intriguing enough to lead to a two-hour discussion between the stranger and Peter. Basically, the offer was this: if Peter purchased shares at a discounted price from one of the existing partners, he and the man who approached him with the idea would gain control of the company.

The proposal wasn't without its concerns. Peter, after all, knew little about both the man and the company. Although these matters became clear over time, it is a measure of Peter Jacyk's vision and management abilities that he not only overcame the difficulties, but turned them to his benefit. Unlike the bookstore and furniture retail operation, this one directed him toward the path that eventually led to his success in property development and management. First, however, he had to deal with those eighteen shareholders and a situation that his new partner had failed to reveal.

7

Prospects and Promises

*Being good in business is
the most fascinating kind of art.*

ANDY WARHOL

AMONG HIS VARIOUS observations of life and business, Peter Jacyk wrote: "Nothing can replace straightforwardness and honesty in dealing with people." It is a guideline that he chose to follow in his business career. Others, however, were not as loyal to the concept of fairness, and their actions challenged him through the course of his career. His partner in the woodworking operation was only the first.

"I was used to doing business on the basis of mutual trust," Peter commented later. "Almost a simple handshake was enough to seal an agreement." Within three days of meeting the man in the furniture store, Peter purchased half the shares owned by one of the woodworking shop's eighteen partners for $3,600 cash, about $40,000 as measured in 2010 currency values. He later remarked that he was "not even suspecting that some people have no basis for their claims and believe only in their dreams."

Fortunately, he balanced his misplaced trust with the wise decision to work in the firm's office, where, within three days of becoming a partner in the company, he discovered the operation's true state of affairs. Accurate Builders Ltd. produced no quality cabinets—in fact, no furniture at all beyond simple cupboards and boxes. Nor could they. Not one cabinetmaker was on staff; the workers were, for the most part, rough carpenters and finishers with limited skills. The company's primary products were storm windows, doors, and various wood products, in competition with the house building industry.

It was a near-hopeless goal. Although the employees appeared diligent in their work, they lacked both the production knowledge and the management direction to do anything except generate just enough income to cover expenses and pay low wages. Every worker was a shareholder in the company, and each believed with some justification that he would earn more money and enjoy control over his working career through the investment. Under normal circumstances, this is a reasonable expectation. Unfortunately, few of them knew how to function in such a partnership. Despite the fact that the number of shares owned by each employee differed widely, according to the amount of money they initially invested, the employees believed they were equal partners entitled to an equal influence on the company's direction. As a mark of this impossible situation, seven different people had filled the company's management position in recent years. All had thrown up their hands in frustration and departed, unable to provide the company and its employees with proper direction.

Peter wanted out. He contacted the firm's accountant and the bank manager, seeking to withdraw his investment. Both commented that, had he approached them for detailed information before buying the shares, they would have warned him away. They also revealed that the shareholders, trying to earn as much from their investment as possible and failing miserably, kept blaming each other for their situation. If Peter remained with the company and succeeded at turning it into a profitable operation with good future prospects, he would demonstrate that he possessed both good knowledge of psychology and effective management skills—and perhaps profit from them sometime in the future.

It may have been true, but it was not encouraging. Now fully understanding the situation, Peter preferred to rescue as much of his initial investment as possible and chalk up the loss to experience, along with the realization that he could not expect to be paid the agreed-upon salary for his office work. "After three weeks on the job I told my partners, the man who proposed the deal and the one who had sold me half his shares, that what he had sold me was not worth even one dollar," he reflected. He wanted out and suggested that he would hand the shares back in return for just half of the money he had invested. Their reply was to refuse to buy back his shares, even at half-price. They also began to belittle him, calling him someone who could not think big and was unable to accept a loss. If Peter was such an astute businessman, they taunted, maybe he should prove it by trying to turn the company around instead of running away with his tail between his legs.

He had little choice. He would hold on to his shares and accept the challenge of turning a disastrous business into a profitable corporation. "My father had a way of rolling with the punches," Peter's daughter Nadia recalls. "He would often say, 'There's nothing bad that doesn't turn out good,' and he honestly believed that." His experience with Accurate Builders justified this attitude perfectly.

SOCIOLOGISTS, ECONOMISTS, INVESTORS, and anyone associated with business on a large scale have pondered for years the problem of determining the true qualities of a successful business leader and their source. They are not found in the textbooks of MBA studies and they are not always passed genetically from one successful business person to another. The only universally agreed-upon aspect of the debate is that business leadership is immediately apparent in those who apply it successfully, whatever its source and pedigree. In that sense, Peter Jacyk demonstrated his business abilities almost from the moment he chose to remain at the woodworking firm instead of writing off his cash investment as an expensive lesson in life.

Years later, he recalled his feelings at the time, providing some insight into both the Canadian culture he had recently joined and the attitudes of immigrants attempting to fit into the culture and achieve financial success.

He had endured "culture shock" when first encountering Canadian values, he acknowledged. As we saw earlier, his first six months or so in Canada were marked by some distrust and disagreement with aspects of his adopted country, and he found it difficult to abandon his conviction that the standards and methods familiar to him from his upbringing in Ukraine were superior.

Once he overcame this barrier, he chose to learn the Canadian methods of doing business before launching a venture, a path that few immigrants appeared to follow. "Whether people admit it or not," he surmised, "I believe that practically everyone in the world wants to earn more money." Most immigrants arrive in Canada with little cash, and although freedom of expression and security from oppression may represent primary goals for many of them, these motives are soon eclipsed by an urge to live well, accumulate assets, and improve their lives, especially the lives of their children.

They are usually successful. "In Canada and the United States," he noted, "a first-generation immigrant who has a good head on his or her shoulders, and is willing to work, can climb from a low social status to a much higher one. Some even manage to reach the very top of the social ladder through honest hard work." This opportunity, he stated emphatically, does not exist in most other parts of the world.

Looking back from the year 2000, when he had achieved extraordinary business success and prominence in the Ukrainian community, Peter Jacyk remained remarkably direct in his criticism of some immigrant attitudes. Many of his comments, no doubt inspired by the memory of his experience with Accurate Builders Ltd., were surely meant to assist recent immigrants in their efforts to succeed, and he was sometimes blunt in his comments.

Consider his observations on negative attitudes that immigrants may harbour about Canada and its citizens, especially during (but not limited to) their first few months in their new home: "To a large extent, new immigrants who come from various cultures that are based on deeply ingrained local customs, traditions, religious beliefs, view Canadians as selfish people who love cars, big houses and expensive clothes, and who are preoccupied solely with materialistic things." In assessing the response of some immigrants to the different values of their new home, he admits that he had been as guilty as anyone. "It took me two years to overcome my prejudice against Canadians," he wrote, "despite the fact that I, just like them, arrived in Canada with the desire to earn more money. But some people never get over their prejudices."

Immigrant prejudices, he suggests, may be linked more to matters of scale than to an immediate aversion to the mores they encounter. As he explains it: "Another difference between life in North America and other parts of the world is the scale and perception of wealth. In many countries of the world, a person who owns ten acres of land is considered rich. Yet, in North America if you own a two-thousand-acre ranch you may be considered poor. Such preconceived notions of wealth and value, brought by immigrants from their culture, can become a serious obstacle on the way to acquiring wealth and influence in North America. They often stand in the way of accepting and developing a tried and tested Canadian approach to work and cooperation."

From time to time, he would choose to be more specific about his analysis of immigrant attitudes and actions—and find ways to rationalize them. Ukrainians in Canada, he suggested, were not seriously interested in business ventures—at least, not as much as other ethnic groups. He had an explanation for this. Ukraine had been invaded and dominated by other cultures for generations, most recently by Poland, Russia, and Germany. In a 1992 interview, he pointed out that the invaders permitted Ukraine to maintain its own literature and art, "but they always kept business and the army in their own hands. So because we were always invaded by somebody, we were permitted to spend our time on literature and culture, forgetting about business, and this developed our values in a particular direction." He continued:

We cannot say that there isn't any value in that, but culture and literature make up only a part of life and life values... For literature, you have to have talent and fantasy, and Ukrainians have a strong sense of fantasy.

The most important value is power [that] comes from education, money and the military. And these are many things which we neglected for many, many years due to our customs, our traditions, our religious beliefs.

Here in Canada we cannot complain that we have not been permitted to move in any direction. Yet, by choice we stick to the old ways. We don't have any manufacturers. We don't have any people with stores. We don't have any businesses... [Ukrainians] still think like their grandfathers in Ukraine did. It is hard for them to get out from our way of thinking and aspire to something more profitable, something with bigger dimensions.

This meant setting aside the short-term need to earn wages and salaries and devoting time and energy to building Ukrainian Canadian–owned businesses, which was important, he suggested, for a number of reasons: "My attitude has always been not to grab something for today but to build something lasting... One person's lifespan is twenty-five years. But a corporation, an enterprise, can last at least one hundred years... [I]t was always my intent to build an enterprise—something lasting."[1]

All of which explains his scathing assessment of the workers in Accurate Builders Ltd. and the manner in which he applied his exceptional abilities to achieve success in business. "My previous experience had been to discuss business on a one-on-one basis or among as many as three people," Peter Jacyk explained. "Here I had to deal with eighteen people, each of whom had equal rights to make decisions." He quickly learned the maxim that it's easier to start a new company than it is to correct the failings and repair the reputation of an existing firm on the brink of failure. If he were to succeed with Accurate Builders, he would need to achieve two vital goals almost overnight: first, find a means of fostering cooperation among eighteen people, each of whom had a different view that he believed was as valid as everyone else's; and second, to improve the company's image and credibility with its customers, suppliers, and bankers.

Surveying the situation, Peter Jacyk quickly identified key problems and their solutions, which had eluded everyone else associated with the firm. Suppliers, for example, were insisting on COD terms before agreeing to ship materials. On that basis, the company could place only small orders that prevented it from earning quantity discounts, often paying higher shipping costs per item. Credit terms would save Accurate Builders substantial amounts of money

---

1. "Formula for Success," *New Perspectives* (May 1992), 3.

each month, but the suppliers refused to extend credit without an assurance of payment. Peter's first major move was to negotiate a $2,000 line of credit with the bank and use the LOC to obtain new payment terms with suppliers. The result: an immediate reduction in materials cost and a boost to the company's bottom line.

Next, he began assessing each employee's work and their contribution to the company's profits. Much of the work, he discovered, derived from custom orders in which doors and windows were built according to unique specifications established by the customers. The amount of time needed to measure, cut, assemble, and finish each custom-made product was never recovered in the higher prices. Meanwhile, a local housing boom was building a demand for standardized windows and doors to fit tract houses in developments of a hundred or more homes. In response, Peter phased out custom products to gear up for mass production of door frames, entry doors, and window sashes. Construction companies bought entire sets in large volumes, each priced with a healthy profit margin.

The result was not an overnight turnaround for the company, but within a few months, the firm was no longer in danger of collapsing. When Peter began ensuring that supplier invoices were paid on time, suppliers offered improved service and volume discounts. Word spread that Accurate Builders did good work at fair prices, and soon private homeowners approached the company to perform major renovations on their houses.

This appeared to be a logical step and it was, until Peter took a closer look at things and discovered that the employee handling renovations may have known carpentry but he did not understand business practices. "He was so good to customers that he charged them for materials and labour, but failed to include overhead in the price," Peter said. "If he had to go back and do repairs to the job, the company suffered a loss. In fact, when I reviewed all the renovation contracts he handled, I realized that we lost money on every one!"

The discovery produced a new method of pricing home renovations and a new approach to measuring the company's profitability. Expenses were closely monitored to determine how much each square foot of product, for example, cost before it was shipped out the door. When necessary, price and cost adjustments were made, and profits improved. He also managed to blend these business decisions with effective marketing, reaching out to potential customers in a sales manager capacity.

Meanwhile, he was absorbing new business knowledge from various sources, not all of them admirable. "On one occasion, I delivered a load of window frames to a builder," he explained. "It was our third delivery to him, and when I asked for payment on our account he told me to come back the following day, when he would have a cheque signed by his partner."

The next day, Peter arrived at the job site and waited two hours for the builder to appear, without success. He returned two days later, looked around, and still couldn't find the builder. Finally Peter asked one of the carpenters on the job if he knew where the builder, whom Peter identified simply as Joe, could be found.

"You're trying to get money from him, aren't you?" The carpenter smiled. When Peter replied that was exactly what he wanted, the carpenter revealed that whenever someone arrived on the site looking for money, Joe the builder would hide in an unfinished basement waiting for his creditors to leave before emerging again.

It seemed a silly, even demeaning act for a builder, especially one who everyone knew could afford to pay his bills. "Then I understood for the first time how he made his money," Peter said. "I have to pay people every Friday and pay suppliers every 30 days, borrowing money from the bank to cover these costs and paying the bank interest on the loans. He didn't." By delaying his payments to creditors and leaving his money in the bank for 60, 120, or even 180 days, the builder won two ways—he paid no interest on loans, and he earned interest from bank balances of several thousand dollars owed to his suppliers. The builder was making money off the backs of his suppliers, a lesson that Peter Jacyk absorbed with some distaste and a technique for maximizing profits that he refused to apply.

Two years after assuming the management role at Accurate Builders Ltd., Peter handed the company's financial statement to their bank manager. The manager was so impressed that he emerged from behind his desk to shake Peter's hand and congratulate him on a job well done, an unusual gesture in a period where bankers were generally viewed as aloof and undemonstrative.

The following year, the company posted a healthy 10 percent profit, and in its fourth year with Peter Jacyk at the helm, Accurate Builders scored a 25 percent profit, which Peter distributed to the eighteen shareholders, proportionate to the number of shares held, at the company's annual meeting. At a time when bank savings accounts were paying around 4 percent annually, returns of 10 and 25 percent on their investment represented a significant bonus.

This should have won the permanent trust of the other shareholders in Peter's business abilities. Unfortunately, it did not. Paying every penny it earned as dividends left the company with no growth opportunity. The employee/partners didn't care; they wanted all the company's earnings in their pockets without exception. And when Peter suggested that the company divert some profits into a cash reserve fund, building its equity and preparing for future downturns in the economy, the shareholders rejected that as well.

The downturn arrived in 1957. Housing slowed, demand dropped off, and the company encountered serious financial difficulties. This was precisely the event that Peter had asked the shareholders to anticipate and handle with a reserve fund. With no cash in the bank, Accurate Builders Ltd. began stumbling financially, prompting the same shareholders who had revelled in their 25 percent annual dividends to demand their original investment be returned. "They wanted to sell their shares for repayment of their capital," Peter said. "They cared only about their own self-interest."

It wouldn't happen. The company's assets were tied up in inventory, machinery, trucks, and equipment. Selling any of these assets to buy back the investors' shares would cripple the company and prevent any recovery. "During good times they were collecting dividends of 15 to 25 percent a year," he recalled, "and with one market slowdown they immediately wanted their money back." Their actions were not only foolish and unfair; they were egotistical. "I understood they were interested only in the profit I could make for them, while all the responsibilities of running the company fell on my shoulders."

When the shareholders realized they would have to ride out the difficult times instead of pocketing their original investment, they directed their frustrations at Peter. But he had had enough. Within a year, still holding on to his financial investment in the company, he stepped aside from day-to-day management to launch a home-building division of the company, under his personal direction. The move marked another stage in Peter Jacyk's journey toward financial success and defined much of his formula for this achievement.

He had joined Accurate Builders knowing little about the manufacturing of home components; his formal training and previous experience, after all, had been in dairy management and locomotive maintenance, two activities as unlike each other as can be imagined. As he had with the Arka Book Store and the furniture retailer, Peter Jacyk added to his fount of knowledge, extending his abilities both wider and higher. His move into the field of property development and home building proved another example of his ability to transfer his business expertise to the most promising and available opportunity.

SELLING DOORS and windows to home builders provided an insight into the business, and he quickly identified an opportunity to be seized. The federal government, in response to a need for new housing, had launched the National Housing Association (NHA) in 1938, adding the Canada Mortgage and Housing Corporation (CMHC) in 1945. The CMHC guaranteed home mortgages offered by investors, making mortgage investment far more attractive and creating a pool of cash to encourage home building. All well and good, but Peter noted a special feature of the CMHC-backed mortgages. Under the NHA, the mortgages covered 90 percent of the cost of building a new home. The payment schedule dictated that 10 percent would be paid when the basement floor was completed, 25 percent when the roof was installed, and the balance when the house was finished.

"If a builder built fast and sold fast," Peter pointed out years later, "he practically did not need any money except for the cost of the land. The secret was speed." Speed in home construction involved good planning and preparation. The process was complex: choosing a house design that appealed to the market; locating and negotiating with suppliers of materials and labour; dealing with lawyers, architects, NHA/CMHC representatives, and local bureaucrats; and settling all these matters quickly and favourably. He believed he could achieve this with sufficient levels of time and energy, and he set out to prove it by purchasing ten building lots with a cash deposit and an obligation to pay the balance twelve months later.

He had seen his future not among the eighteen constantly grumbling employee/shareholders of Accurate Builders but as an independent businessman carving his own path in a language and culture he had entered fewer than ten years earlier. Still, he had financial interests and personal obligations with Accurate Builders that demanded his attention and drew upon his patience. Fortunately, they often provided valuable lessons in business management and human nature that he applied throughout his life.

"I remember that one of the partners at Accurate Builders, an engineer by training, was doing the books Old-World-style," he said many years later. "Despite his duties he was called Mister Engineer, not Mister Bookkeeper." The same man maintained the books for both the workshop and the home construction activities, and as Peter Jacyk soon discovered, his experience with "Mister Engineer" would hand him a costly lesson.

The purchase of the ten building lots, with the obligation to pay the balance owing in full within a year, had been based on the assumption that the subdivision developer would provide services—water, electricity, sewer—for the lots within six months. This would leave Peter six months to complete the properties, a schedule that he was confident he would meet. Completion of the homes would put the balance of the CMHC mortgage in his hands, enabling him to pay the amount owing on the building lots.

All well and good, until the developer and property owner, a man named Davidson, failed to provide the services by the scheduled deadline. Without the services, Peter and Accurate Builders could not obtain building permits, and without building permits, he could not begin construction. The only solution was to obtain an extension of the closing date, a move that Peter's lawyer proposed, suggesting that the closing date on the property be extended by five months. It seemed a reasonable request, on the basis that the cause of the failure to make the final payment lay with the vendor, not Peter. The vendor's lawyers failed to see it that way.

"The answer was 'No,'" Peter said. "We were told by the developer's lawyer, 'Pay up or we foreclose on you,' which would mean losing the deposit plus the opportunity to make a profit on all our hard work."

The bad news was delivered by Mister Engineer (the term is used derisively by Peter in his unpublished memoirs), who, when Peter expressed his dismay, shrugged and assumed that the money and opportunity were already lost.

Peter refused to admit defeat and suggested that he personally meet with Davidson, explain the situation, and negotiate an extension.

"Mister Engineer said, 'No, you can't go,'" Peter said. "'You're so rough in your manner that you'll only make things worse.'"

How, Peter demanded, could he possibly make things worse? The bookkeeper and lawyer had spent five months trying to reach an agreement and failed completely, meaning his deposit would soon be lost. How much worse could things get?

Characteristically, Peter Jacyk refused to admit defeat. A telephone call to Davidson's office secured him a meeting the following day. Davidson was an apparently highly successful developer. Peter recalled being impressed by the office décor, the big desk, the expensive furniture, and the framed paintings on the businessman's walls. Instead of intimidation, however, it appears that he absorbed some inspiration from the visit: "I felt a desire to see myself behind such a desk one day."

The meeting with the developer proved both instructive and rewarding, thanks in a large degree to Peter Jacyk's directness and openness. Reminding the developer that he had purchased the building lots on the understanding and condition that Davidson's company would install the necessary services, Peter recognized that the developer may have encountered problems of his own and that lawyers on both sides had been unable to resolve the situation.

"Perhaps our deposit does not seem like a lot of money to you," Peter concluded, "but that money was all I have saved in seven years in Canada, using my own head," and he held up his hands for inspection, "and these ten fingers." He punctuated his tale with a harder edge: "If you do what your solicitor told us, which is to foreclose on the deal, I would have to defend my rights with all the means accessible to me."

Almost fifty years later, Peter Jacyk did not know if it was his determination, his displaying his hands to illustrate the hard work it took to earn the deposit, or "a spark in my eyes" that did the trick. He only knew that the developer, without saying a word, called in his secretary and informed her that the mortgage on the ten lots was to be extended for a full year without interest. Then he turned to Peter and asked if he was satisfied.

He was more than satisfied. He thanked the developer, shook his hand, and left. "From that moment on," he said, still with apparent gratitude, "I have remembered that there are still good, honest people in the world. I also became even more convinced that nothing can replace straightforwardness and honesty when it comes to dealing with people." This observation could be applied to both sides; what his lawyer had not been able to achieve in six months, Peter Jacyk achieved in less than an hour.

Soon he had another opportunity to prove his point. Instead of relying upon a developer to prepare land for houses whose construction Peter would fund and supervise, he purchased land to be divided into eleven lots, assuming the task of providing services himself. Before the land could be separated into individual building lots, the municipality's bylaws dictated that developers—this time Peter and Accurate Builders—had to provide security to guarantee the installation of the required services. This is a routine service provided by banks and insurance companies, which issue a bond guaranteeing that the funds will be available.

Once again, the responsibility to obtain the bond for $250,000 became the responsibility of Mister Engineer, who approached the insurance company with whom Accurate Builders had been dealing for some years. After four months of back-and-forth requests for the bond, the bookkeeper informed Peter that the bond had been turned down. "We're too big a risk for them," Peter was told.

Peter refused to believe it. If the insurance company sensed a risk in providing the bond, Peter suspected, it had nothing to do with the company or Peter or the development and everything to do with the manner in which the request had been presented. Demanding to know the name of the insurance company executive who had refused the bond, Peter announced that he would make the request directly, face to face. Again, the bookkeeper cautioned that if the agent could not convince the insurance company to issue the bond, what chance did Peter have? He repeated his earlier fear that Peter "might speak rudely and only make things worse." And again Peter said, "How can things get worse?" With the bond application refused, the lots could not be made available, and his investment in time and money would be lost.

Peter obtained the insurance executive's telephone number, called him, and after asking the executive to be patient with his broken English, got to the point: "I said, 'Your company insured my house four years ago. Then you insured my business, Arka Bookstore, and the building where it was located. Now you insure our company and twenty buildings we constructed. We intend to build eleven houses, but the municipal bylaw insists on security from us.' I reminded him that he did not need to give us $250,000, only to guarantee that we would install all the required services. He had known us for four years and knew that we never let anyone down." If the insurance company would help him, Peter added, both firms would grow. If it refused to help, neither firm would grow.

It sounds like a basic business pitch, and it was. No fancy footwork, no complex exchange, and no quid pro quo complicated the direct appeal. Which may have been the deciding factor, along with Peter Jacyk's evident blend of sincerity and determination.

Whatever the cause, the insurance executive responded with a question: How soon could Peter get to his office? "In two hours," Peter replied, and two hours later, after an exchange of pleasantries, the executive removed a sheet of paper from a drawer and handed it across to Peter. It was a fully processed bond for $250,000, guaranteeing that Peter and Accurate Builders would provide all the necessary services for the eleven building lots and opening the way for another development site.

Back at the office of Accurate Builders, Peter handed the bond to the bookkeeper, followed by a question: Since when is an honest and open conversation rude, and why is diplomatically beating around the bush without success considered delicate?

All he received in reply was a smile.

8

The Realization
of Dreams

Money can be lost and made again. It is seldom
possible to do the same with one's good reputation.
PETER JACYK

PETER JACYK FOCUSED on his business abilities and began to
hone his ambitions accordingly. The young man who had witnessed the carnage of the departing Soviets, the onslaught of the
invading Germans, the confusion of their retreat, and the devastation of a wartime Europe, had with some irony become a builder of
homes and dreams in Canada. Most of his associations remained
linked with other Ukrainians. Over time, he would expand his
sphere of contacts and partners, managing to maintain the con-
nections with his native country while fitting into the Canadian
mosaic.

Despite his remarkable success, he continued his quest for
knowledge. He wanted to know more about the business practices
in which he was already engaged and more about the Canadian
society that he was working within, and he absorbed a good deal of

both from the various professionals with whom he worked. Meeting with architects, engineers, lawyers, and politicians revealed to him, if not to others, his limited understanding of deeper aspects of life and business. Seeking the formal education that had been denied him in Ukraine, he enrolled in a fairly extensive business course at the University of Toronto. Two nights each week for twenty-six weeks, Peter Jacyk attended two-hour classes on the U of T campus.

The experience must have been both trying and fulfilling. He was still, apparently, conscious of his perceived weakness in spoken English, a serious challenge when he realized that each class consisted of a one-hour lecture by the instructor, followed by another hour's discussion on the topic among the students. To complicate things, approaching age forty, Peter was among the older students in attendance. He may also have been the least experienced where complex corporate matters were concerned; in his estimation, other students boasted a minimum five years of experience working in a true corporate climate, in positions that included personnel management, public relations, and other specialized functions. In contrast, Peter's experience, besides his ongoing construction and development activities, was limited to his continuing struggles with the shareholders of Accurate Builders, the vast majority of whom appeared to resent his success.

Without revealing to what extent he engaged in the discussions—which, he recalled, became so interesting that the second hour often stretched well beyond its sixty-minute limit—Peter clearly absorbed a great deal of new wisdom from the experience. Over time, he began to view both Canadian business practices and Canadian society in a different light. The process had begun, of course, in his Montreal discussions with Steve Roshko, who advised him not to attempt to change his adopted country to meet his expectations but to adjust his expectations to suit his new environment. During his night business classes at the University of Toronto, the process accelerated significantly.

"After about ten lectures I again began to see Canada and Canadian business in a new light," he wrote, adding that he was speaking of the prevailing Protestant work ethic, consideration for others, and the sense of cooperation and compromise he witnessed. Canada, he acknowledged, was a young country with a culture still based on English and French customs and tradition, influenced by an Americanized approach to life and business.

Although the influences may seem obvious to us today, this realization had a profound effect on Peter Jacyk. He saw himself and his goals in a far different light and began to understand more fully both the position of immigrants in Canada and the attitude of those they encountered. "The majority of immigrants come to a new country such as Canada with the hope of finding a better life than the one they left behind in their own country," he observed. Immigrants to Canada were also rather poor, almost by definition. The aristocracy and others in the wealthy upper class had no need of emigrating in search of a better life. They had, or should have had, no concerns about the lifestyle they enjoyed in their own country, so why travel elsewhere? "But in order to have a better life," Peter concluded, "one must make one's life better."

The statement is simple and almost overly obvious. Its deeper implications, however, are immediately apparent. The best way to achieve this, in material measures at least, is to understand the system and learn the values of one's adopted country. Attempting to maintain and emulate the system and values of one's native country in the Canadian environment was likely to prove unsuccessful and frustrating. "No matter what country an immigrant is from," he noted, "at the beginning he or she continues to live according to the principles and habits based on their native culture, the one they were born and matured within. I was like that."

At the completion of the business course, Peter acknowledged that he had once again altered his view of Canada and his role within the country's business and social environment. The challenge to immigrants that Peter did not directly address in these comments concerned the matter of heritage. Was it necessary for immigrants to shed their language, customs, and legacy, replacing them with Canadian equivalents? He remained equivocal. Regardless of Peter Jacyk's assessment of Ukrainians voiced in Montreal some years later, when he labelled them "immature children who liked to play, sing, dance, drink, eat and recall the good times," he valued both his own heritage and that of others. Moreover, he proved his point in later years through not just words but actions, by making substantial donations to organizations dedicated to preserving the Ukrainian language and history.

He also praised Canada's policy of fostering multiculturalism, creating a society in which newcomers to the country were not forced to abandon their heritage and cultural values. Canada's tolerance for other languages, other faiths, and other practices, he believed, represented a more advanced and humanitarian approach than the "melting pot" approach of the United States. For all the challenges multiculturalism created, Peter Jacyk still believed it represented the best alternative. And for all the concerns he harboured over the years regarding some aspects and attitudes of Canadian political leaders, he never wavered in his love for Canada and his belief in its values, traditions, and people.

For the meantime, however, he absorbed not just a new understanding about Canada and business, but ways in which he could apply this knowledge to his own advantage. Along with drawing attention to many aspects of Canadian values and business practices, the U of T classes also revealed key weaknesses in the operation of Accurate Builders. Among other matters, the company's bookkeeping practices continued to concern him. Studying the ledgers, he was unable to determine the levels of profit and loss applied to the firm's construction activities and to its woodworking shop. He suspected that the bookkeeper, the still-employed Mister Engineer, intentionally kept the books in a confusing manner. Or perhaps it was unintentional yet unaddressed. "More and more often," Peter wrote, "I began to notice Mister Engineer would be looking for papers on his desk that were covered with other papers, and the result was not very productive." Planned scheming or mere incompetence? It really didn't matter. Whatever the motive, it was preventing Peter from managing the company effectively and growing his side of the business efficiently.

Fortunately, he had encountered several wiser, more experienced business people by this time, and he began to draw upon their acquired wisdom. One of these sages was a man named Sus, an immigrant Czechoslovakian Jew whose company, Weston Lumber, supplied much of the construction materials Peter used in his home-building activities.

Their relationship was obviously very close, because at one point Peter began relating his problems with Mister Engineer to Sus, despairing of the man's incompetence. "On the other hand," he added, in an effort to be fair and perhaps explain why the bookkeeper remained in his position despite his failings, "he is educated and honest. He doesn't drink and wouldn't steal. He is basically a quiet, soft-spoken man who is very obliging to people."

Mr. Sus held up a hand to interrupt. "There is one thing to consider," he said. "You tell me he would not and does not steal. But if he spends a third of his time at work looking for papers and generally being confused and confusing others, you are paying one-third more than he actually earns. If he is earning six thousand dollars a year and wasting a third of his time, he is getting two thousand dollars for doing nothing. What is the difference, whether he steals two thousand dollars a year or you overpay him two thousand dollars a year? Either way, he is costing you two thousand dollars a year."

"Mister Sus, of course, was correct," Peter agreed. "If I had discovered that Mister Engineer had been stealing two thousand dollars every year from the company I would immediately have fired him. He wasn't stealing directly, I was sure of that. But the cost, as my friend pointed out, was the same, and I had to take steps."

The man named Sus was not the only Jew who provided helpful insight and advice. Through all of his business life, Peter drew upon the wisdom of several Jewish business colleagues and acquaintances. He respected their direct and straightforward manner and valued the counsel they offered from time to time.

Despite the logic of his Jewish friend's advice, Peter could not easily dismiss "Mister Engineer," replacing him with someone more productive, because the engineer was also a shareholder in the company. Instead, Peter launched a new company, Horizon Wood Manufacturing, to handle the woodworking operations; Accurate Builders now became the construction arm. He also located an office manager for Horizon Wood, a man fluent in both English and Ukrainian. More importantly, he possessed bookkeeping skills. The new individual lacked cash to purchase shares in the company, so Peter guaranteed a $2,000 loan to cover the cost of a reasonable number of shares in the new corporation, to be paid back from the Horizon Wood manager's salary.

Two separate companies meant two financial statements each year, making it easier for Peter, or anyone else, to determine the relative success of each firm. Jacyk also expected the new office manager to inject a level of professionalism into his work that might rub off onto Mister Engineer. When Peter resumed placing his full attention on house building, with twenty new home sites launched, he felt at least hopeful that he had improved the situation with both companies and reduced the tension between himself and others. With time, he discovered he had... and he hadn't.

"At the end of the year we prepared financial statements," he explained, adding: "The manufacturing company made some profit, but I discovered that the two managers had raised their salaries so high that the profit turned into a deficit." The move was outrageous, especially in view of Peter's direct assistance in providing a loan enabling the Horizon Wood manager to purchase shares that provided voting rights. Now the man had used those rights to increase his own salary (there is no indication that he made any early efforts to pay back the loan). "I argued that these salary increases were higher than we agreed upon," he continued, "but the new manager and shareholder retorted that the Board of Directors were authorized to set their own salaries."

Legally, perhaps, the decision was correct. But it was morally flawed. It broke the trust between Peter and the other shareholders in the firm and ultimately destroyed Peter's commitment to the success of the businesses and the income of the shareholders. In fact, it was more than morally wrong; it was fiscally stupid. After all, if directors were able to vote themselves salaries that exceeded the corporation's profits, they were drawing capital out of their own pockets. Eventually all the capital would be withdrawn and the company would be broke, unable to pay salaries of any level to anyone. "So now the situation did not become less tense," he mused. "It became unbearable."

He had traded one dilemma for another. Earlier, he had been dealing with an incompetent if trustworthy manager. Now he had added a competent manager of dubious honesty, and he wasn't sure which one was worse.

The situation drove Peter to struggle within himself between his expectations as a budding capitalist and his sensitivity about the welfare of others, between legal values and moral values, and most pointedly between the Old Country and New World philosophies of employment and wealth. The Old Country tradition held that a rich man was rich because he was basically corrupt, whereas the New World approach declared that hard work and dedication ultimately yielded success and reward. The other shareholders were disciples of the Old Country attitude; Peter Jacyk was substantially wealthier than they were, thus he must be dishonest. Working together in the wood shop, building calluses on their hands while he drove in his car from place to place and met with well-dressed lawyers, architects, bureaucrats, and politicians, they supported each other in this belief. When it came down to choosing sides, it was sixteen against two (one of the shareholders, a man named Myroslaw Bihus, who owned just 5 percent of the company, sided with Peter).

"These people could never agree on anything," Peter wrote with obvious distaste, "but they united against me for two reasons: I demanded greater productivity, and I had more money than any of them." Had the employees reflected on it, they might have acknowledged that more productivity meant more earnings as shareholders. Apparently this concept did not occur to them, and they continued to oppose any of Peter's attempts to manage the company more efficiently. They also apparently ignored the reality that, while their investment had been valued at $40,000 when Peter assumed management duties, its value was now estimated at ten times that amount. For his part, Peter refused to accept the idea that his own investment and overall business success could remain in the hands of people whose attitude he found unacceptable.

An older and perhaps more conniving man might have drawn upon both his knowledge and energy to manipulate the sixteen workers, winning over enough to gain support. But Peter had not acquired this degree of cynicism, nor was there any evidence that he had the heart and soul to carry out the kind of manoeuvring needed to set one partner against the other to his advantage. (In later life, he still refused to employ such tactics, though he was careful from the outset to avoid their need in the first place.)

The conflict over the two companies marked Peter's first serious business challenge, one that he realized he had to resolve on his own. In that sense, dealing with the problem established a method and style he maintained through his future business interests and, most significantly, in his efforts to establish and promote Ukrainian culture. It also deepened his sense that too many immigrants to Canada valued their ethnicity more than their opportunity to succeed in, and contribute to, their adopted country.

Over many months, Peter underwent a good deal of reflection and soul-searching before dealing with the situation. He consulted several people whose business acumen he admired and weighed various alternatives. The biggest challenge, he realized, involved determining the precise nature of the problem.

"I saw that these sixteen people, like myself, wanted to work for themselves and profit from their work," he wrote. "There was nothing wrong with that." How could there be? This was Peter's goal as well. So why couldn't they agree on what needed to be done? The frustration grew palpable. "For months, I drove in my car and yelled at myself, asking why I was so different from the rest of my partners. I was looking for mistakes in my reasoning, but I couldn't find any."

The textbook response would be to call a shareholders' meeting, present the facts, emphasize the need for a businesslike approach to the problems, and expect that at least enough shareholders would side with him to correct the situation. This, he suspected, would be pointless; no one would discuss the realities of the situation. They preferred to resent his success and even his efforts to create similar opportunities for them.

He finally resolved the situation with a blend of hard-nosed business sense and measured generosity, in a move that could serve as a case study for business students wishing to learn how to make the best of an intolerable partnership. When the employee/ shareholders continued to mismanage until Horizon, the wood-working operation, was unable to pay its rent to Accurate Builders, Peter's response was to place padlocks on the doors of Horizon. He informed the employees that they were locked out of their work, a decision that the employees soon learned was entirely within his legal rights.

He had forced a showdown. A general meeting was called to resolve the issue, resulting in the predictable conclusion that the partnership be dissolved. An appraiser was enlisted to calculate the assets of both companies, Horizon and Accurate Builders, and pro-pose dividing the companies according to the number of shares owned. Peter suggested that all employees of Horizon keep their shares in that company; shareholders of Accurate Builders, which Peter wanted to continue running, could either retain their shares or sell them to him, which was his recommendation.

It appeared to be a reasonable proposition, even to the other shareholders, until they saw the results of the appraiser. The shares of Accurate Builders, they claimed, had been judged too low in value, and they should receive more money than was being offered. Peter must have bribed the appraiser, they claimed, an accusation that renewed his outrage at them. "You have worked against me for years," he told them, "and now you accuse me of falsifying the results of a professional appraiser. Any one of you can call an inde-pendent appraiser to repeat the procedure, but you can be sure of one thing: every day that passes reduces the value of our shares." He added that he was not going to wait around for this to hap-pen, before reminding them of the unfairness of their demands. "You want me to accept losses on my shares because you unjustly demand more money for your shares? On what basis?"

The man Peter had dubbed "Mister Engineer" spoke for the others, noting that even if Peter accepted less money for his shares, he would still be wealthier than any of the others. Peter's reply: "At least you have the guts to express your opinion openly."

He had had enough. Now he wanted a settlement at any cost. "I am prepared to take less money per share that I own today [rather] than to quarrel with you and bring the value of the shares down anyway." He would pay the other shareholders more than the appraised value, take the loss, and be done with it.

Eventually they settled on a price of $1.34 per share for the other employees and just $0.93 for each of Peter's shares, despite the fact that each share applied to the same asset base. It was a ludicrous approach, yet carefully considered in light of the alternative.

Peter could easily have purchased enough shares, with the assistance of Myroslaw Bihus, the lone shareholder who sided with him, to provide him with the necessary 51 percent of outstanding shares to do as he pleased with the company and its employees. His first move, had he done so, would have been to fire all the employees and replace them with workers more manageable and productive. The move, however, would produce consequences that he found unacceptable, not because of legal or moral measures but based on cultural concerns.

All the employees were members of local Ukrainian organizations, and all attended local Ukrainian churches. He envisioned the disgruntled workers claiming to everyone who would listen that Peter Jacyk had ruined them with his greed, that he had treated members of his own ethnic group callously. It would take years for him to clear his name, and the image of him as a rapacious boss would perhaps never vanish. "Money can be lost and made again," he reflected, "but it is seldom possible to do the same with one's good reputation." His decision to agree to the demands of the other shareholders cost him about $35,000, an enormous sum at the time, but he considered it a bargain: "I was a free man, and my name was clear." It was 1961; Peter Jacyk was forty years of age and a full-fledged entrepreneur on a scale he probably could not have envisioned ten years earlier.

Along with his ally, Bihus, Peter focused his attention on Accurate Builders and its hard-working employees. The others were free to work as they pleased at Horizon, no longer subject to Peter's concerns about poor productivity and excessive expenses. For a time, the Horizon owners gloated in their success. They bragged about outsmarting Peter Jacyk and about all the money in their pockets, placed there thanks to the inflated share price. Peter, they claimed, had held them back with his careful planning and his fuss over accounting procedures. Now they could work the way they wanted and someday become as wealthy as Jacyk himself.

Flushed with pride, they leased larger warehouses to hold bigger inventories and signed more contracts with larger commitments. But the warehouse leases drained their cash, the inventories sat unused, and the contracts grew less profitable. Meanwhile, their arrogant comments about Peter continued to reach his ears. He found the comments unpleasant, despite his attempts to dismiss them, and he balanced their effect with patience. Time, he believed, would yield rewards. And it did.

The shareholder dispute had tarnished the names of both companies to a degree. Peter neither cared nor could do anything about Horizon, but he decided that the best way to deal with Accurate Builders was to clean the slate and begin building a first-class reputation for the company. The opportunity soon presented itself, along with a new means of growing his asset base.

Prombank Investment Ltd. dated back to 1958, when its partners placed deposits to purchase land for future development. Four years later, during a market downturn, the owners were forced to abandon their deposits and offered the charter for sale. Peter liked the name Prombank; he must also have liked the opportunity that the company provided. Investing $250, he purchased the charter for $249, leaving one dollar as the company's assets against a recorded $14,000 in losses. Operating as Prombank, he purchased empty lots, added water, sewers, electricity, and roads, and sold them as serviced lots, ready for construction. He also built twenty houses on land he already owned, selling them quickly.

Prombank's first annual report under the ownership and management of Peter Jacyk showed a profit of $50,000. Subtracting his initial loss of $35,000 left him with $15,000 in profit that he did not have to share with sixteen other people who constantly criticized his abilities and fairness. It must have been a satisfying moment for him. If it was, he spent little time basking in it. A few years later, he purchased the outstanding shares of Accurate Builders held by Bihus, who had stood by him during the tumultuous time spent wrestling with shareholders.

His first major project with Prombank proved a startling contrast with his previous experiences. He went from juggling the petty concerns of sixteen shareholders in a struggling company to dealing, at a distance to be sure, with one of the world's most powerful financial institutions, purchasing thirty-five acres of land from a two-hundred-acre package owned by England's Rothschild management group. The original Rothschild investment had been a disappointment to them and they sold the remaining land as a means to cut their losses, and Peter humorously viewed the deal as a can't-lose proposition. "If I don't make any money on this deal," he joked, "I will be only as good as the Rothschilds. But if I make a profit, I will have proved that I am better than them."

Indeed he was, employing a strategy that went well beyond mere number crunching. Local zoning for the Rothschild property had designated it suitable for light-density development, limiting the size and value of the buildings that could be constructed. By severing four acres from the parcel and donating it to the municipality as parkland, Peter Jacyk persuaded the municipality to rezone the land for medium density, opening the door to substantial profit opportunities.

The success of this venture caused him to reassess the risk factor in real estate development, leading to another refinement in his business strategy. After the success with the thirty-five-acre Rothschild property, he focused on something still larger, offering a proportionally larger potential profit. Like any other investment, the larger the anticipated profit, the bigger the risk, and Peter Jacyk disliked risk. His matter-of-fact, step-by-step approach to business had evolved directly from his insistence on anticipating and reducing risk before committing the first dollar to the venture, which in this case involved acquiring a fifty-acre parcel of land.

Purchasing fifty acres of raw land would entail the usual financial arrangements: give the vendor a 10 percent deposit and assume a mortgage on the balance to be paid off in five to ten years. Should Peter encounter financial problems, with a major reduction to his cash flow before the mortgage was cleared, he stood to lose his total investment to that point, because of foreclosure, including the initial deposit. If the fifty-acre parcel of land was priced at $100,000, he would require $10,000 cash at the beginning as well as sufficient cash flow, beyond his other needs, to carry the mortgage for several years.

"I am not a good sport," he admitted, "in the sense that I do not like to lose." What he needed, to cut the risk, was a new approach to land development. Instead of residential construction, he would look to industrial and commercial developments, leasing the space to individual businesses. "If I have ten buildings with a different firm in each building, I will still have big financial obligations," he commented, "but the obligations will be spread across ten different clients. It would be almost impossible to imagine all ten companies failing simultaneously. If even five failed, rent from the remaining five would be enough to carry the project cost."

Peter Jacyk had been looking for a means of building wealth while reducing risk. With this decision to change the direction of Prombank, he found it.

The move consolidated two qualities that became hallmarks of Jacyk's business practices. One was the ability to recognize imminent developments and the opportunities they presented. The other was to maintain a high level of ethics in his business dealings.

The imminent development in this case grew out of the changing nature of Peter's adopted country. Canada was well on its way to shifting from a broadly based agricultural and resources economy to one based on industrial, commercial, and financial activities. Residential home construction remained important, but the demand for appropriate business facilities in and around major metropolitan centres was growing just as rapidly. Satisfying this demand appeared less competitive and perhaps less risky as well. He began shifting to commercial-industrial projects in 1964, with three relatively small industrial buildings of just three thousand square feet each. He rented two and sold the third, rolling his profits from the sale into new land purchases for development and applying rent payments against the original mortgage.

The pattern was established. Moving speedily, he needed only to invest the standard 10 percent deposit to purchase the land, construct the buildings, rent them to established commercial or industrial tenants, and direct the rental income against the outstanding mortgage balance to retire the mortgage as quickly as possible. "It was not enough to build more," he explained. "It was better to profit more by saving every penny on the mortgage interest."

Within four years of striking out on his own, free of the constraints and complaints of partners, Peter Jacyk had quadrupled the size of his company, while rewarding himself with a healthy salary and paying his employees and suppliers on time. Once it had taken a personal meeting with a bank manager to secure a loan of $500. Now he had access to a $50,000 line of credit.

He was also building a reservoir of trust and respect within his own industry. Unfamiliar with legal niceties (and likely trying to avoid the expense and delay of professional legal guidance), he sealed most of his early deals with a handshake. "Somehow, I was lucky and encountered good, honest people," he recalled many years later. Or perhaps he was an effective judge of good character.

In one instance, he entered a deal with two brothers, named Fiksel, who wanted to build a group of new homes under Peter's Accurate Builders umbrella. The brothers' lawyer, an astute man named Murray Payne, warned the brothers against the deal, fearing that Peter would take advantage of them. When the deal was completed to the benefit of both sides, the lawyer congratulated all three for being fair and honest businessmen.

Some time later, Peter agreed to sell two industrial buildings to another firm. As it turned out, this firm, headed by two brothers named Rosenberg, retained the same lawyer, and the real estate agent involved passed the following story on to Peter: "After seeing my signature on the offer," Peter wrote, "the lawyer told his clients to accept it. When one of the brothers pointed out that the lawyer hadn't even read the terms of the offer, the lawyer told them that he knew me and my reputation, and that was good enough for him. He suggested they read the offer for themselves and tell him what they didn't like about it."

The brothers returned to complain that Peter was asking for more money than they had offered to pay. Payne's response was to suggest they raise their offer to match Peter's price. "I know this man well," the lawyer explained. "He is worth every penny he asks. Go ahead and sign the offer—you are dealing with a gentleman."

Not surprisingly, Peter Jacyk took some measure of pride and comfort in hearing this and similar stories. He also realized that

The young man who dodged bullets and bombs in war-torn Ukraine rose to become a pillar of Canadian business and a major philanthropist on behalf of Ukraine and its people.

ABOVE, TOP Peter (*far right*) smiles proudly at the opening of the newly expanded Arka Book Store, which soon became a focus of Ukrainian culture in the early 1950s.

ABOVE, BOTTOM "I don't go to banquets," Peter once told a reporter. "I work."

FACING, TOP Finding his entrepreneurial niche in building construction and development, Peter Jacyk launched Prombank.

FACING, BOTTOM Peter with his mother, Mariana, who in his words "was very much in favour of learning."

FACING, TOP Professor Frank Sysyn (*left*) and Mark von Hagen (*centre*) with Peter.

FACING, MIDDLE Peter's frequent visits to Ukraine enabled him to meet and chat with people...

FACING, BOTTOM ...and often attracted coverage in Ukrainian media.

ABOVE, TOP Dr. Jeanette Bayduza (*second from left*) became a treasured and frequent companion on Peter's visits to Ukraine and elsewhere.

ABOVE, BOTTOM Business success provided comfortable quarters and security for Peter, seen here in the den of his Mississauga home.

ABOVE Among Peter's proudest accomplishments was the launching of a nationwide effort to encourage the reading of books in the Ukrainian language among schoolchildren, seen here (*above and below*) receiving their awards and recognition.

FACING No single event generated more pride in Peter, seen here with Frank Sysyn, than the honorary doctorate of laws bestowed by the University of Alberta during its spring 1995 convocation.

ABOVE, TOP The proud grandfather: Peter with his granddaughter Andrea.

ABOVE, BOTTOM Peter's daughter Nadia worked closely with her father through much of his career and assumed the management of Prombank following his passing.

his reputation made it somewhat easier to continue expanding his business. "After this incident," he said, "the real estate agent, a very active professional, accepted the conditions of our offers without reservations. It cannot be stressed enough to what extent honesty, and not suspicion, helps a person through life."

He also began assembling a library of observations that, had he expanded and published it, might have generated impressive sales as a guide to creating partnerships in business. Among his points of advice:

· Focus not on how much your prospective partner knows but on what they have done in the past and how much money they will put into the business.

· Put all possible expectations on paper.

· Decide what happens when a disagreement occurs and the partnership must be dissolved—who pays whom, and how much?

· Remember that, at the beginning, it is easy to get into a partnership or marriage, but it is much harder to get out of either one.

HIS FORMER PARTNERS at Horizon were not doing nearly as well. Inspired by their profitable settlement with Peter, they had continued to rent larger premises, negotiate bigger contracts with little regard for profits, and purchase excessive amounts of raw materials on credit. When the company's profits dwindled and it was not able to generate sufficient cash flow to cover its obligations, leaving them unpaid for several months, the shareholders of Horizon called a creditors' meeting.

The meeting served only as an opportunity for Horizon shareholders to request an extension of the credit terms. The creditors asked to see the company's financial statements, which revealed a large inventory of materials. But when one of the creditors visited the company's premises and asked to inspect the inventory, it could not be found. The claimed asset did not exist, which was enough motivation for the creditors to force Horizon into bank-ruptcy. Within four years of choosing to manage it on their own, the shareholders had reduced a company once valued at $400,000 to zero.

The same Ukrainian community that had been hearing about the business abilities of the Horizon shareholders, and how they had outsmarted Peter Jacyk, could now assess things for itself. Horizon was no more, and its owners/employees were out of work. Meanwhile, Peter Jacyk's firm was continuing to expand and his reputation for honesty and integrity was beyond reproach. The $35,000 loss he had accepted four years earlier represented a small price to pay when it came to keeping his name clear.

The experience provided him with more than a source of justi-fiable pride. It inspired a dedication on his part to educating new immigrants about the prospects available to them in Canada and how to avoid what he saw as serious errors. Many, he believed, tried to attain wealth too quickly and assumed they could use the same techniques familiar to them in their native land. "Instead of learning Canadian methods first," he wrote, "they resort to negative and dishonest business practices. Very often, instead of helping themselves they hurt themselves."

To his native Ukrainians, he demonstrated a disciplined and demanding attitude while simultaneously contributing enor-mous amounts of time, effort, and money to defending and uplifting the awareness of Ukraine and its people. For a man who unquestionably loved his country and its people, and who wanted wider recognition for Ukraine's strengths and achievements, the opinions he expressed from time to time were undoubtedly dev-astating to some, especially when he questioned their ambition and realism. His remarks reveal, perhaps, not so much his true feelings as his inability to recognize his own strengths and accept the fact that few others, of any national origin, could match them.

His attitude appeared to be that since he had achieved exceptional success, others with a similar background and heritage could do just as well. It took a former Communist to point this out to Peter Jacyk and modify his often harsh views of Ukrainians.

John Kolasky was born to Ukrainian parents in Cobalt, Ontario, in 1915, and his struggle to survive through the years of the Great Depression radicalized him. He joined the Communist Party of Canada, earned an MA in history from the University of Toronto, and worked on behalf of Communist causes through the post-war years. In 1963, he was sent by the pro-Communist Association of United Ukrainian Canadians to Ukraine to attend the Higher Party School of the Communist Party of Ukraine.

It was in Kyiv that his Communist philosophy encountered Soviet reality. When Kolasky began asking embarrassing questions and pointing out flaws he perceived in the Communist administration, he was arrested, questioned, and expelled. Back in Canada, he wrote *Two Years in Soviet Ukraine*, a devastating indictment of Communism, and *Education in the Soviet Ukraine*, covering the Soviets' covert agenda to essentially eliminate the Ukrainian language in Soviet Ukraine. The books drew Peter Jacyk's attention, and the two men became colleagues in their anti-Communist activities: Jacyk through his support of Ukrainian culture and language and Kolasky through his authorship of various books and his fundraising on behalf of projects promoting Ukrainian studies and independence.[1]

During one of Peter Jacyk's tirades, in which he repeated his criticism of what he perceived as a lackadaisical attitude on the part of Ukrainian Canadians, Kolasky cautioned his friend. "Peter,"

---

1 Kolasky, despite his early Communist beliefs, set a goal of $1 million for an endowment fund (the Ukraine Exchange Fellowship Endowment Fund) to award scholarships in his name.

Kolasky said, "how come, out of all the Ukrainians who came to Canada, none has made it to the level you have? Obviously, you are a little different, and you cannot expect from others what you expect from yourself."

Nadia Jacyk, who was present when Kolasky made this observation, feels that Kolasky's comment began to change both her father's attitude and his expectations of Ukrainians. "From that day forward, he began to take a little more pride in himself and his achievements," she says. "He realized that he wasn't like everybody else. He was different. He was blessed with higher abilities."

9

Taking Stands

*One should, as a rule, respect public opinion in so far
as it is necessary to avoid starvation and stay
out of prison. But anything that goes beyond this is
voluntary submission to an unnecessary tyranny.*

BERTRAND RUSSELL

AS SUCCESSFUL AS Peter Jacyk became as a Canadian businessman during these years, he remained very much aware of
developments in his home country, and through the 1960s and
1970s these were not encouraging, on the whole.

The Soviet Union continued to take actions that could only
be interpreted as a means of undermining Ukrainian culture and
identity. During this period, one historian noted, "Ukraine was
already a country of two languages and cultures, with the Ukrainian half in retreat."[1] The Russian language was still favoured in
public schools, and although Ukrainian teachers were permitted to
fill some teaching posts, Russian-language teachers continued to

---

1. Andrew Wilson, *The Ukrainians: Unexpected Nation*, third edition (Newhaven and London: Yale University Press, 2009), 152.

be paid substantially larger salaries and selected to fill senior posts. As a result, many Ukrainian children grew up speaking and reading Russian more than Ukrainian and became far more aware of Russian history and culture than of their own country's.

The situation doubtless made many Ukrainian citizens uncomfortable, but to effectively judge their response requires an assessment of their situation. After almost half a century of foreign invasion and domination, some observers speculated, the country appeared settled and secure, notwithstanding or even because of the continued presence of Soviet political and military power. The sense of peace, relative safety from invasion, and comparative prosperity were clearly attractive to a generation of Ukrainians to whom decades of war, foreign threats, and famine remained painful memories. In this context, the dilution of national identity may have appeared a reasonable price to pay.

Others were not so sure. During the de-Stalinization of the late 1950s and the short thaw of the early 1960s, Ukrainian intellectuals and cultural leaders strove to revive Ukrainian culture and defend the Ukrainian language. Resistance to pressure by Moscow to assimilate the entire country grew widespread with time but remained generally ineffective. The notorious KGB (Komitet gosudarstvennoy bezopasnosti, or Committee for State Security) infiltrated and harassed Ukrainian dissidents more than any other group within the Soviet Union. Statistics confirm this observation. During the mid-'60s, Ukrainians comprised half of all political prisoners in Soviet jails and camps.[2]

The KGB's retaliation against protests during the Khrushchev and Brezhnev regimes precluded widespread public resistance. While Ukrainian dissidents chose not to charge the barricades, however, they also refused to be silenced by the Soviets' efforts.

---

2. Ibid., 153.

Opposition to Russia's authority where language and culture were concerned focused in two locations: within the existing legal and political system and via the distribution of *samizdat* (in Ukrainian, *samvydav*, or "self-published"), uncensored publications reproduced by hand and passed surreptitiously from reader to reader.

On the surface, the legal/political route may have appeared to be a means of surrender or collaboration in the face of dominant military power and a lack of effective support from beyond the country's borders. In fact, it had some basis in legal rights, which granted republics within the Soviet Union the right to secede under certain conditions, though these rights, like most within the Soviet Communist system, existed almost entirely on paper and virtually never in reality. The prospect of a potentially peaceful solution kept the dream of Ukrainian independence alive and in the public eye, but discussing such ideas risked drawing the attention of the KGB. The use of *samizdat* was more effective—but also far more dangerous. Anyone caught copying, distributing, or in possession of censored materials faced harsh punishment from Soviet authorities.

It was in *The Right to Live*, one of the more widely circulated *samizdat* publications, that writer Yuri Badzo stated, "The route to the creation of a 'single Soviet nation,' that is, to deepening the Russian nation [by absorbing] the national ethnos of the USSR... will sooner or later lead to a change in ethnic consciousness."[3] The awareness and rejection of this possibility, especially among the generation reaching maturity in the 1960s and 1970s, may have been helped by Soviet Russia's efforts to assimilate Ukraine through an educational system dominated by the Russian language. Many Ukrainians managed to hold on to the language and

---

3. Ibid., 152.

customs, even as they absorbed an education better, for the most part, than the one that had been available to their parents. One Ukrainian historian noted: "Despite the increasing dominance of Russian forms in Ukrainian political, social and cultural life...the Soviet system at the same time produced a highly educated and nationally conscious stratum of the population."[4]

Against this backdrop of change and threat in his home country, Peter Jacyk began to form and express his personal political viewpoints. In step with other Canadians of various origins, he grew intrigued by the rise of Pierre Trudeau in the late 1960s. Clearly the most polarizing of recent Canadian federal politicians, Trudeau appears to have impressed Jacyk at the outset of his career, later sliding to less than admirable status. "Pierre Elliott Trudeau, as he was presented to the public before the election," Jacyk wrote in an apparently unpublished letter in early June 1971, "appeared to me as one of the smartest men of our time. Unfortunately, the longer he remains a public figure, the more he convinces me that he is a mixed-up, spoiled product of wealth and theoretical knowledge with no understanding for anybody or anything."

The spark for this extended vilification of Trudeau was the prime minister's controversial May 1971 visit to the Soviet Union. Ostensibly to discuss the development of the Arctic by both countries, and perhaps to probe the first budding shoots of détente, his visit remained a politically dangerous journey. Soviet Russian tanks had wreaked destruction in Prague barely three years earlier, a fact that Trudeau overlooked while in Russia, even as he criticized the domineering presence of U.S. interests in Canada. This might have been ignored had Trudeau avoided stating, on his return to Ottawa, that "my position in the Soviet Union

---

4. Paul Robert Magocsi, *A History of Ukraine: The Land and Its Peoples* (Toronto: University of Toronto Press, 2010), 713.

or in Canada is that anyone who breaks the law in order to assert his nationalism doesn't get much sympathy from me." Made barely six months after the FLQ October Crisis, the comment was directed at extreme Quebec separatists as much as anyone, but its application to groups seeking legitimate freedom from tyranny—specifically in this case Ukrainians—generated an angry response from Peter Jacyk.

"Being leader of the best country in the world is not a light responsibility," he wrote in a letter to the PMO, "and it should not be squandered in signing treaties with Soviet Russia—treaties that are so restricting and so binding that the Ukrainian nation has never been able to rid itself of the imperialistic effects of one signed 317 years ago." He was referring to the 1654 Treaty of Pereiaslav, also known as the Council of Pereiaslav. The infamous agreement resulted from a meeting between Prince Vasili Baturlin, representing the Russian tsar, and Bohdan Khmelnytsky, on behalf of the Cossack Hetmanate, a nationalist movement that had succeeded in leading central Ukraine's breakaway from Polish domination.

The Hetmanate's motive in signing the treaty had been to secure an ally in its continued independence from Poland, protecting Ukraine from future attempts by Poland to recover its domination of the country. Unfortunately, its primary impact was the replacement of a Polish upper class in Ukraine with a Russian upper class. The long-term results were even more devastating and included the Ems Ukaz,[5] an 1876 decree by Tsar Alexander II that banned the use of Ukrainian in printed documents, the hiring of "dangerous" pro-Ukrainian teachers, the importation of Ukrainian documents, and the production of Ukrainian-language plays and

---

5. Translated as "Ems Decree," from the German city of Bad Ems, where the text originated.

lectures. An understandable attempt to seek help had led to devastating control over the nation's language rights. Russia drew upon the terms of the Ems Ukaz for three centuries as legal justification for its dominance of Ukraine and its severe limitation on the rights of its citizens.

In that light, it is easy to understand Peter Jacyk's outrage at Trudeau's comment. Recognizing the likely influence of the FLQ experience on Trudeau's statement, Jacyk lectured: "How could a man of your reported knowledge consciously compare Ukrainian nationalism with FLQ nationalism? Each is a combination of the circumstances and political situations of its respective country. The cause and effects of nationalism in both Canada and the USSR are totally unrelated. Therefore, what has brought you to lump the striving for acknowledgement and freedom of Ukrainians with the violent insurrection and illegal methods of the FLQ?"

The blistering attack continued for four pages, noting that a declaration of nationalistic support for Ukraine (or for any state within the Soviet Union) by an individual would likely result in a sentence of ten years to be served in a Siberian gulag. His letter also became scorchingly personal. "It is hard to believe that such an ignorant statement could have been uttered unintentionally [by you]," he continued. "One has to assume either of two outlooks on your actions in Russia: That either you admire and agree with the Russian form of government and would like to see [it] installed in Canada... or that you are a hypocrite." He concludes his tirade to Trudeau with: "I think it is high time for you to awake to the realities of a treaty with Russia, before generations will have a reason to blame you for their suffering!!!"

Peter Jacyk was hardly the only person, inside and beyond Canada, to criticize Trudeau's words. Forty years after the incident and ten years after his death, Trudeau's remarks following his visit to Soviet Russia were called "frankly, wrong and foolish" by arguably his most sympathetic biographer.[6] It is doubtful, however, if anyone exceeded Peter Jacyk's commentary in vehemence and relevance.

Although he made campaign contributions to both major federal parties, Peter's dislike for Trudeau remained unabated. Eight years later, in an another unpublished letter, he once again drew attention to Trudeau's ill-advised remarks after visiting Russia ("Through his rose-coloured glasses, Mr. Trudeau discerned similarities between our system of democracy and the Soviet system of autocracy during his visit to Moscow in 1971"), closing with the observation: "For a man who criticizes others on the basis of their credibility, [Trudeau] seems to have done very little in more than a decade to safeguard his own."

These and other comments are notable not for their unique point of view—Trudeau attracted more than his share of such severe criticism from other sources after all—but by the way they demonstrate the political awareness and deep passion for Canada that Peter Jacyk acquired during his years of business dealings. His political views extended well beyond personal attacks on leaders with whom he deeply disagreed. By the early 1980s, he was setting his sights on various drawbacks of Canadian society, especially when they made an impact on the country's business and financial performance.

In a published letter to a trade journal in 1983, he attacked Canada's poor record of productivity. "The best example of our unproductivity," he wrote, "is the fact that other nations are able to take any one of our raw materials, load it, transport it overseas, manufacture it into many different forms of finished product, bring it back, pay our import duties and still, after all this, manage to undersell us here or anywhere else in the world."[7]

---

6. John English, *Just Watch Me: The Life of Pierre Elliott Trudeau: 1968–2000* (Toronto: Knopf, 2009), 166.

7. *Cost & Management Journal* (April 1983), 16.

Here and elsewhere, he picks up a theme that represented the man Peter Jacyk had once been, the man he became, and the man who remained at the centre of his soul: a distinctly practical man who repaired steam locomotives, managed dairy operations, and cleaned blood and offal from butcher shop machines to support himself. Despite all the admiration he held for the denizens and practitioners in the field of academics, he was a blue-collar man at heart, suspicious of those who proposed strategies or solutions in arenas where they had yet to dirty their own hands. Canadian values, he lectured, had been eroded in the years from the end of World War II to the early 1980s, adding: "Productivity has declined, unemployment and welfare rolls keep growing, as does the national deficit. Unfortunately, our theoretical geniuses do not know what to do." Then, to a series of steps he feels Canada must take to become more productive ("Return to realistic values… abandon the indifferent attitude… curtail stifling overregulation"), he adds: "Redirect our educational systems toward more practical and applicable programs."

It is essential to understand the dual allegiance Peter Jacyk believed he owed to Ukraine and to Canada. He loved both countries equally, if for different reasons, and expressed his love by voicing unease whenever he saw either country failing to meet its potential. He considered it his duty to speak up whenever he encountered instances and actions that he believed were not in the country's best interests. To remain silent or passive achieved nothing. He preferred, where appropriate, speaking out and taking action. The sin, after all, was not in making mistakes; it was in not doing.

WITHIN A YEAR of vilifying Pierre Trudeau for his visit to Soviet Russia, Jacyk was horrified by a violent incident involving Ukrainians and their supporters that occurred not on the steppes of Ukraine but in a parking lot in Toronto.

Toward the end of 1972, Soviet premier Alexei Kosygin made a state visit to Canada, with stops in Montreal, Ottawa, and Toronto. When protestors in Ottawa, many of them Ukrainian, expressed their disgust with Kosygin and Soviet Russian policies toward Ukraine and other nations, Toronto police grew concerned about the potential for violent attacks that might occur in their city.

On October 25, as Kosygin, his party, and various Canadian dignitaries dined at the Ontario Science Centre, a crowd of protestors estimated between three and four thousand in number gathered outside, waving placards and lighted candles. More than a thousand Toronto police officers, including twenty on horseback, confronted the crowd until, in a coordinated charge, the entire police contingent attacked the protestors, swinging riding crops and police batons. The resulting mayhem tarnished the image of the Toronto police force and enraged Ukrainian Canadians, including Peter Jacyk, who saw intimations of the kind of police brutality he had witnessed as an adolescent in Ukraine.[8]

His response, in a letter addressed to politicians at municipal, provincial, and federal levels across the country, revealed not only his justified outrage at the police response, shared by a majority of citizens, but his ongoing distrust of Soviet Russia and all that it stood for. After noting that the demonstrators had gathered "to warn Canadians against what they could expect from associating with the Russians," he added, "This method of police action may

---

8. The outrage spread throughout the city, prompting a Royal Commission to investigate charges that the Metropolitan Toronto Police had used excessive force upon a basically peaceful demonstration. After thirty-four days of public hearings and the testimony of 214 witnesses at the enquiry, provincial judge Ilvio Vannini concluded "that the problems were started by a small group of unidentified youthful demonstrators, that there should have been more policemen at the rear of the crowd, that there was inadequate communication by the police with the crowd, that the Mounted Unit should have been used first as a show of force rather than to directly charge the crowd, and, finally that the Mounted Unit was not justified in endangering the lives of other persons by attempting to disperse the agitators."

be the first fruit and influence from Russian trade with Canada. The second Russian method consists of lies by government agencies to the public." The latter comment referred to early press reports that the police officers had faced an angry crowd of twenty to twenty-five thousand, greatly exaggerating the size and intent of the protestors. "I witnessed something that makes me scared and ashamed for the future of Canada," he concluded.

The letter reveals not only the degree of anger the incident generated but also the determined passion to fight injustice that continued to burn within Peter long after he had escaped post-war Ukraine and built a successful business and comfortable life for himself and his family in Canada.

Earlier that year, he had engaged in a protest with the Catholic Church, prompted by the Vatican's treatment of Joseph Cardinal Slipyj. The event revealed Peter Jacyk's commitment to battling Soviet Russian injustices, as well as his continued support of his Catholic faith.

Cardinal Slipyj, born in Galicia/Halychyna in the late nineteenth century, when the region was ruled by the Austro-Hungarian Empire, became head of the Ukrainian Greek Catholic Church in November 1944. It was not an auspicious time to assume the role. The Greek Catholic Church had been closely associated with Galicia for some time and, despite a hostile attitude toward the institution that dated back at least to the time of Tsar Nicholas I in the early nineteenth century, it remained dominant. The church's vaunted leader, Andrei Sheptyts'kyi, died shortly after the arrival of Soviet forces in mid-1944, elevating Slipyj to the church leadership. In 1946, the Soviets announced that the Ukrainian Greek Catholic Church was to step aside and its parishioners were to enter the embrace of the Russian Orthodox Church, led by the patriarch of Moscow, an order unacceptable to Ukrainian church leaders and their congregations.

In response, most Ukrainian church leaders and many priests fled to the West and maintained the institution there. Slipyj remained in Ukraine as a measure of defiance, and he and the Greek Catholic hierarchy were arrested and charged with having "accept[ed] Hitler's yoke" during the war years. The only course to be followed now, the message said, was for Ukrainian Catholics to "hasten to return to the embraces of our own mother—the Russian Orthodox Church."[9]

Slipyj was accused of collaborating with the Nazis during their occupation of Ukraine and was sentenced to eight years of hard labour in a Siberian gulag, a period that extended while copies of his writings, critical of the Soviet regime, circulated within Russia. He was finally freed in early 1963, thanks to political pressure applied to Nikita Khrushchev's government by Pope John XXIII and U.S. president John F. Kennedy.[10]

Following his release, many Ukrainian bishops began petitioning the Vatican to appoint Slipyj a patriarch of the church. Pope Paul VI refused, much to the annoyance of the bishops and Ukrainians generally. The pope also named bishops in the cardinal's region without the cardinal's knowledge or consultation, an action that many Ukrainians considered disrespectful to a man they revered.

The final complexity to the situation involved the Vatican's efforts to placate Soviet Russia and, by extension, the Russian Orthodox Church. Too much recognition for Slipyj, the Vatican believed, could position him as a rallying point for Ukrainian political,

---

9. Bohdan Rostyslav Bociurkiw, *The Ukrainian Greek Catholic Church and the Soviet State*, 1939–1950 (Edmonton: Canadian Institute of Ukrainian Studies Press, 1996), 119.

10. His life story inspired Morris West's 1963 novel *The Shoes of the Fisherman*, in which a Slavic priest, released after serving twenty years in a Russian work camp, is called to Rome and eventually elected pope. The book became that year's top bestseller and in 1968 was adapted into a movie starring Anthony Quinn and Sir Laurence Olivier.

cultural, and religious agitators, both within and beyond Ukraine, and risk offending Soviet Russia. In Rome, the church reached a decision, and soon the Russian Orthodox Church, with Moscow's approval, effectively absorbed the Ukrainian Orthodox Church, forcing Ukrainian Catholics to either join the Russian church or go underground. The Vatican, faced with annoying either Soviet Russia or Ukraine, chose the safe option of insulting Ukraine.

The question of Ukrainian independence regarding what otherwise would have been a purely internal Vatican affair drove Peter Jacyk to draft a letter to Pope Paul VI, protesting the treatment of Cardinal Slipyj. The letter, if it was read at all by those in the higher levels of Vatican management, is insightful for its declaration of Peter's faith. After reviewing Cardinal Slipyj's persecution and imprisonment, Jacyk wrote, "It grieves me deeply to know that the Holy See in its wisdom and knowledge has not raised its voice to stop the persecution and oppression on the part of your church by the Russian communists... It is hard to believe that countless ranks of clergy and faithful who offered their lives to build this bastion of truth and justice in the past... became weak-minded well-wishers and so [do] not seem to realize the nature of the Soviet creature." In case the Pope believed that Soviet Russia was lessening its attacks on Christians in the post-Khrushchev age, he added, "One should not blame scorpions for behaving like a scorpion, but it is naïve to pretend that a scorpion will become a budgie bird."

A SELF-MADE MAN who eventually assembled more than a million square feet of industrial and commercial buildings in his company's portfolio, Peter Jacyk took a dim view of those who appeared to choose a laissez-faire approach to life and work. By the 1970s, he felt strongly enough (and articulate enough) to express his opinions openly and with some force, though most of his views were expressed directly to assorted public officials.

He continued his opposition to the policies of Pierre Trudeau through various elections, decrying Trudeau's excessive government spending and deficit budgeting. His targets extended beyond one man and one party, however. In an extensive letter published in the *Mississauga News* in mid-1981,[11] he praised, with some reservations, the Canada that had welcomed him and other displaced persons thirty years earlier. "A comparatively small number of people, some 10 million at a time," he wrote, "were able to do so much to build up a vast territory with highways, hydro-generating rivers and bridges... The friendly spirit and strict adherence to the motto 'An honest day's work for an honest day's pay' seemed to travel throughout the country."

The intervening years, he suggested, had weakened the Canadian spirit that he once found so inspiring. He continued, "With more industrialization and more formal education came a more comfortable life," adding that, in his opinion, "we lost the balance between our input of productivity and our demands for compensation in the form of money." He had little sympathy for organized labour, reacting as many Canadians did to the constant waves of strikes, especially in the public service, sweeping across Canada. Labour unrest in Canada Post was especially upsetting to him due, without doubt, to both the militant attitude of the labour leaders and the widespread impact on his business activities of constantly interrupted mail service. In the same *Mississauga News* letter, he commented: "Even if a striker does succeed in obtaining a little more money, this increase does not justify the constant disruption in services and the deterioration of mutual respect. If we take the average post-office worker, he is no better off today than he was 30 years ago, only 30 years ago he or she had national respect and today he does not."

---

11. Peter Jacyk, letter to the editor, *Mississauga News* (August 15, 1981), 7.

His leanings were decidedly right wing. The resignation of Pierre Trudeau overjoyed him, and shortly after the selection of Trudeau's successor, John Turner, in June 1984, he wrote Liberal Party president Iona Campagnolo to observe, "The Liberal Party, for the last fifteen years, has tended to support the weaker and the disabled and to penalize the stronger, more innovative, creative people, thereby taking away the incentive to produce more. As a result of such practices we have high unemployment, deficits and taxes, and Canada finds itself in the category of the least productive western country."

These and similar statements may suggest a somewhat grumpy individual unresponsive to the needs of the unemployed, underemployed, and disabled, revelling in his own achievements and urging others to duplicate his success. If so, it is an erroneous assumption. Although he clearly believed in the ability of determined individuals to rise, as he had, above the challenges that life may have handed them via their ethnicity, economic status, and lack of education, he was not the inflexible plutocrat that such a description suggests.

Walter Jacyk confirms it. Now retired from Air Canada, the former electrical engineer arrived in Toronto from Montreal in 1973 and, becoming aware of Peter Jacyk's presence, called to see whether they were related. They were not, even though their fathers both grew up in the same township of Galicia/Halychyna, but the meeting launched a friendship that extended for almost thirty years to Peter Jacyk's death.

Gathering in Peter's home, they would sip single malt Scotch, a favourite periodic indulgence for Peter, and discuss any of a wide range of topics that might arise. Ten years after his friend's death, Walter Jacyk, relaxing in his comfortable Toronto home, recalls a man whose persona was very much at odds with the view some might have of him based solely on his personal correspondence. "He was a friendly, down-to-earth, and unpretentious man," Walter

Jacyk offers, "and I enjoyed his company very much. Which is not to say that we agreed on everything. In fact, we had some pretty serious disagreements on social and political topics from time to time." Peter did not suffer fools lightly, Walter Jacyk admits, but emphasizes that his friend's criticisms were never malicious, despite the force with which they might be delivered.

One instance remains firmly fixed in Walter's memory. "One day Peter, his daughter Nadia, a visiting businessman from Ukraine, and I were having lunch in a local restaurant," he recalls, "and Peter and I began discussing something. I can't even remember the topic, but I remember he gave an opinion I disagreed with, and I responded with a fact." Instead of accepting the fact or disputing its relevance, Peter expressed his deep differences where Walter's view was concerned. "I thought he was just having a bad day," Walter Jacyk smiles, "so I backed off and we parted in a friendly manner as always."

That evening, Peter called Walter at home. "He said, 'Walter, I want to apologize. I was out of line and I'm sorry.' And I said, 'Peter, you're even a bigger man than I thought you were.' He was like that. At heart, he was a fun-loving man who wouldn't waste time hating anybody." Instead of hating people, Walter Jacyk says, Peter would advise others to study their adversaries, learn from them, and try to be better than they were.

Jeanette Bayduza, who grew as close to Peter Jacyk in his later years as anyone did, noted that he "had this deep belief that if something bothered you, you should bring it out in the open and deal with it. That was how you solved a problem. You didn't keep it inside and hope it would fade away. You dealt with it then and there, but this didn't mean you made it personal. It was just an opinion."

Either in spite of or because of his horrendous wartime experience, Peter Jacyk considered hate a negative force to be avoided at all costs. This attitude coloured his approach to those who were in need of support. "He would say, 'I don't believe in giving a hungry man a fish,'" Walter Jacyk says. "Peter always proposed giving the man a fishing pole, teaching him how to fish, and encouraging him to stand there on his own two feet."

The departure of Pierre Trudeau from the federal political scene in 1984 and the ascension of the Progressive Conservatives under the leadership of Brian Mulroney inspired some friendly advice in a letter to Mulroney's newly appointed minister of finance, Michael Wilson. Among his observations regarding unfair practices by Canadian banks, a need for greater Canadian patriotism, and nostalgia for a lost work ethic, Peter noted: "Academics should not only impart knowledge but should also put stress on teaching how, through this acquired knowledge, one can serve his or her community better." [12]

When considered among his other observations in this letter (which was accompanied by copies of various articles and letters to the editor under Peter's name), the comment defined what Peter Jacyk expected of those in academia, government, and other sectors of society dependent upon public funding or private endowments. In a word, he expected excellence. In addition to theorizing, he submitted, they should also reveal how to put their theories into practice. Unproven and unapplied theories, after all, offered little value until they produced some kind of tangible and ideally beneficial effect. Tied to this concept was the principle that everyone, in his or her own way, should strive for the best achievements of which they were capable.

Or, as he was often heard to say: "I don't want 'nice.' I want *good*."

---

12. Peter Jacyk, letter to Michael H. Wilson, December 18, 1984.

10

Setting His Own High Standards

Leave them alone and pretty soon the Ukrainians
will think they won the Battle of Trafalgar.
STEPHEN LEACOCK,
MY DISCOVERY OF THE WEST, 1937

ALMOST UNPRECEDENTED levels of inflation drove bank and
mortgage interest rates beyond 20 percent annually through
much of the ten-year period between 1975 and 1985. Yet they did
little to slow down the growth of Toronto into Canada's largest
and most influential city. The shift in the country's centre of grav-
ity that began after the FLQ crisis of 1970 saw many corporate head
offices relocate from Montreal to Toronto. The expansion into
Canada of firms from the U.S. and elsewhere helped accelerate
the swing when these companies located in and around Toronto,
preferring to avoid the political instability that they perceived in
La Belle Province. The result was a boom in the construction, sale,
and leasing of industrial and commercial facilities throughout the
Greater Toronto Area.

With rapid expansion and high interest rates came a flurry of
questionable transactions in construction and real estate. The

most notable and scandalous of these events concerned three trust companies and 10,931 Toronto-area apartment units. Through a series of financial manipulations, back-room deals, quick real estate "flips," and alleged thuggery, the principals in the affair attempted to sell the apartment buildings to Arab investors for an astonishing $230 million profit.[1]

Peter Jacyk was as irritated as anyone when the events unfolded, in part because he suspected the situation tainted everyone in the commercial real estate and development industries. When some observers suggested, perhaps tongue in cheek, that the individuals involved could be recruited to deal with the country's growing deficit problem, Peter drafted a letter to a Toronto newspaper that did not treat the event nearly so lightly. "Some are suggesting that these kinds of people should be running our country because 'they know how to create dollars and jobs,'" he said, adding, "I agree that profit should not be a dirty word, but *dirty profits* should be banned." The remark reflected his values, to be sure, but he was also interested in confirming his reputation among a range of potential partners, clients, and tenants who viewed him as both a shrewd and honest businessman.

Among cynical observers, aspects of the property development industry are assumed to involve shady dealings or simply outright greed. Peter Jacyk encountered these attitudes from time to time and grew intent on preserving his good name as well as the reputation of other honest developers. He could not deny that bad apples existed in the industry, as they did everywhere, and recounted one incident in which a salesman for a building materials firm proposed a deal that would net Peter about ten times his annual income. The details remain sketchy, but it appeared to

---

1. Details of the complex crime were summarized in *Public Money, Private Greed*, by Terence Corcoran and Laura Reid (Toronto: Collins, 1985).

involve financiers purchasing one hundred acres of land sold to a numbered company to be founded by Peter. He would subdivide the property, build perhaps five hundred homes on the land, collect deposits on the homes, and declare the numbered company bankrupt. Keeping $400,000 profit, Peter would remit the balance to the financiers, who still controlled the property. After they withdrew their share, the remainder would be offered to the contractors and builders who erected the houses, on a take-it-or-leave-it basis.

"What would I do with $400,000?" Peter asked the man proposing the scheme.

"Who cares?" came the reply. "You could move to Switzerland and live off the interest, which would pay you $40,000 a year for doing nothing."

Peter Jacyk asked for time "to think it over," but in reality he had already made up his mind. When the man returned a few days later and began addressing Peter as "partner," Peter gave his answer. "The deeds and ownership would be in the desk of the financiers," he explained. "I would be the person who requested credit from builders and contractors. These people would entrust their capital to me and work for me." In the end, Peter noted, the builders and contractors would receive perhaps ten cents for every dollar they put into the project, based on Peter's word. "Everyone would know that it was me, and only me, who deceived them. No! My conscience would not permit me to do that."

The salesman called Peter "an idiot" for not jumping at the chance, telling him that not many people were handed an opportunity to make so much money in such a short period of time.

"Call me what you wish," Peter replied, "but if I cannot live with people who trust me and whom I trust in return, I would possibly have lots of money but a very poor life."

There is no doubt that the incident is true; whenever and wherever substantial sums of money change hands among a large group of people, someone often suggests a means of sliding much of the cash into his or her own pocket. Peter Jacyk remained adamant. Whatever conflicts anyone might have with him in business or elsewhere, they needn't question his basic honesty.

Maintaining his good reputation was clearly the motivator for avoiding such deals, but it may have been spurred by other concerns where partners were involved. "I was simply afraid of working in a group again," he said with characteristic directness. He knew the benefits of shared investment and responsibility through business partnerships, but perhaps they were more applicable to others. "When I looked back and questioned whether I would have been better off in business and socially if I went with a group, I find no clear answer. Yes, by now I would have been 'one of them,' but I am my own man…and isn't that good?"

Despite his achievements in building substantial material wealth while maintaining his reputation, the spirit of the Ukrainian boy from the Galician peasant farm continued to reside within him. "I still make much more than I need to support myself and satisfy my basic human needs," he noted. "I have plenty of food to eat, I live in a big house, I drive a comfortable car. So what is life and what is a big business? Is it better to own half the world without a penny to your name, or better to own one property with a clear title to ownership?"

Peter knew the answer: "It seems to me that I belong to the people who prefer this second alternative."

His openness, almost to the point of naïveté (though he was anything but naïve at this point), proved both rare and welcome in the higher levels of finance where he sometimes found himself. In the early 1980s, he was invited by directors of the Bank of Montreal to a luncheon, along with presidents of various substantially sized Canadian corporations. Over cocktails with a bank director from one of the Maritime provinces, Peter was asked why he had settled in Ontario instead of venturing to Alberta, where, as the director put it, "most Ukrainian farmers went." On the surface, it was mildly insulting, playing on the stereotype of Ukrainians as rural peasants, not shrewd urban developers. Peter ignored the suggestion and replied, "In my village, there was a saying: go to the forest for wood, go to the village for brains, and go to the big cities for money. I didn't need wood and I didn't need brains, so the only thing left was money."

The line both amused and impressed the bank director, who asked him to repeat it a few times to other attendees. Peter Jacyk's Prombank Investments, as the bank director confirmed later during the luncheon, was not yet a large corporation, but it was quite clearly a growing one. He was by now a wealthy man, but there are no absolutes when it comes to measuring personal material wealth. Someone else will always have a larger home, a more expensive car, a more prestigious personal jet. Peter Jacyk remained as determined as ever to expand his company and its value—what business person is not?—but at this point in his life, he began setting his sights on other achievements. Recognizing this juncture, he offered his earliest and perhaps most concise definition of the personal goals he set for himself in the later years:

> I am happy with what I have done, and I am still trying to do more. I think that this "more" is the need for growth and achievement in any profession and walk of life. [It's] what "life" represents for any ambitious person after he or she secures the basic necessities. As for personal happiness and self-contentment, at my age I am more content with the money I give away than with the money I make. I am especially happy when I donate part of my earnings to educational institutions, because I believe that more education means less confrontation.

There is truth to the image of immigrants representing those who have more ambition than education and are more determined to make a better life for their children than they experienced themselves. Why would they not encourage their sons and daughters to gain an education? In Peter Jacyk's mind, however, the concept of supporting education and extending its benefits to others reached well beyond his immediate family, and beyond Ukrainian Canadians generally, eventually stretching to Ukraine itself. "My business absorbed half of my life, making a living and [making] money," he wrote some years later. "The other half of my life was dedicated to working with education and academics for bettering my community with the understanding that, by contributing to the growth of knowledge, I was also contributing to Ukraine and the world."

Peter Jacyk did not view higher education as an end in itself. In discussions with friends and colleagues, he would remind them about the importance of thrift and hard work, delivering his thoughts with all the stern conviction of a Calvinist preacher. Nor did he seriously entertain the idea of multiplying his earnings and savings by assuming unnecessary risk. He knew the hazards involved in property development and investment, but they were risks he could weigh and, to a degree, control. He did not accept risk controlled by others, and this included stock market investments on a substantial scale. He did not like to keep cash in the bank but rather invested it in land and buildings as much as possible. On a shorter-term basis, he favoured investing his cash in bond portfolios and bankers' acceptances rather than equity-based mutual funds or daily plays on the stock market. The earnings on these products may not be impressive, he agreed, but he took great comfort in their guaranteed status. He worked very hard at minimizing risk in his business ventures, and he insisted on the same approach when it came to the stewardship of the money he earned.

"One should not forget that I would not have been able to donate funds to support education had I not learned how to make money in the first place," he continued in his unpublished memoirs. "Personally, I believe that the key element for every immigrant is to work and save at the beginning. This saving of every penny at the beginning allows [you] to spend the interest from these pennies in the future."

The approach, he realized, demands self-discipline: "Every fool can spend money, but not every smart person can make money and hold on to it."

PETER JACYK earned the largest portion of his income from industrial construction, selling or leasing properties to quality tenants. Each development provided two steps toward his ultimate success: it provided experience in negotiating and pricing the buildings he constructed, and it encouraged him to raise his sights even higher with the next project. Having begun with compact buildings of 3,000 and 7,000 square feet (280 and 650 square metres), eventually his Prombank Company was building structures of more than 100,000 square feet (9,300 square metres). In the burgeoning western sectors of Toronto, especially in Mississauga and the environs surrounding Pearson International Airport, Prombank became a major force in the commercial and industrial building projects.

Although he had launched his move to commercial and industrial developments ten years earlier, he accelerated work in this area from the mid-1970s forward, and both his timing and strategy proved brilliant. Not only was this region of Canada experiencing a growth phase it had never encountered before, but in the inflationary environment of the period, quality land development was proving a safe and profitable hedge against rising prices. Soon the Prombank tenant list consisted of more than two hundred individual firms. Not all were burgeoning successes, but most were able to meet their monthly rental payments, spreading the risk of any serious financial failing across a wide cross-section of industries and business categories.

Among his strengths was his refusal to allow the bureaucracy encountered by developers to overwhelm or deter him. Municipalities represent a push-pull challenge to developers in many instances; they welcome the growth in employment and the wider tax base that new projects provide, but they often simultaneously attempt to control this same growth and monitor the business practices of the developers. Peter Jacyk considered the challenges of municipal bureaucracy to be part of a game and found ways to work within them. "We don't make the rules," he said, "but we have to follow them. And the red tape is what it is. We can't avoid it. We just have to treat it like another problem and find a way to solve it."[2]

Mississauga's burgeoning growth was driven in large part by new immigrants who chose the community as both a residential and an employment centre. The city became such a wide cross-section of new Canadians that Peter Jacyk joked he could deal globally with virtually every nationality in the world without leaving Mississauga. The substantial immigrant quotient added another element to his remarkable business success. "It was easy for new immigrants to communicate with me," he explained, "because, due to my heavy accent, they accepted me as an immigrant as well." Their landlord, the tenants understood, had overcome many of the same kinds of challenges they were facing. The realization generated immediate empathy and trust on the part of the new Canadians, qualities that Peter Jacyk encouraged with his own standards of integrity and fairness.

These are admirable qualities in anyone, especially someone dealing in projects requiring substantial amounts of cash and involving various stakeholders. Failing to accurately assess the risks involved, originating either with other participants or with

2. Conversation with John Zdunic, November 30, 2010.

economic conditions, has ruined countless other developers. How did Peter Jacyk manage to stickhandle around obstacles created by the vagaries of the market and the frailties of human nature?

"He was ultra-conservative in his planning and totally driven to examine every detail before going ahead," says his daughter Nadia. "When he was projecting the income and profit on a project, he would review every detail over and over again before deciding how much money he could make from the deal. Then, after he had subtracted all the costs and allowed for all the things he could possibly imagine going wrong, he would divide his projected profits in half. If it still made sense, he would go ahead with it."

No one played a larger supportive role in Peter Jacyk's business success than his daughter Nadia. After obtaining her university degree in science, Nadia Jacyk became a teacher, but after two years, she discovered the classroom was not a wholly satisfying environment for her. Peter began floating the idea of Nadia stepping out of the classroom and into the boardroom at Prombank. Her value to him in that capacity appeared sealed during a discussion at the family cottage, when he mused about making a substantial contribution to Harvard University's Ukrainian studies program. The amount—$2 million—represented a substantial portion of the family assets.

When Peter asked Nadia her opinion of his plan, she replied, "If you feel that way about it, then don't give it another thought. They need the money, so give it to them."

"Do you realize," he replied, "that the more I donate to different causes, the less will be left for you and your sisters?"

Nadia assured him that she indeed grasped the situation. "You came to this country without any knowledge of the Canadian system, without anybody to give you advice, and without any money," she replied. "Yet you've made your success here. We were born here, were educated here, and have friends here, and if we can't make it on our own, your money can't help us." Before long, she joined her father at Prombank.

Years later, Peter Jacyk admitted that he tried to conceal just how deeply her words touched him. Meanwhile, to better prepare herself for the transition from education to business, Nadia enrolled in the MBA program at York University and later transferred to Harvard to earn a graduate degree in business. After receiving her Harvard degree, and with several years of experience working at Prombank, she commented that her father's business philosophy and strategies were not much different from the practices taught at Harvard. Soon Nadia became more important than anyone else on the Prombank team when it came to assisting her father in making major decisions. There were few conflicts between father and daughter along the way. Her words had carved a soft spot in Peter's heart that remained throughout his life.

"He thought the world of Nadia," Walter Jacyk says, echoing the opinions of others, "and she of him. They could resonate so well in their decision-making—anyone could see that."

HIS DAUGHTER'S steady hand along with his at the helm of the corporation became an asset whose value could not be overestimated. Although he and Nadia did not agree on every aspect of the business, her observations provided him with a sounding board, a means of testing his own opinions and decisions on a source he could trust completely. In truth, he needed all the qualified opinions he could access, because he began encountering problems that often had little to do with basic business decision-making and much to do with human nature.

Prombank, after all, was no longer a builder-developer but a landlord dealing with tenants ranging in size from local retail outlets to international corporations. Peter Jacyk's relationship with a client did not end with a bill of sale; it extended over many pages in contractual obligations and five or more years of tenant/

landlord exchanges that, as often as not, encountered difficulties based as much on personality conflicts as on legal differences.

As in the past, he determined that the key to dealing with these kinds of problems lay in education, and he began absorbing wisdom from various books on business practices, psychology, and public relations. These, he acknowledged, could take him only so far. "Even if one has a university Business Administration degree," he wrote later, "one still has to learn to deal with people face to face, to negotiate, to agree and disagree, and often to make decisions right on the spot." Honest discussions and patient explanation, he believed, would lead to agreements that could be defined precisely, and once both sides understood and accepted their respective rights, serious problems could be avoided.

But not always. From time to time, his trust in other parties would be broken by their actions, prompting him to observe, "An agreement is only as good as the two parties involved." And when difficulties appeared pegged to ethnic characteristics or behaviours, he often found himself assessing the situation by linking it to the subject's origins. It was never done in an overtly racist manner, or even by assuming that some members of one ethnic group demonstrated certain negative characteristics shared by all. Instead, it was used as a means of understanding different values rooted in national origins, an attribute that, given Peter's early life experiences in the mélange of eastern Europe, was perfectly natural.

Still, while he obviously enjoyed assisting new Canadians where practical, he remained realistic about the nature of people generally. "All nationalities and all religions produce both good and not so good people," he commented. "At the beginning, I tried to limit myself to dealing with people whose ethnic and religious background was similar to my own. With time and experience, I understood that one should not focus on nationality and religion, but rather on professionalism and good business ethics. Every country has its specific features, and each new immigrant should

learn those in his or her new country, and look for ways to cooperate with others." He made these comments after several years'
experience dealing with immigrants. Most of these experiences
were both profitable and gratifying. A few, however, tested his
patience as well as his wisdom.

An example arose out of a dispute between two tenants in the
same Prombank-owned building. The larger of the two, an electrical wholesale and distributing firm employing three hundred
people, occupied twenty thousand square feet of one building. A
tool and machine shop company leased a much smaller space in an
adjacent building. The two companies shared a common driveway,
which led to an incident igniting a serious quarrel.

One morning, workers at the electrical firm were unloading
materials from a large trailer blocking the shipping door of the
machine shop in the neighbouring building. When the owner of
the smaller company complained that his supplier had arrived to
find the entrance blocked and demanded the adjacent firm's trailer
be moved immediately, he was asked to wait until the unloading
was completed. Angry that his request was ignored, the machine
shop owner flattened all four tires on the trailer. When the electrical wholesaler discovered the flattened tires, he called the police.
The other tenant went beyond admitting to police that he had
disabled the vehicle; he loudly boasted about it, declaring that the
next time any truck or trailer blocked his receiving dock he would
use an axe to chop the tires. Hearing that threat, the officers placed
him under arrest.

The large electrical firm was a long-established Canadian company whose employees, while representing a cross-section of
Canadians generally, were primarily white and English-speaking.
The smaller tool and machine shop was owned by Sikhs, who
employed people of their own origins and faith.

Peter Jacyk admired the two young Sikh men who ran the
machine shop. He respected their education—one was a lawyer,

the other an engineer—and the work ethic displayed by the owners and their employees. "They were both handsome men, very hard-working and always on the job," he recalled. "They had a number of older Sikh people who were always busy, it seemed. Whenever I came into their machine shop, they greeted me pleasantly and with respect."

The Sikh was quickly released on bail, but the problem remained. The owner of the electrical wholesaling firm, unable to resolve things with the Sikhs, asked Peter to step in and settle the situation. It was not a duty that he welcomed. Fully prepared to deal with tenant issues involving himself and Prombank as the landlord, he preferred that any conflict between the tenants be addressed by themselves or some appointed arbitrator. Playing the role of honest broker between two valued tenants, especially when the problem was rooted in emotions rather than rights, risked alienating at least one side and possibly both. Reluctantly, he agreed to listen to the electrical wholesaler's argument. "He said that the trailer drivers often had to drive all night long bringing in supplies," Peter wrote, "and both of them often arrived at the same time each morning. When that happened, they had just enough room to squeeze next to each other in the driveway, but sometimes the bigger trailer left no room for the smaller one, delivering materials to the machine shop."

Later that day, Peter visited the Sikh-operated machine shop to hear their side of the story. Although they greeted Peter warmly at the beginning, his descriptions of the wholesaler's position and his suggestion that they attempt to solve things in an equitable manner created an angry response from the Sikhs.

Peter described in detail his efforts at playing peacemaker:

The older brother started to raise his voice, and said "Next time I will do what I promised. My religion tells me that if someone hurts me, I am to repay him ten times over!" I responded in the same tone, asking him who was the judge to determine who hurt whom? Was it him alone? I said, "You accuse people of hurting you and then you feel you have the right to retaliate?" I explained to him that the wholesaler had three hundred employees, and if all of them began letting the air out of the tires of any trucks arriving at the machine shop, the Sikh would spend all of his time refilling tires. "Can you make money doing that?" I asked.

When the Sikh replied that he could not change his religion, Peter's response was classic Jacyk philosophy, couched in terms only a successful immigrant, proud of his achievements and pleased to be living in Canada, could articulate so effectively: "When he said that, I asked, 'Why did you come to Canada then? To make money or to make trouble? Everyone has only what he or she has made for themselves. If you make money, you will have money. If you make trouble, you will have trouble. Make up your mind.'"

As much as anyone, Peter knew that disagreements over religions and their values never resolved anything. While the Sikh engineer and his brother pondered Peter's words, Peter reminded them that their lease agreement included a nuisance clause, and Peter was prepared to exercise it and evict them from the building if the brothers continued with their threats. Then he turned on his heel and left.

The encounter is revealing because once again Peter framed his position as someone who had arrived in Canada owning nothing and expecting nothing except an opportunity. Having received the opportunity and made the most of it, he refused to tolerate the complaints of others who refused to acknowledge all that Canada had provided for them, especially when they leaned on values and traditions rooted in their native country to justify their actions and attitudes.

This time it worked, helped along perhaps by his threat to evict the Sikh brothers and their firm. The following morning, the younger of the two brothers approached Peter with a broad smile. He had been angry over Peter's comments about his religion until he realized that his attitude was the reason for such widespread poverty in India. "It is the oldest democracy in the world," he explained, "but instead of making money and cooperating with each other, our people tend to make trouble for each other."

According to Peter, the two sides found a method of handling the trailers as they arrived without causing difficulties for each other. The Indian brothers remained good tenants for some time before purchasing their own building, eventually acquiring 100,000 square feet of space on their own. "Now they are big millionaires," Peter wrote in 2000, "and have no need to fight anyone."

Another tenant experience was not nearly as gratifying. This time, the tenants were Lebanese people who, employing a clause in the zoning bylaws, opened a retail food store in a Prombank location originally zoned for industrial use. Peter agreed to the lease, at rentals substantially lower than would be charged in a commercially zoned property.

He admired the Lebanese owners for their cleverness and was impressed by the attention and the investment spent on finishing the store's interior. Flooring, lighting, décor, and equipment were all first quality. Selling Canadian food, supplemented by Lebanese meats and groceries, the store initially attracted a large customer base, most of them Lebanese. From time to time, Peter purchased some food products for his evening meal, until he realized the owners were not being entirely fair in the pricing of their produce. "They sold small one-ounce bags of baking soda for fifty cents," he recalled, "which added up to eight dollars a pound. But the same baking soda was less than a dollar and a half a pound in other stores. Their vegetables were priced much higher than other stores as well, and I could tell their meat was not very fresh."

Calling the owner one day, Peter observed that the pricing seemed far too high, especially considering that the meats and vegetables were hardly the best available. "Do you think this is okay?" he asked the store owner. The response was disturbing. "Our people don't know the language very well," the owner said, "so they prefer to come to our store. Besides, they are used to this kind of practice."

Peter responded by suggesting the owner was mistaken to judge his own people in this manner. "They may not know the language today," he suggested, "but their children who attend schools will teach them the language, and they'll know the difference in the future. Instead of building trust with your customers, you will turn them away."

The owner's response: "Don't worry. By then I'll be rich and have another store."

Soon the store's traffic began falling off rapidly. Peter's observations about failing to build customer loyalty were proving prescient. Lebanese customers refused to patronize a fellow countryman when they realized he was taking advantage of their ethnic connection. The owner made a few changes to stem the drop in sales—but without success.

It all ended with a 1:30 AM telephone call to Peter's home from the fire department. His building was aflame, and when he arrived a few minutes later, his fears were confirmed. Someone had spread several cans of gasoline inside the grocery store before setting it ablaze and closing the door. When sufficient pressure built up from the heat of the flames, the resulting explosion literally blew the roof off the building.

Prombank's insurance covered damage to the building. The interior contents, including food inventory and equipment, had recently been insured for $400,000 by the owner. In an ironic twist, however, most of the interior damage had been caused not by fire but from the resulting explosion, an event that the policy did not cover. The owners collected nothing.

SUCCESS, AS IT DOES with most people, brought both satisfaction and challenges to Peter Jacyk. The satisfaction could be measured in various ways—enjoying the comfort and security that a large income could provide, turning his visions of new buildings into brick-and-mortar reality, earning the respect of colleagues and competitors, and enabling him to support causes near to his heart.

The challenges most often were rooted in the response of others who, for whatever reasons, chose to exploit or denigrate him for his success. "When one grows in business," he noted, "one becomes more and more visible. When that happens, people want to associate with you and try to share your success. Some are honest people, some are dreamers, and some are con artists." Most, of course, wished to tap into his wisdom and his wealth, especially the latter. He wrote:

> Various proposals come so well prepared and presented that it is often difficult to recognize which is realistic, which is fantasy, and which is a pure con. You cannot reject all of these people, but even if you accept only the ones that sound honest you spend a lot of time listening to other people's needs. And this does not mean that he or she will be good in business. To be successful in business, you often must give one hundred percent of your time, and this requires change in your relationship with others.

Dealing with these challenges, he recognized, meant building a protective shell of sorts, without insulating himself from those he valued and needed. His observations may not be unique among those who rise from poverty to heights of success, but they bear reflection to understand not only the man and his values but the substantial and unglamorous price that must be paid. In Peter Jacyk's own words:

When one grows successful, one has to reduce one's social contacts and friends, and relate to a new environment. This is a hard shift to make for most people. My former friends complained that, when I was poor, I had been a good man. Now that I am rich, I ignore them.

They do not realize two things. First, I have little time for myself as well as for them. Second, their way of life, if it is not a constructive and positive life, is a waste of time. I am convinced that most successful people share my opinion.

To some, this may sound like pronouncements from a man obsessed with business and the need to keep growing it. It's a false impression, however. Peter Jacyk understood the need for a balanced life and appreciated the opportunity to step back from his business activities from time to time. Whether relaxing at his simple cottage a hundred kilometres east of Toronto in Grafton, Ontario, or occasionally travelling to distant countries, he demonstrated his ability of knowing when to work and knowing when—and how—to relax.

"Can you imagine," he said to friend and business partner John Zdunic one evening, "if you were to buy a car that had everything, every feature and every option and every comfort you could ask for, but it did not have any brakes? How far do you think you would go before you crashed? This is something that I keep repeating all of my life." You must have the drive, you must have the education, you must have the stamina, you must have all the other qualities needed to succeed in whatever you choose, he explained. But you must know as well when to slow down, and when to stop and rest, maybe just to look around a little.

11

The Halls of Harvard

*I came to realize that giving money to
causes I considered worthwhile
was just as satisfying as making it.*

PETER JACYK

TWENTY YEARS AFTER his arrival in Canada as a virtually pen-
niless immigrant, Peter Jacyk had achieved a remarkable level
of success in his business endeavours. His dedication to building
Prombank into a substantial corporation was as strong as ever, but
with his financial future secure, he began shifting some of his energies and attention elsewhere—not to new business opportunities,
but to educating the world about Ukraine.

Through most of his adult life, Peter Jacyk celebrated two separate but linked qualities: his Ukrainian roots and his Canadian
identity. Neither was permitted to interfere with or denigrate
the other; each represented a different facet of his pride. His success in Canada enabled him to express his love and concern for
Ukraine, initially through funding various projects and ultimately
through his own energy and example for others to emulate. The

first substantial contribution occurred in 1970, when he donated $1,000 to funding for a Ukrainian textbook to be used in Canadian schools. This was followed the next year with a significant donation to Ukrainian schools and churches in Brazil.

Ukrainians had emigrated to Brazil in three waves: prior to 1914, between the two World Wars, and immediately following WWII. Most arrived from Galicia/Halychyna and settled in the hilly southern state of Paraná, often referred to as "the Brazilian Ukraine." They soon came to represent a substantial portion of Brazilian society and culture; by the year 2000, an estimated 500,000 Brazilians could trace their ethnic roots back to Ukraine.[1]

Hearing of the need for educational materials among these largely unacknowledged members of the diaspora, Peter Jacyk played a major role in providing assistance, travelling to Brazil to confirm that the investment was paying dividends. He was also supportive of many activities conducted in Ukraine by the Catholic Church, though he expressed some criticism of the apparent lack of balance between religion and education in the rebuilding of post-Soviet Ukraine. "We spend four hundred and eighty-nine million dollars on our churches," he noted at one point, "but only eighty-five million dollars on education."[2] The comment should not be considered evidence of Peter Jacyk's lack of religious faith but rather testimony to his high opinion of the value of education.

Where Ukrainians were concerned, he wanted them to view education as a means to success, broadening their goals and

---

1. University of Alberta press release, "Scholars Impressed with Ukrainian Life in Brazil," June 29, 2009.

2. No record is available to substantiate the figures quoted by Jacyk. Various observers, notably Magocsi, have contrasted the growth of churches and religious factions in post-Soviet Ukraine with limited achievements in the country's educational system. See Paul Robert Magocsi, A History of Ukraine: The Land and Its Peoples (Toronto: University of Toronto Press, 2010), 739–41.

expectations. He had a point. In 1971, only 3.6 percent of Ukrainians in Canada were owners and managers. Of the balance, 10.6 percent worked as professionals and in technical fields, 13.1 percent in clerical work, 9.2 percent in sales, and 12.5 percent in service fields.[3] Ukrainians clearly had come a long way from the stereotype of them as labourers and farm workers, but Peter Jacyk wanted his people to advance more quickly. Twenty-five years after the end of World War II, too many Ukrainians, in Jacyk's view, still considered themselves "suitable for work that required strong backs," and it disappointed him.

"Peter loved Canada and saw it as the true land of opportunity," Nadia Jacyk explains, "and with all that opportunity available, he didn't want them to keep seeing themselves as labourers. He wanted them to aim higher, to take full advantage of Canada as he had done." In Jacyk's view, many Ukrainians and other immigrant groups were aiming too low when it came to achievements. He was familiar with the traditional portrait of immigrant parents working long, hard hours at mundane occupations, boasting that they were sacrificing their lives "so our children won't have to work as hard as I did." This, he believed, was wrong-headed. In a country as filled with opportunities as Canada, they should be building something beyond their family, creating businesses and enterprises that, one way or another, benefited and were recognized by all of Canada, not just the immediate ethnic community. As long as Ukrainians chose not to set their sights higher and refused to consider themselves potential entrepreneurs, many of the sacrifices made for their children would be in vain. Peter Jacyk wanted more—more from himself, more from Ukrainians within Canada, and more from those who remained in his native land.

---

3. W. Roman Petryshyn, ed., *Changing Realities: Social Trends among Ukrainian Canadians* (Edmonton: Canadian Institute of Ukrainian Studies Press, 1980), 62.

In 1986 he established the Petro Jacyk Education Foundation, a step that facilitated a number of initiatives on behalf of Ukraine and the Ukrainian language. In a recollection written some years later, he explained his motivation for the creation of the foundation with words that, in a different context, would sound like a combination of manifesto and call to arms:

> At the time that I was formulating the principles of my Foundation, I attempted to look toward the future in redefining the traditional Ukrainian viewpoint. Ukrainians have always constituted part of the world's working class, and the world (through taxes) has always profited from their labour. The time has come for Ukrainians to break out of the mould of hired workers and passive consumers of information, to become equal partners in the process of global development and active shapers of international public opinion.
>
> We must attain influential positions throughout the world, which is impossible without a proper education. We must also provide the world with objective information about Ukraine's past and present through the establishment of high-level scholarly programs in Ukrainian studies. This information will determine the world's attitude toward us. A generous and intelligent financial investment strategy is necessary for the realization of these objectives.

Peter Jacyk accumulated substantial assets from the mid-1980s forward, but his generally conservative approach to finance and to life meant he was more concerned about the things his wealth permitted him to do than the things it may have said about his business success. "People come to know you after an accumulation of material wealth," he wrote, "but [they] don't see that one is rich not by what he has, but by what he or she gives to others."

Like so many goals Jacyk chose to pursue, his contributions to Ukrainian studies and culture outpaced everything else in the field, and by the end of the 1980s, he would be recognized as the biggest contributor to Ukrainian studies in the western hemisphere. His efforts and generosity were not always universally commended, however, especially at the beginning. Some people doubted his motives, calling him a self-promoter. Others believed his generosity was not wholly reflective of his ability to fund these projects, suggesting that he should give more. Nevertheless, he pressed on.

In the draft of the unpublished memoir completed just a few months before his death, Jacyk traced his major contributions to educational and cultural causes. He concluded: "It is hard to estimate the value of this work in dollars, but I am convinced it produces better individuals than any stock market."

Peter Jacyk's respect for higher education was tempered by his expectation that everyone, in every position in society, should be expected to make a meaningful contribution. Academic studies and research were important activities to be sure, but he appears to have had little patience with unproductive "blue-sky" dreamers, especially when they were drawing income from limited financial resources—and most especially when the resources had been provided directly from his own bank balance. This led to periodic sparring with individuals whose work he encouraged with his financial aid but whose attitude toward managing finances differed from his own. None was more telling than a series of disagreements with the Ukrainian Studies Fund (USF), which raised funds in support of Ukrainian programs at Harvard.

Ukrainian students in New York had first begun pressing for a field of studies on their native country at an American university in the mid-1950s. Some scholars and faculty countered that Ukraine was merely a province of Russia, and the Ukrainian language itself was a dialect. In their view, Ukraine deserved no special status as a nation; all Ukrainian studies could be conducted beneath the umbrella of Russian-oriented courses.

The students rejected this concept and continued their efforts. Many expected that a chair for the study of Ukrainian history and culture would, once sufficient funds were accumulated, be established at Columbia University under the aegis of the Harriman Institute. This made a good deal of sense. Harriman was highly regarded, with a deep background of study in that region of the world, and the New York area was home for a large contingent of Ukrainian-born residents.

In Cambridge, Massachusetts, however, Professor Omeljan Pritsak had other ideas. Pritsak declared that a chair in Ukrainian studies should be established at Harvard, where he was an influential lecturer and professor in Turkic and Central Asian studies as well as a specialist on Ukraine. Pritsak lobbied for a faculty group dedicated to Ukrainian studies that would provide a true perspective on the field. Harvard authorities agreed. An endowment fund of $1.8 million was to be raised to fund chairs on Ukrainian history, language, and literature, and additional funds were to be raised for an institute. In the 1960s, that sum was an enormous amount of money. But an even larger amount would be accumulated through contributions from a broad cross-section of Ukrainians in North America, ranging from auto workers in Detroit and Windsor to highly successful business people—among them, Peter Jacyk.

Peter took justifiable pride in his association with the renowned university. "At Harvard, academics make no differentiation to colour, nationality or religion," he wrote. Then, suggesting that Harvard represented the pinnacle of the West's approach to education, he added: "Knowledge in the Western world is shared and everyone values it, contrary to Russian or Hitler's Nur für Deutschen!, only for Germans… [In the West] someone can be recognized worldwide by his or her discipline. Professor Pritsak was known in the world for his knowledge in Arabic, Chinese and 53 languages. I felt respect [from] the other professors in his presence."

Peter quickly established a close rapport with the celebrated Professor Pritsak. "For some reason he respected my opinions and I greatly appreciated his," Jacyk wrote.

Among the views they shared was a judgement of some aspects of their own people. Recalling a visit with Professor Pritsak, Jacyk wrote:

> One evening at his residence he pointed out how our community leaders wasted time and money to portray themselves as great patriots. People in the newspapers, radio and books mistakenly point out how we organize protests and demonstrations… Instead of wasting time and money for protests, is it not better to write an objective book and question some statements or ideas? By joining our strengths, we can become strong [and] be prepared for a larger reality, but our language is weak.
>
> What interests will any foreign scholar have to learn Ukrainian? With our Ukrainian knowledge we can reach at the most 20 million people. By knowing the English language and communicating, we can make ourselves known to 300 or 400 million readers. How many interesting translations do we have from Ukrainian to English? You see, the world doesn't hate us—it doesn't know us! How can one love something that it doesn't even know? We have not even translated our own history into the English language!

Peter Jacyk assumed a leading role in raising the endowment funds for the Harvard Ukrainian program through the USF, and the Harvard Ukrainian Research Institute (HURI) was launched in 1973, with Omeljan Pritsak as its first director. The institute was almost immediately attacked by Soviet Ukrainians, who called the Harvard group and its supporters "bourgeois nationalists" and criticized Peter Jacyk for being "against the real Ukraine,"[4] a claim that may have amused him but could hardly deter him.

The choice of Harvard as the locus of Ukrainian studies in the West was not universally admired. Many Canadians wondered why they should be expected to contribute funds to an institution south of the border. Couldn't similar achievements be scored by a Canadian university? The answer was twofold. First, no university operates within a more prestigious aura of ethics, integrity, and scholarly standards than Harvard—an important factor when seeking funding. An estimated ten thousand Ukrainians in the U.S. and Canada initially donated more than $4 million to establish the three Harvard chairs and the research institute.[5]

Second, Canada would soon have its own centre for Ukrainian research. The Canadian Institute of Ukrainian Studies was founded at the University of Alberta in Edmonton in 1976 to support research in Ukrainian history and culture, publish books and other materials in these fields, and provide scholarships and bursaries. The Alberta centre's significance would be enhanced to at least some degree through its association with Harvard. Peter Jacyk explained, "If you have two books on the same subject and one lists any publisher you wish to name and the other lists Harvard, which will people trust and reach for? We must begin with Harvard to create our credibility, then expand our works where we find the best people for the job."

Among those who encountered Peter Jacyk in the early days of his activities on behalf of Ukrainian studies was Frank Sysyn, who arrived at Harvard in 1969 to pursue postgraduate studies and was

---

4. *The Stone Cross of Peter Jacyk (Kamyianiy hrest Petra Yatsika)*, produced and directed by Edward Zaniuk, Ukrainians in the World video series (WETI Telehrupa (Telegroup), 1998), videocassette (VHS).

5. Ellie McGrath, Bruce Van Voorst, and Christopher Redman, "Education: Wanted: More Kremlinologists," *Time* (November 29, 1982), 98.

soon caught up in the fundraising effort. "While it was apparent that he lacked formal education beyond a basic level," Sysyn recalls, "he was always prepared to listen carefully to the most arcane kind of academic discussion and then challenge the academics, just as he would challenge the intelligentsia, the educated Ukrainians who represented a kind of bourgeoisie of culture." Jacyk's challenges were never disdainful, Sysyn emphasizes. "He had enormous respect for knowledge and learning. One of his most common sayings was, 'I can make money, but I can't create ideas in people's minds, which professors can do.' But he also made it clear from the beginning that he had a higher ambition than most." Peter Jacyk impressed Sysyn as a man who, though not notably eloquent in his speech, carefully considered what he was about to say before he said it. "He wanted to test you and question you about things, and he was dedicated to the idea of doing big things. He wasn't interested in wasting his time on small achievements."

Sysyn suggests the respect shown to universities was likely based on the deprivation that Peter Jacyk and his contemporaries suffered under the Poles, who denied Ukrainians the right to form a university and hindered them from attending any institution of higher learning. "For Ukrainians to have a university or to have chairs dedicated to some aspect of Ukraine culture and history," Sysyn adds, "was important not only for the well-being of individuals, but also for the prestige of the group." Being denied the right to higher-level studies for such an extended period created a substantial amount of dedication to supporting the opportunity when it appeared. "He also loved history," Sysyn continues, speaking of Jacyk. "He had lived through some of the great upheavals of history, after all."

Toronto in the 1970s was, in Frank Sysyn's phrase, already a "full-service community" for Ukrainians. Community facilities in his chosen city were important to Peter Jacyk, who backed their activities as much as anyone did. He contributed to and volunteered his time to assist in youth organizations and sports teams. He enrolled his daughters in Saturday schools to study the Ukrainian language, history, and other cultural endeavours. He wanted more, however. He wanted to reach the "outer world," the one beyond the Ukrainian community itself, to tell the story and describe the achievements of his homeland. HURI proved the perfect vehicle for that.

As a member of the executive of the USF, the fundraising organization and charity that had begun the drive to establish a chair at an American university, Peter was responsible for fundraising in Canada. He worked within a group of mostly Ukrainian immigrants who dedicated their efforts to the Fund of the Chair of Ukrainian Studies, or FKU, as the USF was known in Ukrainian.

As an outstanding donor and leader of fundraising efforts in Canada, Peter was also invited to join the Harvard Visiting Committee for Ukrainian studies at Harvard, comprising prominent scholars, businessmen, community activists, and supporters of Harvard. The committee was appointed by the university's Board of Overseers, and its role consisted of speaking with professors and students to review activities, discuss projects, provide an off-campus view of the work, and advise on Ukrainian studies at Harvard. Its findings were then submitted to the Board of Overseers as a means of assessing the relevance and value of these various activities. Over the years, distinguished members of the Visiting Committee for Ukrainian studies have included Zbigniew Brzezinski, the noted academic and statesman; the well-known columnist Joseph Alsop; Neil Rudenstine, dean at Princeton University and later president at Harvard; and Charles Francis Adams, a scion of the family who gave the United States two presidents. Peter Jacyk was in essence the USF representative on the Harvard Visiting Committee, and he often served as a channel for the fund's views. Nevertheless, he remained very much his own man and was not bashful in expressing his opinions.

Service on the committee may have left Peter Jacyk with mixed emotions about academia, though it apparently banished to a large degree any feelings of inadequacy he felt about his lack of higher education. He expressed his initial misgivings when he wrote: "There must be a reason why the general opinion is that those who teach in universities sit in ivory towers. The atmosphere in an academic world is quite different from the rest of the world. I have to admit that, at the beginning, I felt very strange towards the titles and everyone's reserved expression."

The interviews conducted by the committee involved extensive note-taking; at the end of the day, both committee members and the relevant faculty members had the opportunity to express views and opinions. "From the first interview I noticed that nothing was more important at Harvard than getting results," Jacyk wrote. "If something was not good, their main goal was to improve it. Whether one's English was broken or well-spoken, it did not matter. When my time came to express my observations on the interviews, I did not know if the professors noticed my accent."

Recalling this first encounter with the venerated Harvard faculty and its roster of graduate students, Jacyk noted that his own lack of formal studies soon stopped intimidating him. "I did not even come close to their knowledge or intellect, but my knowledge of real life, and the real world, was what impressed them, and they complimented me. This made me feel more at home with these academics, and after three days I felt that, overall, I was not inferior." Then he added a confident prediction: "Next time, we would meet as colleagues."

Any remaining inhibitions that Peter Jacyk experienced in the presence of Harvard faculty and administrators were swept aside when the subject of financial management arose. He contributed millions of dollars over the years to Harvard and other institutions to strengthen the impact and raise awareness of the Ukrainian language and the country's history. He expected these contributions to produce measurable results. When they failed to do so and funds began to run short, he expressed his concerns in typically direct fashion.

During Peter's term on the Harvard Visiting Committee, and in his years on the executive committee of the USF, two major issues arose relating to finances of the Harvard endowments. The first was the question of whether the $1.8 million donated to Harvard by the USF in the early 1970s guaranteed the existence of three endowed chairs. "Most of his financial contributions were for endowments," Nadia Jacyk explains. "This meant the money would generate income for use by the university and as a means of funding programs in perpetuity. When he learned that there were income deficiencies causing operating shortfalls at HURI for the years 1981 and 1982, he delved into the matter wholeheartedly in an attempt to analyze the source of the problems, looking for ways to improve the situation." What soon became apparent was that Harvard was acknowledging only one chair. As a result, more money would be needed to ensure that all three chairs were funded in perpetuity.

Not surprisingly, Peter expressed deep disagreement with this prospect. "Some fourteen thousand people donated their money on the understanding that the Chairs would be endowed forever," he wrote to Professor George Gibian, head of the Harvard Visiting Committee. "To approach these same donors, eleven years later, with a different interpretation will be an immense discredit to Harvard University in general. Not trusting Harvard, these same people will no longer donate a penny to the Harvard Ukrainian Studies program."[6]

---

6. Peter Jacyk, letter to George Gibian, May 11, 1981.

Peter worked closely with the faculty at Harvard and with Professor Gibian to press the case that the three chairs had been endowed in perpetuity according to a written agreement in 1968 and confirmed in a 1973 letter. The university, Jacyk insisted, must honour its agreements. In October 1981, the Harvard administration apologized for the deviation from the agreement and confirmed that there would be full funding of the three chairs, with retroactive income remitted to HURI for the entire period extending back to 1972–73.

On October 29, 1981, Peter wrote with pleasure to Professor Gibian, "I think we succeeded in straightening out the matter concerning the three Chairs at Harvard University, with many thanks to your three years of persistence."

The other troubling financial issue was the relatively small return the endowment of HURI was realizing at a time when interest rates and returns were very high in the business world. The financing problem, Peter Jacyk believed, could be traced to two factors: an inadequate return on invested endowment funds and an imbalance in Harvard's distribution of these funds between educational purposes and administration costs.

In 1981, the institute was expected to receive $88,000 from its $1.8 million endowment fund from the Harvard administration via Harvard Management Company, fund managers for the university. This represented an annual return of less than 5 percent during a period in which the annual interest paid by major banks hovered at almost 20 percent. The low rate of return surprised Peter Jacyk. According to his calculation, HURI was spending 25 percent of its available funds in the endowment on education while 75 percent of the earned income went back into the endowment fund held by Harvard. "If this trend is allowed to continue for another five to ten years," he wrote, "there will be no practical value left for the $2 million collected and endowed for education. I am sure that the overall intent of Harvard is for education and only a certain portion of the total expenses should be for administration. Strangely enough, it seems to be the contrary in our case."[7]

When Peter met with the executive of the USF, he was more direct in presenting his concerns. In a draft letter to members afterward, he vented his frustration in unmistakable language:

> Disappointment is what I felt upon my return from the meeting held in New York on the 9th of January 1982. I was disappointed in the people who spoke empty words and to whom I had entrusted endless hours of my time and $260,000 of my own money. These same people did not even take a little time to consider if my argument had some validity. They simply treated me with prejudice and distrust. I had considered resigning from the board but felt it would be the easier way out. In order not to leave the cause in which we all believe, and to prevent the deterioration of it, I shall try once more.

The draft letter lifted the curtain on what, from Peter Jacyk's point of view at least, must have been an emotional encounter between various strong personalities, including people who believed that another approach should be adopted in dealing with Harvard and the USF.

"Peter always believed that there is nothing in life that can't be improved upon," Nadia Jacyk says about her father's problems with the situation at Harvard. "He was never tolerant of poor management of any kind—or at least what he perceived as poor management. He realized that universities functioned in a different fashion from businesses, and he respected the fact that universities can do things that we could not do." In Peter Jacyk's view, however, Harvard's leadership was more interested in the

---

7. Peter Jacyk, letter to George Gibian, October 29, 1981.

functioning of the overall university than in the success and achievements of individual units, including the Ukrainian studies program. Another factor entered the equation, according to Nadia Jacyk: "The Harvard fund also included a large amount of money collected from the Ukrainian community, and I think he felt responsible for the way that money was being spent."

Peter claimed to hear one member of the USF declare that the $2 million endowment fund "went toward paying for the name of Harvard,"[8] an approach he rejected with some vigour. Expressing the unease he felt as a result of these comments, Peter Jacyk enunciated his concerns and proposals in characteristically straightforward language, concluding: "Perhaps it was a mistake to invite me to sit on the Visiting Committee, because otherwise I might still be buying [another USF member's] fantastic plastic gimmicks and ploys on how to collect money, how to place it into a 5 percent self-liquidating program, and never question the more important side. And that is: what are we getting for our collected monies, and for how long?" He ended his letter with a detailed financial analysis illustrating how, should the management continue unchanged and costs maintain their upward trend due to rising inflation, the "in perpetuity" endowment fund would vanish.

In response, one USF member's rambling letter contained the following comments:

> The purpose of your unbridled criticism is very questionable, and we sincerely hope that in the future such criticism be tempered with justice and understanding.
>
> You leave us with the impression that you would like to change everyone into your own image. This can never be... At

---

8. Quoted in Peter Jacyk's letter of February 1982 to members of the finance committee of the USF board.

all times, we aspire to do our very best but there are times when we fall short of our expectations. If we fail to perform your way, it does not necessarily mean that we have no respect for your ideas and opinions. However, we do not take kindly to a dictatorship or verbal abuse… There is no doubt that improvements can be made in the financial structure of the Ukrainian Studies [endowment]. Inflation is slowly consuming the base of the Institute. We have to find means to assure the financial future of the project.[9]

The tone of the response ("we aspire to do our very best but there are times when we fall short of our expectations") seems at odds among serious adults dealing with a financial crisis at an institution in which the Ukrainian community had invested so much. It also appears to illustrate the reason for Peter's repeated frustration with the USF, which, in his view, preferred to talk about problems rather than take action to solve them, including making an attempt to negotiate better terms with Harvard. His annoyance grew more pointed when, instead of responding to his concerns directly, the other members chastised him.

Peter's answer was to repeat his calculations indicating that the endowment fund had lost 35 percent of its capital value over three years, presumably based on the impact of high inflation at the time. Doing nothing for another three years, he suggested, would effectively end the program, and its "perpetual" endowment income, forever.[10] Then he added: "Action is always stronger than fatherly philosophy."

---

9. Joseph Iwaniw, letter to Peter Jacyk, February 22, 1982.

10. Peter Jacyk, letter to Joseph Iwaniw, March 5, 1982: "For three years I have tried to correct [the problem with the financial structure] between Mr. Tarnawsky and myself before taking the present step. In those three years, through inflation, we lost on $1,500,000 approximately 35%. This amounts to about $600,000 and you tell me this is just a minimal crisis."

He had not ended a disagreement. He had launched a saga.

Almost a year later, in mid-December 1982, Peter Jacyk sent an extended letter to George Yurchyshyn, senior vice-president of the First National Bank of Boston, who had attended a meeting of the Harvard Visiting Committee for the Ukrainian Institute. Yurchyshyn, whose day-to-day work involved high-level financial and investment matters, had grasped Peter's concerns, and according to Peter, his "in-depth analysis of the situation and delivery at the meeting were definitely a step forward." Peter's letter ended with the request: "Since we are all very busy, I suggest you hire a local independent accountant to look into [these] matters quite critically, and prepare the statements as quickly as possible."[11]

Peter may have hoped the view of a neutral observer would pacify USF members who were upset by his criticism. It did not. Whether he pressed his case too strongly or other members of the USF resented "an outsider" questioning their decisions, Peter evidently touched a nerve in at least one executive committee member who threatened to launch a criminal investigation against Peter and who found Peter's correspondence "opinionated, self-serving and short on courtesy and good taste. I have no patience with that kind of nonsense [sic]," adding: "Since your inclusion in the USF, you behaved with superior insolence and arrogantly insulted anyone who dared to differ with you. As far as I am concerned, the money you contributed is not worth the grief you inflicted."[12]

Later that month, Peter detailed his position in a four-page letter to USF members. Given the charges directed his way by the USF member quoted above, his letter is worth reviewing in some detail. This is a man determined to make his point, keenly

---

11. Peter Jacyk, letter to George B. Yurchyshyn, December 15, 1982.

12. Joseph Iwaniw, letter to Peter Jacyk, February 18, 1983.

interested in the long-term success of the institute, and refusing to be cowed by anyone:

To the "so-called" USF Executives and the USF Board Members:

The reason I address you as "so-called" is because it is unfortunately so. When and where were you elected and re-elected; by whom and by how many votes? Have you ever seen a report on the annual meeting? Were minutes ever read from previous meetings? Did anyone ever approve or disapprove any financial statements? Was there ever any supervisory committee or chartered accountants appointed? The answer to all these questions is No. In my opinion, the [list of] so-called Executive Board members... on the letterhead is only a deceit of the public...

From personal experience I know that money which is inherited, won in a lottery or collected through fund-raising is one thing. To manage and obtain the most [value] for the collected money is another matter. It is the management aspect that I am concerned with...

If any difference of opinion should occur among the members of any board, which is an absolute normal occurrence, the only mature way to handle the difference is to bring the members to one table, discuss the difference, and resolve it by a majority of votes... To permit (if not to instigate) the board members to fight each other, the manager sits on the fence... This further supports my previous statement of there being a lack of managerial skills and abilities to manage a group of people and keep records straight...

In the present situation there isn't any co-ordinated decision-making body nor any communication among the group members. Therefore, in addition to my previous letters, I feel obligated to inform all of you of my observations with regard to USF management. It is up to you to decide what you want to do. There are many of you from the States and only myself from Canada. Sometimes, I question my rights. Why must I continually aggravate you all? I promise you, no more.

At several previous meetings I stated that, "My time was too expensive to collect money from the Ukrainian Community." Therefore, I applied my time to my business and instead of collecting $5 or $10 from the public, I donated much larger sums of my own money. It would be unwise of me now to use my time, travel to Harvard, go through customs, etc., only to hinder, not help, the people who cannot see the correct way of administrating. Instead of thanking me, they oppose me in not a very agreeable way.

In view of all this, please take my name off all USF stationery. My only wish is that I am mistaken in my analysis of the USF situation.

Peter's impatience was with the USF, many of whose members were neither academics nor associated with the Harvard administration itself and were not dedicated to providing the degree of transparency in their dealings Peter expected. Nonetheless, his commitment to supporting Ukrainian studies remained unshaken. While he ended (temporarily) his role in USF functions, he continued to participate in activities of the prestigious and influential Harvard Visiting Committee.

There was nothing miserly about Peter Jacyk. His substantial contributions to causes both related and unrelated to Ukraine prove the folly of that portrayal. He was simply a man who understood the value of a dollar earned through hard work and sacrifice. While the contrast in scope between the two situations is dramatic, he might have compared the money he helped solicit and provide to Harvard with the funds he awarded to the struggling educational system in Brazil. In one case, he could see with his own eyes the benefits his largesse provided; in the other, the money appeared to vanish into a private bureaucracy where his queries about its application were rebuffed.

The short explanation for Peter Jacyk's challenge to the situation at Harvard is simply that he refused to waste money—any money, for any purpose. Uliana Pasicznyk tells the story of institute members gathering in Miami, Florida, in 1982 to celebrate the twenty-fifth anniversary of the launching of the USF. The gathering was also planned as an opportunity for the group to streamline its fundraising efforts. Travelling in her capacity as a member of the institute's staff, Pasicznyk flew to Miami along with two graduate students and a co-worker.

"Mr. Jacyk had arrived earlier, having flown in from Toronto," she says, "and offered to pick us up at the airport. He had rented a compact, a hatchback, that was probably the least expensive model available from the rental car company. And he was a big man!" All five crammed themselves into the small two-door vehicle, and as Peter drove them to the homes of Ukrainian studies supporters and other accommodations where they would stay during their conference, thus avoiding costly hotels, he glanced over his shoulder and said, "I know you're crowded back there, but the next model up from this one—well, it's expensive!"

Peter Jacyk continued to communicate directly with university management at Harvard, particularly recording secretary Schuyler Hollingsworth. In a 1984 letter to Hollingsworth, Peter noted that he had spent some time "in an effort to find out what has been and is being done with the money collected. What I found out instead is that when I give money, I am glorified and as soon as I ask what is accomplished with the money, I become an intruder on [the USF's] authority and personality."[13]

---

13. Peter Jacyk, letter to Schuyler Hollingsworth, June 26, 1984.

Time eventually resolved Peter Jacyk's concerns about the USF and Harvard's endowment investment policies. The rectified funding of the three chairs in perpetuity helped bring in more income for the operation of HURI, and diminishing inflation levels reduced to some extent the 5-versus-18 percent endowment income dilemma in the face of rising operating costs. An individual gift from Peter created a chair titled the Petro Jacyk Endowment Fund in Ukrainian Bibliography. In a letter dated May 30, 1995, to George Grabowicz, director of HURI, Peter remarked on the fact that his gift had grown considerably because of favourable economic conditions and wise investment by the Harvard Management Company. "It is gratifying to find out that my fund has grown to the present value of $830,337," he wrote, noting perhaps facetiously that the Harvard management group deserved a Nobel Prize for its excellent investments.[14]

In a later letter to a prominent publication directed toward Ukrainians, Peter even rose to the defence of Harvard in response to some members of the community who had questioned the value of supporting the university. "I personally know every professor, librarian and staff member working at the HURI as well as many non-Ukrainians associated with Ukrainian studies at Harvard," he explained. "They are pro-Ukrainian, and I have always been pleased that we have such an institution that stands out above all our small-minded groups that call themselves 'political.'"[15]

In January 1998 Peter topped up his Harvard donation to $1 million, adding to the existing Petro Jacyk Bibliography Chair. The newly launched Petro Jacyk Distinguished Fellowship would be awarded to gifted Ukrainian scholars, scientists, artists, and politicians and was also to be funded "in perpetuity." The contribution

14. Peter Jacyk, letter to Professor G. Grabowicz, May 30, 1995.

15. Peter Jacyk, letter to the editor, *Ukrainian Weekly*, September 6, 1998.

prompted Robert Franklin, Harvard's director of development planning, to acknowledge Peter's donation as the largest at HURI, representing "a splendid example for other donors of international studies."

Peter Jacyk's affection for his homeland and his people extended well beyond his extensive contributions in time, energy, and money at Harvard and elsewhere. He often spoke openly and directly as a means of encouraging Ukrainians to look at themselves critically and realistically. Then, recognizing the problem, they would be prepared to deal with it and move forward and upward. "He believed that to remain passive," his daughter Nadia notes, "was not the way to make a positive contribution to the communities he loved and to which he belonged in both Ukraine and Canada. He wanted to encourage people to find solutions to problems."

12

—

The Many Schools
of Jacyk Support

*A university has as its main aim to supplement
the weakness of the individual by the strength of the race.*
JOHN WATSON, QUEEN'S UNIVERSITY, 1950

HARVARD REPRESENTED THE pinnacle of Peter Jacyk's efforts
on the academic stage to advance the cause of Ukraine in
North America. As he had indicated, reference to Harvard elevated
a project or an entire program in the minds of people everywhere.
On its own, however, Harvard would not be sufficient to achieve
his goals—nor, perhaps, to contain all of Peter's ambitions where
his mother country's identity was concerned. When it came to
Ukrainian studies, Harvard might have achieved the highest profile among North American schools, thanks in large part to the
pioneering work of Dr. Pritsak, but others were at least as active.
Chief among them was New York's Columbia University, which
broadened its Ukrainian studies program under the aegis of the
Harriman Institute.

The first academic centre in the U.S. devoted to the interdis-
ciplinary study of Russia and the Soviet Union, the Harriman

Institute had been founded in 1946, supported by the Rockefeller Foundation. The institute, based in Columbia's School of International and Public Affairs (SIPA), is the oldest major university centre in the U.S. for graduate study of Ukraine and the former Soviet Union. Among its primary goals is to teach specialized knowledge of Ukraine to graduate students preparing for professional careers in government, diplomacy, business, journalism, and non-governmental organizations—people who, in the program description, "hold the key to public understanding of Ukraine and to Western policy towards Ukraine."

Mark von Hagen, now director of the School of Historical, Philosophical and Religious Studies and history professor at Arizona State University, warmly recalls his association with Peter Jacyk. Previous to his Arizona State posting, von Hagen was a professor in the Department of History at Columbia University, where he taught modern Russian, Ukrainian, and Eurasian history. Von Hagen first encountered Peter Jacyk while lecturing at Columbia in the early 1990s. In 1993, Jacyk committed a total of $500,000 to endow the graduate program in Ukrainian Studies there, and von Hagen was named its director.

At the time of the program's launch in October 1995, von Hagen noted that the funds provided by Jacyk would enable the Harriman Institute to develop a permanent commitment to Ukrainian studies, calling Jacyk "one of the most generous and farsighted patrons of Ukrainian studies." "After his experience at Harvard, Peter Jacyk was looking for a new avenue to carry out his goals," von Hagen adds. "I think he was especially impressed that, even though I am not of Ukrainian background, I was interested in developing Ukrainian studies."

Von Hagen's background may indeed have represented the core of Jacyk's espousal of him. An expression of deep interest in the history and culture of Ukraine by non-Ukrainians was considered by Peter Jacyk to be a compliment to his heritage and community, and he valued such attention. He was also, in all likelihood, aware that outsiders bring a unique, often enlightening point of view to the study of any group, whether cultural, social, or ethnic.

In many ways, Columbia was a more attractive location for a school of Ukrainian studies than Harvard. Its Institute on East Central Europe, founded in 1954, is the oldest academic institution dealing exclusively with that region of the world. Together with the Harriman Institute, it was designated an East European, Russian, and Eurasian National Resource Center by the U.S. Department of Education. The development of Ukrainian studies at Columbia reflected the reality that the New York City region, including neighbouring New Jersey and Connecticut, has a greater concentration of Ukrainian diaspora residents than anywhere else in the U.S.

"The immediate area around New York is kind of a homeland for Ukrainians," von Hagen notes. "We were getting more and more Ukrainian-heritage students coming to Columbia, but there was nothing for them to do. They took Russian-language classes and Russian-history classes, but nothing else, not even Ukrainian language studies." It was Professor Alexander Motyl, a Ukrainian lecturing on political science at the time, who launched the first series of studies on Ukraine in the early 1980s, attracting the attention of Peter Jacyk. "When Peter Jacyk began making enquiries, we had at least the basis of a program," von Hagen adds.

The earlier Harvard experience had altered Jacyk's approach to funding universities and educational projects. He decided that he could best fulfill his goals by striking out on his own as the lead fundraiser for programs that he believed in. On a practical note, as the primary motivator for Ukrainian contributions to programs funded by the community, he had exerted enormous effort drafting, printing, mailing, and coordinating appeals, followed by the

necessary bookkeeping and paperwork to track and credit donations that were often little more than $20 or $30 each. "The money
I collect gathering these funds isn't worth the work I put into it,"
he told his daughter Nadia at one point. After the Harvard experience, he appears to have determined that, if cash were to be raised
for projects he believed in, the source would be his own bank
account, eliminating the time-consuming fundraising process and
providing him with the justification to exert as much direction as
possible on the manner in which the funds were applied.

"He decided it would be more efficient to plough all his energies
into the business," Nadia Jacyk explains, "and maximize his earnings that way. Then he could afford to give directly to many causes
without depending on others."

The endowment Peter Jacyk awarded Columbia spawned a
number of additional activities on behalf of Ukrainian studies. It
funded undergraduate courses for students who wanted to pursue Ukrainian projects, covered expenses for one visiting faculty
member per year to teach on various subjects related to Ukraine,
and provided the basis for other fields to be explored. "Once these
activities began, they inspired others to become involved and support the programs," von Hagen says. It seems that Peter Jacyk's
relationship with Columbia was warmer than with Harvard in at
least some aspects. In a speech to the Ukrainian study group at
Columbia in 1994, he stated:

> I believe that money and education make a most constructive
> combination. If I had more money for myself, hardly anybody
> would notice. But contributing to people who will do some-
> thing good with that money gives my life more meaning and
> satisfaction.
>
> This fulfillment I would not be able to achieve without you
> people who have dedicated your lives to academics, teaching

younger generations to strive for excellence making a better world for us all.

In legal terms, no agreement is valid unless supported by the dollar. To prove that I practice what I preach, I am providing an additional fifty thousand dollars to Columbia University for Ukrainian studies.[1]

Without question, Peter Jacyk's support of Columbia's Ukrainian studies generated a wave of interest in and support for activities on the topic, most of them occurring within the vaunted Harriman Institute. Perhaps most influential was a series of conferences in the mid-1990s titled "Peoples, Nations, Identities: The Russian-Ukrainian Encounter," which created extensive debate in the international press. Administrators of the Columbia program recognized Jacyk's devotion to the school's programs by electing him in 1996 as a member of the Harriman Institute National Advisory Committee, assigned to formulate an overall strategic plan for the organization.

Across the border, the University of Toronto became a centre for important Ukrainian studies and resources not only in Canada but internationally as well. In 1985, Peter Jacyk sponsored the publication by the University of Toronto Press of Robert Magocsi's *Ukraine: A Historical Atlas*. This was an important project in the continuing effort to establish Ukraine as an independent nation with a history and culture distinct from that of Soviet Russia. Its thirty-five maps of Ukrainian lands in various periods of history were supplemented with extensive commentary that underlined the shaping of the Ukrainian nation over several centuries. The atlas was the first of its kind to be published in English in addition to Ukrainian. The initial $55,000 contribution by Jacyk subsidized

---

1. Peter Jacyk, speech to Columbia University, April 26, 1994.

the printing costs of the full-colour atlas. The book would prove vital in defining the difference, geographically and by other means, between Russia and Ukraine, and quickly sold more than fifteen thousand copies.

The creation of the Petro Jacyk Microfilm Collection of Ukrainian Serials facilitated the transfer to microfilm of Ukrainian newspapers and journals originally published between 1848 and 1918 that were held at the Austrian National Library. Its inauguration represented a major achievement in providing historical resource material. The collection, launched in 1982 and extended through 1989, soon became among the most heavily consulted collections in the Microtext Section of the University of Toronto Robarts Library, and it proved invaluable for researchers working on the English-language edition of the *Encyclopedia of Ukraine*.

This donation was followed by Jacyk's support to the Robarts Library to establish the Petro Jacyk Central and East European Resource Centre in 1994. The Jacyk collection provided a centralized location for more than five thousand reference volumes in twenty languages, along with special collections in paper and microfilm. Staff members offer reference service and instruction, produce printed and online research, and host workshops and seminars.

"I think of Peter Jacyk as the most consistent supporter of academic work on Ukraine anywhere," says Professor Peter H. Solomon Jr., former director of the Centre for European, Russian, and Eurasian Studies (CERES)[2] at the University of Toronto. "He has had a tremendous impact on studies of Ukraine and helped make enormous progress in Canada and elsewhere." Jacyk also, in Solomon's

---

2. Originally known as the Centre for Russian and East European Studies (CREES). The title and objectives were changed when the original program merged in 2005 with the European Studies Program, the Joint Initiative in German and European Studies (JIGES), and the Institute of European Studies.

view, "wanted to get things accomplished, he wanted something to happen," reflecting an oft-employed description of Jacyk.

Established in 2001, the Petro Jacyk Program for the Study of Ukraine functions within CERES and was created to encourage scholars at the University of Toronto and Ukrainianists at other North American institutions to develop joint projects. As described in the program's mission statement, its primary goal is "to promote scholarly understanding of the government, economy and society in contemporary Ukraine, as well as the country's history and culture, through the encouragement and support of collaborative projects—typically involving workshops, conferences, lectures and seminars, and visiting scholars—and through the support of graduate students studying Ukraine at the University of Toronto." In addition, a graduate student exchange program in conjunction with Kyiv-Mohyla Academy in Ukraine hosts visiting scholars from Ukraine at U of T for a one-month period, and Ukraine's most prominent leaders and cultural figures are invited to speak in its guest lecture series.

Although the launch of the Toronto program may chronologically have trailed those at Harvard and elsewhere, Peter Jacyk's timing was superb from a financial standpoint. "The university was in one of its phases where it was providing matching money for endowments relating to the support of students," explains Solomon. As a result, the initial $350,000 contribution from Jacyk was doubled by the university's matching contribution. Jacyk added a further $650,000 to cover, on an endowment basis, other activities, such as attracting visiting scholars, hosting conferences, and producing associated events.

Through the impetus of Nadia Jacyk, the initial program was expanded with the introduction of the Petro Jacyk Post-Doctoral Fellowship in Ukrainian Politics, Culture, and Society. Launched in 2008, the fellowship is open to PhD students of any nationality who focus their studies on Ukraine and who wish to continue their research on the subject. Although successful candidates perform their work at U of T, the fellowship provides for twelve months of research, study, and teaching, with six to eight weeks in Ukraine itself.

From the outset, the programs have been broadly based, drawing upon the participation of Ukrainian specialists at the U of T as well as various universities in Ontario, while collaborating with other institutions engaged in the study of Ukraine. The participating organizations often join forces to co-host or co-manage programs related to Ukrainian history and culture in a manner that would likely not be practical were each to function independently of the others. "There is a lot of synergy in the relationships," Solomon emphasizes.

PERHAPS JACYK'S most notable and satisfying support for Ukrainian causes through educational facilities was the Petro Jacyk Centre for Ukrainian Historical Research at the University of Alberta.

In 1976, the university had launched its Canadian Institute of Ukrainian Studies (CIUS), on the Edmonton campus, as a response to requests from Ukrainian community leaders and academics in Canada. The role of CIUS was to provide an institutional home for Ukrainian scholarship in Canada while supporting similar studies on an international scale.

Peter grew impressed with the achievements of CIUS. Here was an academic arm that appeared focused on achieving significant and measurable results without being bogged down in the "ivory tower" mentality. In addition to publishing books and journals, CIUS developed other materials for Ukrainian-language education; organized conferences, lectures, and seminars; awarded graduate and undergraduate scholarships, along with research grants; contributed to the cultural and educational development of Ukrainian community groups; and fostered links with international organizations after the late 1980s, primarily in Ukraine, that benefited Ukrainians the world over.

CIUS, Jacyk determined, would be the ideal facility to administer his long-planned translation and publication of Mykhailo Hrushevsky's *History of Ukraine-Rus'*, along with other future publications relating to Ukrainian culture. He also discovered, and took advantage of, an opportunity provided by the provincial government, which provided two-for-one funding of approved educational programs in partnership with private supporters. As a result, the $1 million initial funding from the Petro Jacyk Education Foundation ballooned to $3 million with the assistance of the Alberta government.

Located in Athabasca Hall on the university's Edmonton campus, the centre opened in August 1989, with Dr. Frank Sysyn as its first director. In his speech at the centre's opening ceremony, Peter Jacyk characteristically noted that his business involved making money, and he liked to see that money from whatever source (but especially his) was put to good use.

This indeed proved to be the case at Edmonton. In subsequent years, in addition to the enormous task of supervising the translation of Hrushevsky's work, the centre assumed sponsorship of an English-language monograph series and a Ukrainian translation series entitled Ukrainian Historiography in the West. Centre scholars are regular participants at international conferences, often as panel organizers, and the centre arranges academic exchanges with institutes of the National Academy of Sciences of Ukraine. Other activities include the awarding of research grants and doctoral fellowships in Ukrainian history. The effect on Edmonton generally and on the local Ukrainian community has been stunning. Jacyk's $1 million gift to the institute went on to make such an impact that he was declared an honorary Edmontonian.

Peter's daughter Nadia extended the impact when, in 2008, she inaugurated the Petro Jacyk Program for the Study of Modern Ukrainian History and Society through a donation from the Petro Jacyk Education Foundation, with matching funds from the Province of Alberta. A cooperative venture between the University of Alberta, the Ivan Franko Lviv National University, and the Ukrainian Catholic University in Lviv, the program publishes the academic journal *Ukraina Moderna* and organizes international symposia on topics in modern Ukrainian history.

The arrangements reflect the insistence by Peter Jacyk, and later by Nadia, that the foundation's contributions bear no political or religious bias or aspect. The Ukrainian Catholic University was the successor to the Greek Catholic Theological Academy, closed at the outset of World War II.[3] Established in the wake of the Soviet collapse as the Lviv Theological Academy, the university had its cornerstone blessed by Pope John Paul II in June 2001, and the institution remained closely associated with the Ukrainian Greek Catholic Church. To avoid the appearance of bias, the Ukrainian Catholic University's administration was broadened through an association with Ivan Franko National University, a state university that traces its origins back to 1661.

In 1979, Peter Jacyk had agreed to head the fundraising committee for the Ukrainian-language encyclopedia to be published by the Shevchenko Scientific Society in France. This project represented a challenge to the Soviet authorities, and many believe that the Soviet authorities later permitted the publication of a Ukrainian-language encyclopedia in Soviet Ukraine primarily as a response to it. This first Ukrainian-language work served as the basis for the English-language *Encyclopedia of Ukraine*, published by CIUS, and it became an authoritative source that continues to fill a vital need for scholars, diplomats, business people, journalists,

---

3. The academy's rector at the time was Cardinal Slipyj.

and the general public. The publication of the Ukrainian-language encyclopedia marked a major personal accomplishment for Peter Jacyk, and he took considerable pride in his role of supporting it. Expressing his delight in this achievement, he noted: "Russians can no longer claim that Ukrainians do not exist."

More daunting for all the parties involved was the English translation of Mykhailo Hrushevsky's monumental *History of Ukraine-Rus'*. Written between 1894 and 1934, with the final volume published in 1937, Hrushevsky's magnum opus is both the most comprehensive account of the ancient, medieval, and early modern history of Ukraine and the definitive declaration that Ukrainians constitute a nation, not an adjunct of Poland, Russia, or any other claimant. One observer noted that the translation of Hrushevsky's work would "open for the English-speaking world a kind of window onto Ukraine."[4]

Some years later, Peter Jacyk would explain the need for a translation of Hrushevsky in this manner:

> In the ex–Soviet Union in the 1970s, an historical library was burned down in Kiev in an attempt to ruin the possibility of [Ukrainians] knowing other cultures. This incident instilled in me [an] understanding, respect and appreciation for the Canadian mosaic of tolerance and freedom. The [event] nurtured what a destructive force could do to ruin my former homeland. We had to rebuild our losses in this free, loving constructive country... To undertake such a project, a translation of eleven volumes of Hrushevsky's history would be needed.

In the beginning, Peter had suspected that the task would be beyond even his organizational capabilities, not to mention his not inconsiderable wealth. He found a vehicle for translating

---

4. Petro Jacyk Education Foundation data accessed at www.infoukes.com/pjef/pjef_e6b.html on February 11, 2011.

the *History* through his endowment of the Petro Jacyk Centre for Ukrainian Historical Research at CIUS. It would take an exceptional team of scholars, translators, and editors; a substantial infusion of outside cash, much of it through sponsors of individual volumes; and many years of intensive labour to realize the dream. But it was well worth the investment.

Mykhailo Hrushevsky, too little known in North America, was a man of remarkable achievement. In addition to organizing and leading the two most honoured centres of Ukrainian historical studies—the Shevchenko Scientific Society of Lviv and the Institute of History of the All-Ukrainian Academy of Sciences— he produced more than two thousand works in history, literature, and other fields of study. Although the institutions he nurtured were destroyed in the vortex of Stalinism, most of his *History of Ukraine-Rus'* weathered the assault on Ukrainian culture because no one within the Soviet bureaucracy was capable of producing a comparable work. Hrushevsky's work remains unsurpassed, in part because Soviet policies through to 1990 discouraged the study of pre-modern Ukrainian history. The widespread destruction of Ukrainian archives in the twentieth century, caused by wars and revolutions, frequently left Hrushevsky's work as the only qualified information source. Exiled to Russia in 1931, he died there in 1934 while undergoing surgery. Many Ukrainians suspect his death was no medical mishap but the result of one of Stalin's purges of intellectuals.

Peter Jacyk recognized that Hrushevsky's work needed translation into English so that the extent of the author's genius and the impact of his thought could be appreciated beyond Ukraine. "The world knows about Ukrainians only from Russian history translated into English," he explained. "Russians do not have a good name in the cultural world; however, they have presented us as something worse: that of small Russians...Once we put Ukrainian history in English and place it on the shelves of libraries, governments and universities, the world will find out we are not small Russians—we are Ukrainians!"[5]

Hrushevsky's original text covered ten volumes of densely written prose that would stretch into twelve books when translated into English. A noted member of the team of translators and editors assigned to the project, Uliana Pasicznyk had experience in scholarly publishing extending back to 1973, when she joined the staff of the new Ukrainian Research Institute at Harvard University. In 2011, she was serving as managing editor of the Hrushevsky Translation Project of the Petro Jacyk Centre for Ukrainian Historical Research, working through the CIUS office at the University of Toronto.

"I remember Mr. Jacyk as a tall, attractive man who had a commanding aura about him," she recalls. "He felt that the international scholarly community needed to know about Ukraine's history, and that the translation and publication of Hrushevsky's work would help achieve this." Her opinion of the multivolume work and its place in Ukrainian scholarship and culture is clear. "The book is fundamental for a knowledge of Ukraine's history and an understanding of the development of the Ukrainian people. Because the story of Ukrainian history involves events and developments in Poland and other countries of central and eastern Europe, along with the Crimea, Russia, and the Ottoman Empire, it also represents an enormous contribution to historical study generally."

Through her work at HURI and with the Hrushevsky Translation Project, Pasicznyk gained an impression of Peter Jacyk as a complex man whose passion, as well as his finances, powered his commitment to Ukrainian studies. "He was very thorough in

---

5. Peter, Jacyk, speech to the Canadian-Ukrainian Business Association, Edmonton, March 29, 1996.

his dealings, and he was never timid about asking questions in order to fully understand what was being discussed." Jacyk was also more interested in positive results than in plans and projections, she confirms. "The publication of a book, or having large numbers of students in a class studying Ukrainian history—these were definite results. He wanted results, and perhaps some of his impatience with academic projects or institutions grew out of that expectation."

The quality assessed as impatience by some academics was the response of a man familiar with the results-driven environment of business, confronting the more methodical approach of academia. To miss or ignore a deadline in construction and land development often resulted in the payment of substantial penalties. In most academic endeavours, however, deadlines are necessarily secondary to an approach concerned more with methodology, confirmation, and peer review. But Jacyk understood and appreciated the key role played by PhDs in developing and leading educational and research programs, and he displayed deep interest in their qualifications, abilities, and achievements. "He knew the names of many up-and-coming PhDs and their fortes," Nadia Jacyk says, "and he demonstrated his support by promoting chairs, programs, and fellowships." It was difficult for Peter Jacyk, as it would be for anyone, to step from one environment to the other without grappling with an appropriately altered perspective.

Jacyk's concern about the pace of progress was felt among the teams working on the *History* project, though from the outset he had some idea of the scope and complexity of the work involved. Hrushevsky, one of the most remarkable personalities in world history, served as head of the Ukrainian government in 1917 (Central Rada), wrote a multivolume history of Ukrainian literature as well as the country's history, spoke and wrote in a wide range of languages, and conducted research in many more. His broad spectrum of learning and knowledge influenced his writing, especially the extent of the detail he provided. This made the translation and editing of his work difficult enough, but it proved even more challenging because of one particular weakness in his craft.

"Hrushevsky was enormously erudite and prolific," Uliana Pasicznyk remarks about the master historian, "but he could also cite a source one way this time and somewhat differently another time." Some of Hrushevsky's sources were rare early manuscripts or publications, and in many instances, the project's translators and editors were obliged to check or confirm references and perform other tasks to ensure that the English-language version met scholarly standards. "These are time-consuming processes," Pasicznyk explains, "and whenever the pace of this work seemed to him slow, Peter grew anxious. Preparation of the first volume, in particular, required a good deal of time because it involved deciding matters that would set editorial policy for later volumes, such as the translation of specific historical terms lacking English equivalents, establishing bibliographical format, and so on. He often asked why a volume took so long to produce," she says with a smile. "He would listen to our editorial concerns with understanding but later might inquire again why a volume didn't appear more quickly."

Publication of the first translated volume of the *History* was followed by volumes on the Cossack era. Volume 1 (*From Pre-History to the Eleventh Century*) was released in 1997, followed in 1999 by Volume 7 (*The Cossack Age to 1625*), Volume 8 (*The Cossack Age, 1625–1650*) in 2003, and Volume 9, Part 1 (*The Cossack Age, 1650–1653*) in 2005. The lengthy Volume 9, Part 2 (*The Cossack Age, 1654–1657*) was divided into two books: Book 1 in 2008 and Book 2 in 2010. Volume 6 (*Economic, Cultural, and National Life in the Fourteenth to Seventeenth Centuries*) appeared in early 2012.

Volume 7 of the *History* had its U.S. launch on April 12, 2000, at the Ukrainian embassy in Washington, D.C. Among those attending were the minister-counsellor of the Ukrainian embassy, the librarian of Congress, the director of the co-sponsoring Kennan Institute at the Woodrow Wilson Center, and Dr. Frank Sysyn, all of whom were welcomed by Peter's daughter Nadia. A similar event was held three days later at the Shevchenko Scientific Society in New York City.

Within and beyond the Ukrainian community, the English translation of Hrushevsky's masterwork is seen as a major achievement by various measures. At the Canadian launch of Volume 7, celebrated with a banquet and reception at the Great Hall of Hart House on the campus of the University of Toronto on December 1, 1999, Dr. Roderick Fraser, president of the University of Alberta, said the translation and publication "may well prove to be the most important scholarly project undertaken in the West in the twentieth century."[6]

Other comments were equally laudatory. "This evening is about history," master of ceremonies Dr. Marko R. Stech announced, "and about the relevance of history in our lives; about what history is, and how it shapes our views of the world and of ourselves." Nadia Jacyk, as director of the Petro Jacyk Education Foundation, noted that the current edition of the history had already received international acclaim among specialists in the field, who praised it for being virtually flawless. "Perhaps the most valuable aspect of our cooperation is the high quality of its final product," she added.

Among the guests was Canada's secretary of state, David Kilgour, who declared the book "a gift from the people of Canada to international scholarship and, in particular, to the people of Ukraine" before presenting a copy to Volodymyr Khandogiy, Ukrainian ambassador to Canada.[7] American historian Professor

---

6. "Banquet Celebrates Jacyk Centre's 10th Anniversary and Release of Hrushevsky History's Volume 7," *Ukrainian Weekly* (February 6, 2000), 4.

7. Ibid.

Thomas Noonan greeted the publication of Volume 7 with similar approval: "We do a great disservice to our students and to the public in Canada and the United States as long as we repeat the traditional Great Russian view of Ukraine's history. With the launching of this edition, we begin a new era, a time when the greatest of the histories of Ukraine shall become available to all those interested in East Slavic history."

None of this would have been possible without financial support from an unhesitant Peter Jacyk, a fact that was emphasized throughout the ceremony. "We all should be grateful to Canadians such as Peter Jacyk who never forgot their roots," said Mr. Kilgour, while Dr. Fraser stated: "Through the creation of the Hrushevsky Project, which changes the Western view of the history of Ukraine, Dr. Jacyk is himself creating history."

Peter Jacyk's contributions to fund Ukrainian studies were not limited to North American educational centres. In 1991, he established the Petro Jacyk Lectureship in Ukrainian Studies at the University of London, England. In his speech at the launch of the program, he revealed a degree of affection for his homeland that he often hid behind his criticism of Ukraine and its people, along with some hopes for practical benefits to be earned from his investment:

> Consider that Ukraine and its people were suppressed for hundreds of years, that everything Ukrainian was presented to the free world as Russian, or if it was presented as Ukrainian it was misrepresented or shown in such a light that it was shameful. Really and truly, when we think of how much damage was done by many people and many departments, only then can we realize how much work lies ahead of us to undo the wrongdoings of the past.
>
> Let us all agree that today's lectureship at this university is only a small window opened for a suppressed nation into the free

world. Ukraine is a country rich in natural resources, with a good climate and 52 million people trained to work for next to nothing. With today's transportation and communication, and our help, it should not take long for Ukraine to become one more member of the European Community on an equal basis with the other members...

If we build strong Ukrainian Studies at the University of London, then the next time that Mrs. Thatcher goes to Kiev with her thousand business people, these people will be well informed by the Ukrainian Lectureship about the possibility of doing business in Ukraine. This information, based on good research, will help English business people to establish good businesses in Ukraine. The same information will be open to Ukrainians on how to achieve good transactions with English people, because any transaction is only good when both sides are satisfied. The results from this lectureship should be beneficial for all concerned.

The Petro Jacyk Education Foundation also continued to support Ukrainian schools and orphanages in the Brazilian city of Prudentópolis and to rebuild a burnt-down Ukrainian seminary in Curitiba. This was in addition to financing a Portuguese-language book about Ukraine and Ukraine settlements in Brazil. And in the early 1990s, Jacyk explored opportunities for other Canadian universities, including the University of Guelph and Ottawa's Carleton University, to establish links with higher-education institutions in Ukraine.

Books represented both a source of wisdom and a measure of achievement for Peter Jacyk. To those who authored them, they held the promise of immortality; to those who read them, they signified a means of accessing knowledge, inspiring ambition, and creating identity. It is no surprise, then, that grants from the foundation assisted in the purchase and shipment of several thousand copies of technical, medical, business, and law textbooks into Ukraine, as well as Ukrainian-language children's books, globes, and atlases.[8] Grants from the foundation also enabled the Organization for International Cancer Control to organize a training program for prominent Ukrainian oncologists in several top-rated cancer research institutions in the West.

It's revealing to note that, as a philanthropist, Peter Jacyk played the role of facilitator more than that of pioneer or innovator. With both the interest and the ability to promote Ukrainian culture, he first responded to needs expressed by others, then found a way to meet them.

For example, in the late 1990s, someone suggested a contest to stimulate the learning and use of the Ukrainian language in Jacyk's native country as an effective means of countering the prevailing emphasis on Russian. Earlier efforts to achieve similar goals with schoolchildren had offered rewards of books, watches, and candy.

"Peter believed that in a poor country such as Ukraine, cash is always the most effective motivator," Nadia Jacyk explains, "and he set up the contest so that winners would be rewarded with substantial sums of cash."

Since the end of World War II, through the educational system, the media, and anywhere they could make their point, Russian political and academic leaders had lectured Ukrainians about the inferior nature of their own language. Nadia Jacyk explains it this way: "They said that the Ukrainian language, compared with the Russian language, was like Cockney English compared with the Queen's English, a dialect that nobody else really took seriously."

As a result, Ukrainian youth had grown embarrassed to speak Ukrainian. They viewed Russian as the language of sophisticates, spoken by the fashionable and the progressive, the winners and

8. Mykhailo Slaboshpytsky, "Why did Peter Jacyk Initiate the Ukrainian Language Contest in Ukraine?" *Day Weekly Digest*, May 27, 2003.

the leaders, an international language that commanded respect around the world. Ukrainian, in comparison, was the language of peasants. Peter Jacyk was determined to change that attitude. The awarding of cash prizes represented a conscious move on his part to demonstrate the worth of the language and the value of speaking Ukrainian. You did not receive mere medals or diplomas for being fluent in the language; you received cash.

The impact of his message proved enormous. "The top prize of three thousand U.S. dollars," Nadia Jacyk points out, "was equal to as much money as many parents of the children could earn in three to six years."

The contest started at the school level, where written assignments were distributed to students. Winners were assigned an oral test; those with top marks proceeded first to a district level, then to a regional level, and finally to the national championship series. Ukraine's Ministry of Education oversaw the mechanics of the contest, the League of Philanthropists handled the overall administration, and the Jacyk Foundation supplied a major portion of the funding.

In May 2001, Ukrainian president Leonid Kuchma joined a very proud Peter Jacyk in handing out awards to the national winners, marking another successful step by Jacyk in developing and encouraging wider appreciation for the Ukrainian language.

His remarks at the ceremony addressed both his point of view and the legacy of Soviet Russia's linguistic dominance of Ukraine for so many years. "Many countries smaller than [Ukraine] have preserved their language and are developing it," he commented. "But in our country with a population of 50 million, the majority speak a foreign language thrust upon us. This just does not sound normal. It is akin to dogs meowing."

His "dogs meowing" statement caused quite a reaction. The quote was carried widely on Ukrainian-owned media outlets, both print and broadcast, but was censored by outlets owned or controlled by Russians.

Following the success of the first year's contest, Ukraine's president announced that all children in the country's educational system were to participate in future events. The impact of this decision was massive; the participation of 300,000 children in the first year jumped overnight to encompass a potential 5 million Ukrainian students vying for cash prizes and the national honour of promoting the Ukrainian language. "The news that three hundred thousand had taken part in the first year brought tears to my father's eyes," Nadia Jacyk comments. "The news that 5 million might be involved in the second year was overwhelming to him. In many ways, I believe he felt it was his biggest achievement."

In 2002, Nadia Jacyk travelled to Kyiv to represent the Petro Jacyk Education Foundation and accept Ukraine's Man of the Year Award on behalf of her late father. She also attended the annual meeting for those administrating the language contest, where she reminded the administrators that the foundation's commitment of support had originally extended for just three years, meaning it was scheduled to end in 2003. The foundation, she announced, was pleased to extend the financing for a further three years to 2006. She implored others associated with the language contest to explore new sources of funding, suggesting that Ukrainian business firms would be ideal.

The full impact of the contest is yet to be measured with adequate precision. There is no doubt, however, that its activities have assisted young Ukrainians to more fully employ and appreciate their own language and have turned back, to some degree, many generations of Russian-language dominance.

It is difficult to overstate the value and impact of the multiple contributions Peter Jacyk made to education. His primary goal was to spread awareness of Ukraine and its history and language, but the ripple effect of his involvement and his donations cannot be discounted. The programs he initiated and funded in Brazil and Ukraine have positively affected the lives of literally millions of schoolchildren and their families. The increased funding to Harvard, Columbia, the University of Toronto, the University of Alberta, and others enabled those institutions to build their staff, improve their facilities, encourage research projects, and generally widen their role and impact in various fields beyond those directly associated with Ukraine.

Compared with the horrors Jacyk had witnessed first-hand, the solace of study and the benefits of education represented alternatives for investing in the future. The benefits of his generosity will continue to accrue.

13

The Demjanjuk Ordeal

---

*Man's capacity for justice makes
democracy possible, but man's capacity for
injustice makes democracy necessary.*

REINHOLD NIEBUHR

ANOTHER OF PETER JACYK'S interests was perhaps smaller in its scope—it dealt with insuring that one individual received justice—but proved more extensive in its immediate impact and implications.

For almost a decade, Peter Jacyk worked with a fundraising committee to provide the means for John Demjanjuk to mount a defence against the false accusation that he was Ivan the Terrible, the notorious guard at the Treblinka death camp responsible for the deaths of tens of thousands of Jews.

John Demjanjuk, born Ivan Mykolaiovych Demianiuk, the son of peasants in Dubovi Makharyntsi, became a German POW during Operation Barbarossa, when the Nazis overran eastern Europe. He emigrated to the United States after the war and settled in Cleveland, Ohio, where he worked in an auto plant, raised a family, and led an uneventful life for twenty-five years.

Everything changed in August 1977, when the U.S. Justice Department demanded that Demjanjuk's citizenship be revoked on the grounds that he allegedly concealed his involvement with Nazi death camps on his immigration application in 1951. The request was made on the basis of five Holocaust survivors who identified Demjanjuk in a photo spread supposedly discovered during the investigation of a notorious Treblinka concentration camp guard. Crucial to the charges was an identity card, supplied by Soviet authorities and placing Demjanjuk at a Nazi-established training camp. Demjanjuk denied the charge, and various neutral observers questioned the accuracy of his identification as Ivan the Terrible.

Beginning in October 1983, when Israel issued an extradition request to the United States for him to stand trial on Israeli soil, Demjanjuk's life became a blend of Kafka's *The Trial*, an episode of *The Twilight Zone*, and the script of some outlandish Hollywood production. He was stripped of his U.S. citizenship and deported to Israel in February 1986. The trial, a public event that attracted large audiences and international notice, ranged widely in discussions of World War II and the Holocaust. Emotional eyewitness affirmations by Holocaust survivors of Treblinka that Demjanjuk was indeed Ivan the Terrible generated much drama, and in April 1988, he was found guilty and sentenced to death by hanging.

Peter Jacyk grew concerned at the charges against Demjanjuk and the manner in which the case was handled. Initially, he was not sure of Demjanjuk's guilt or innocence, but in any event he felt strongly that Demjanjuk should have the resources to conduct an adequate defence. In time, Jacyk grew convinced that Demjanjuk was not guilty of the charge, believing the evidence that Demjanjuk had been Ivan the Terrible was severely flawed.

JACYK, AND MANY others, viewed the charges against Demjanjuk as an attempt to blame the entire nation of Ukrainians for the murderous actions of Nazi Germany. The action, in his eyes and those of many others, was bolstered by Soviet Russia, which wished to discredit Ukrainians abroad by associating all of them with the worst atrocities of Hitler's Reich.

To support this latter point, Demjanjuk and his defenders pointed to allegedly forged identity cards provided as evidence by the Soviet KGB. In addition, subsequent revelations suggested that the Office of Special Investigations (OSI) in Washington, D.C., had withheld key evidence that would have exonerated Demjanjuk. To add to the absurdity of the situation, the OSI staff member who had pursued the charges with great conviction was disbarred after it was proven he had embezzled funds from a Holocaust foundation.[1]

Peter Jacyk's actions over the Demjanjuk affair targeted a range of co-conspirators and bystanders. Among the latter were other Ukrainians who, while decrying the treatment of Demjanjuk, chose less involvement and support on Demjanjuk's behalf than might have been expected. Meanwhile, there were the understandably passionate demands of Jews seeking retribution for Holocaust horrors carried out by the man alleged to be Ivan the Terrible. For many Jews, to refute the identification by Holocaust survivors of John Demjanjuk as Ivan the Terrible was seen as an affront to the victims of the Holocaust and a blow to potential prosecutions of perpetrators. What should have been a trial of one individual increasingly involved numerous issues of historical memory and engendered conflict between the Jewish and Ukrainian communities in North America.

Three years after Demjanjuk had been found guilty in Israel and sentenced to death, Peter Jacyk wrote to a New York newspaper that had run an editorial suggesting that prosecution evidence had been doctored:

---

1. District of Columbia Court of Appeals, Board on Professional Responsibility, August 6, 2003 (Bar Docket No. 085-03).

1. In 1969, the Office of Special Investigation had interviews with Otto Horn, Karl Streibel (Treblinka commandants) and over forty Treblinka survivors. None of the interviewed recognized Demjanjuk as Ivan (the Terrible). This evidence was hidden by the OSI from the courts in USA and Israel.

2. Israeli prosecutors did not present one piece of evidence that proved Demjanjuk was ever in Treblinka. (*Sixty Minutes* [sic] proved that.)

3. No Ukrainian state, institution or organization placed any guard at Treblinka. Why were Soviet guards called Ukrainian guards?

4. In the Demjanjuk verdict the word "Ukrainian" was used 307 times. This raises the question, if Demjanjuk killed 850,000 Jews, why does the Israeli Court blame all fifty million Ukrainian people for his action? On the other hand, if there are historical grievances between two nations, is it fair to orchestrate charges and kill one innocent man for the fault of the whole nation? There is something very fishy with the whole case.[2]

Peter Jacyk, along with the Charitable Committee in Defence of John Demjanjuk, travelled widely, to Chicago, Florida, Los Angeles, and other locations, to build support for the position that Demjanjuk had been unfairly tried as part of a wide anti-Ukrainian campaign.

Fortunately, the collapse of the Soviet Union allowed new evidence to surface before Demjanjuk's sentence was carried out. Five years after his sentencing, an Israeli appeals court ultimately agreed that the evidence was not conclusive, and five Israeli Supreme Court judges overturned the guilty verdict, exonerating Demjanjuk of all charges. Their ruling was based on written statements by thirty-seven former German guards at Treblinka

---

2. Peter Jacyk, letter to the editor, *New York Tribune*, April 4, 1990.

identifying Ivan the Terrible as Ivan Marchenko, not Demjanjuk. The case grew even more questionable when it was revealed that U.S. officials had been aware, without informing Demjanjuk's attorneys, of the testimony of the German guards.

Many Ukrainians believed Soviet Russia was behind the entire Demjanjuk affair, a view that Peter did not entirely share. Although he suspected that the Soviets played a role in demonizing Demjanjuk as a means of condemning Ukrainians generally, he felt their actions were likely limited to providing the alleged forged identity card. He was more specific about the importance of unity among Ukrainians who shared his view of the Demjanjuk trial as an orchestrated effort to demean them.

Efforts made on behalf of Demjanjuk involved lobbying activities launched by support groups, as well as cash contributions, often as small as $20, submitted by individual Ukrainians toward Demjanjuk's defence costs. The fundraising committee raised more than $1 million; without these funds it would have been impossible for Demjanjuk to launch any effective defence at all.

Thanking those Ukrainians who had contributed in various ways to Demjanjuk's defence, Peter noted the existence of "universal rules for honesty and fairness that are upheld by religious and secular sectors of society." Those who instigated the charges against Demjanjuk had broken those rules. By standing together, Demjanjuk's supporters had revealed the "underhanded agenda" of his tormentors, and by winning the case against him, had defended the universal right of justice against those who would, in this case at least, abuse it.

After Demjanjuk's conviction was overturned, he returned to the U.S., and his American citizenship was restored. But this merely launched a new act in the drama. Years later, the U.S. government, in a move that many considered retribution, charged Demjanjuk with being a different guard at a different death camp. This time, after many years of litigation, with Israel itself having declared him innocent, he was deported in 2009 to Germany, which wanted to try him as an accessory to the murder of Jews at the Sobibór and Majdanek camps in occupied Poland and at the Flossenbürg camp in Germany. Mortally ill and ninety-one years old, with his wife and son to assist him, John Demjanjuk endured long incarceration in a German prison before facing yet another trial.[3]

To some observers, this was a self-serving action on Germany's part. In Demjanjuk's adopted country, the undertaking would have been impossible because of the U.S. law against double jeopardy: being tried and found innocent of a crime prevents the state from trying the same individual again on the same charge. German law does not rule out double jeopardy,[4] and the Germans' actions in this situation can only be assessed as a means of dispersing at least some of the guilt for perpetrating the Holocaust.

Several disturbing revelations arose during Demjanjuk's German trial, among them the fact that a 1985 FBI report, marked secret for the previous twenty-five years, brought to light a judgement that the Nazi ID card that had been provided to the U.S. by a Soviet source (and had played a major role in the charges against Demjanjuk) was "quite likely fabricated" evidence.[5]

On May 12, 2011, Demjanjuk was found guilty of participating as an accessory in the murder of 27,900 Jews at the Sobibór camp

---

3. The appalling treatment of John Demjanjuk has been recorded in countless magazine articles and books (including a fictional reference by novelist Philip Roth), most notably in *John Demjanjuk: The Real Story*, by Jim McDonald (Beltsville, MD: Amana Books, 1990) and *Defending "Ivan the Terrible": The Conspiracy to Convict John Demjanjuk*, by Yoram Sheftel (Washington: Regnery Publishing, 1996).

4. Nor does Canadian law. Among those who were found innocent by a jury but faced the same charges yet again is Guy Paul Morin, accused of raping and murdering his eight-year-old neighbour. The second trial found him guilty; a third trial finally exonerated him.

5. Allan Hall, "Trial of Suspected Nazi Mass Murderer John Demjanjuk Could Be Based on Fabricated Evidence, FBI Claims," *Daily Mail*, April 13, 2011.

and sentenced to five years' imprisonment. Court records noted, "No evidence was produced that [Demjanjuk] committed a specific crime."[6] In light of his age and length of incarceration at that point (he had spent two years in a German prison and eight years in Israeli prisons), the sentence was suspended pending appeal. In the end, even this was not resolved; John Demjanjuk died on March 17, 2012, age ninety-one, in a German nursing home before the appeal could be launched. His family requested that he be buried near his home in Ohio.

Demjanjuk's trial in Germany occurred years after Peter passed away, and we cannot know what his reaction would have been. Peter Jacyk's interest in the Demjanjuk case demonstrated his high regard for justice and his belief in the value of action over dialogue. Many people discussed the events of the case, doubting the veracity of the charges against John Demjanjuk as Ivan the Terrible. Jacyk did more than discuss them; he publicly stated his concerns and privately contributed to Demjanjuk's defence. It was a classic response by Peter Jacyk, a man who valued fairness as much as he valued his own heritage.

---

6. Peter Worthington, "No Satisfaction in Demjanjuk Case," *Toronto Sun*, May 21, 2011.

14

Russia Pre- and Post-Soviet

Scratch a Russian and you will find a Tartar.

JOSEPH DE MAISTRE

IN 1968, WHEN Peter Jacyk was on the verge of accumulating the economic assets that fuelled his support of Ukrainian cultural and language activities in Canada and beyond, the Soviets brutally subdued Czechoslovakia's Prague Spring. This effort to loosen Soviet Russia's dominance over its satellite countries now stands as the first in the series of events that shook the Soviet grasp in eastern Europe, leading to the total collapse of Russian Communism in 1991.

Through the decades of Brezhnev's rule of Soviet Russia, that country continued to dominate Ukraine, boasting of the Communist Party's supposed achievements and crushing any political opposition. No one spoke of the Holodomor, the Great Famine of 1932–33, except to claim it was a myth spread by Western imperialists.

Looking back from the viewpoint of a world in which Marxist-Leninist philosophy appears as dated and vigorous as dinosaurs,

226

the Soviets' propaganda as it related to Ukraine appears somewhere between farce and tragedy. In a Ukrainian publication from the late 1970s, a Soviet "Doctor of History" praising Soviet Communism declared, "No other political organization in the world has ever reached such grandiose successes or influenced so tangibly the course of world history."

Those familiar with Ukraine's relationship with Soviet Russia during the Brezhnev years knew that waves of arrests and show trials of Ukrainians who dared to criticize Russia took place, beginning in 1965–66 and continuing through the 1970s. Most were dissident intellectuals and journalists whose most apparent crime was daring to promote Ukrainian culture, language, and other causes, qualifying them as perpetrators of the crime of "local nationalism."[1]

By the time hammers began demolishing the Berlin Wall in November 1989, the Petro Jacyk Education Foundation was well established and making major strides in supporting Ukrainian interests. For the next ten years, Peter Jacyk took great satisfaction in watching Ukraine and other Slavic nations that had been ground beneath the Russian boot for several generations assume the rights and responsibilities of freedom. The changeover was not always smooth, to be sure, and many aspects of Ukraine and its citizens continued to trouble him. He could, however, foster the hope and dream that his beloved country would achieve all of its potential, unencumbered by either the insanity of Communism or the imperial ambitions of Russia.

Regardless of Ukraine's status, he frequently visualized Russia as a dangerous bully, prepared to dominate Ukraine and all of its neighbours by political, economic, and, if necessary, military means

---

1. Paul Robert Magocsi, *A History of Ukraine: The Land and Its Peoples* (Toronto: University of Toronto Press, 2010), 711.

at any time. He based his opinion of Russia on more than his war-time experiences in Galicia/Halychyna, travelling to Soviet Russia on various occasions with Canadian trade and cultural missions. In 1989 alone he made three journeys to Russia and returned to Canada each time with few positive impressions. This was the year when Gorbachev's glasnost and perestroika initiatives were iden-tifying him as a different kind of Russian leader, far removed from the inflexible and brutal approach to Russian politics practised by Stalin, Khrushchev, Brezhnev, and the rest. Staunch pro-capitalists such as Margaret Thatcher and Ronald Reagan may have been praising Gorbachev in these years; Peter Jacyk, however, begged to differ.

According to Walter Jacyk, Peter Jacyk saw Gorbachev as one of a new generation of leaders who offered hope but appeared to lack the skills and dedication to deliver on his promises. The Soviet Russian leader's ignorance of capitalist procedures and philosophy appeared to annoy Peter. He expressed his problems with Gorbachev in a published letter to the *Globe and Mail* on March 8, 1990:

> I was in the Soviet Union in 1989 three times looking for pere-stroika [restructuring]. I agree fully… that Soviet leader Mikhail Gorbachev does not understand the system.
>
> He reminds me of Peter the Great who, 300 years ago, recog-nized that Russia was behind the world. He personally went to the Netherlands, bought overalls, tool box and carpenter's tools and joined the carpenters to personally learn how to build ships in order to advance Russia to world level. The poor chap did not know that a carpenter has to follow a plan. A plan has to be drawn by an architect and to develop an architect takes time and talent.
>
> If Mr. Gorbachev would hire someone like [Chrysler Corpora-tion chairman] Lee Iacocca to analyse the system, make plans and

force the apparatchiks to follow the plan, he would have a chance to become a good carpenter.

When Gorbachev's early initiatives led to the collapse of the Soviet Union in 1991, Peter Jacyk was appropriately pleased. Still, there was work to be done. In September of that year, he wrote to William Hogan of Harvard's Kennedy School of Government in support of Hogan's efforts to assist Ukraine in making the transition from Communist to capitalist state. Hogan was serving as director of the Project on Economic Reform in Ukraine, a remarkable endeavour in which academics and private citizens contributed time, energy, expertise, and money to assist Ukraine's move to private enterprise.

The transition presented a challenge. Although other countries within the Soviet structure, such as Poland, Czechoslovakia, and East Germany, had recent "memory" of free enterprise, Ukraine's economy had been Soviet-dominated for three generations. "Unfortunately, few [Ukrainians] have direct experience with non-Soviet ways of doing things," Hogan explained in describing the project's objectives. "The goal... is to provide Ukrainian policy makers with advice and also with data, with texts, with contacts, with communication links to the West, so they can draw on the economic experience of others to aid in crucial decisions."[2] With no direct links to any foreign government, and determined to avoid involvement in Ukraine's political issues of the day, the project set an ambitious goal focused entirely on the practical needs of Ukraine, without regard for ideology.

This was precisely the kind of effort that Peter Jacyk believed Ukraine desperately needed—and one he felt urged to support.

---

2. "Interview: William Hogan on Harvard Project on Economic Reform in Ukraine," *Ukrainian Weekly* (June 16, 1991), 3.

Commenting on the challenges faced by Ukrainian legislators and business people, he wrote:

> Probably Gorbachev is to blame because he wanted to improve the economy but left the management with the Communist Party. He wanted infusion of capital and know-how through joint ventures without giving their new partners some kind of security...
>
> To put infusion of capital and know-how into the hands of people who do not know any different means placing investment at risk. Call them Communists, Nationalists or Democrat, they are the same people and to give them money means they will do [what] they know and that is mismanage.
>
> The only way to help the Soviet Union, Russia or Ukraine is... to get in, set up guidelines that are based on thousands of years of western experience, set in laws for the security of investment, set in government departments strong enough to implement these laws, and only then will the country's individual units such as education, manufacturing, business, etc. get honest.

In support of the project, he ended the letter by noting he was accompanying it with a cheque for $100,000 to serve as "seed money."

Peter Jacyk's attitude toward Russia was complex. He despised Communism, as did the vast majority of people in the West, and he had expressed his dislike for Soviet Communism from the first days of World War II. The animosity, however, was driven not by any visceral hatred for Russia and its people, but by what he saw as a history of unfair treatment of his beloved Ukraine by the larger nation, extending from the Middle Ages through the twentieth century.

In 1994, he noted: "In 1991, little unknown Ukraine gained its independence. Taking advantage of knowledge America had of

Ukraine, Russia started right away to sabotage the former Soviet Union republics through its Disinformation Centres inherited from the Soviet Union... In 1992–93 the USA provided $2.5 billion in financial aid, 63 percent of which was received by Russia and only 5.9 percent by Ukraine, even though the population of Ukraine was 18.19 percent of the former USSR."

Sometime later, in an unpublished essay, it seemed his feelings toward Russia had softened a little:

Human characteristics, developed over hundreds of years, are powerful, and cannot simply be legislated away. The Russian attitude did not collapse when the Soviet Union did. While the Russians are begging the world to help them with food and medical supplies, at the same time they are financing intelligence gathering operations around the world and sending troops into Georgia, Armenia, Azerbaijan and Moldavia, and Commandeering Ukrainian aircraft and Black Sea fleets.

This attitude, passed down from Eastern and Southern tribes (Tatars, Pechenigs and Huns) was never directed towards the production of consumer goods. The attitude was: to organize power and hold on to it; expand, taking over neighbouring countries who are smaller but who had better standards of living; rob them; enslave their people as a non-compensated workforce. With time and education, methods to apply terror and fear changed. Communists would occupy other countries, create laws under which they branded leaders and managers of those countries as bourgeois nationalists, and condemn them to a slow death through inhuman conditions in jails and in Siberia. In addition, the Generals and Commissars exploited the lower masses of these countries with complete disregard to any human rights...

As a practical businessman, someone who began life in the Soviet Union and spent 40 years in business in Canada, traveled three times with the Canadian-Soviet consul to Moscow, I know that Russia has what it takes to be self-sufficient. In fact, the Russian people can do more than this, by eventually acting as leaders in the world community, helping others less fortunate than themselves.

15

Ethics, Achievements, and Disappointments

I remember the first time I had to sign a cheque for a million dollars as part of a development. My hand was shaking as I went to sign it, and I said to Peter, "What if I make a mistake?" Peter replied, "If you learn something from it, it is not a mistake. But if you make a mistake and learn nothing from it, you lose."

JOHN ZDUNIC

PETER JACYK'S EFFORTS on behalf of Ukraine and its citizens were made while he continued to build Prombank into a major developer in the Greater Toronto Area. While the 1980s marked an intense period of support for Ukrainian causes, he continued to manage and grow a highly successful company. Turning his attention back to residential development and construction, he achieved exceptional success, thanks to a combination of careful planning, conservative financial practices, and an insistence on pursuing his own vision.

John Zdunic, a contemporary of Jacyk's who arrived in Canada from Croatia, first met him in the late 1960s. With similar backgrounds that included escaping from war-torn Europe to find opportunity and prosperity in Canada, they gravitated toward each other, sharing their experiences, their views, and their ambitions. The two men remained friends and, in some instances, partners on major projects. Even when they were not sharing a development, John Zdunic sought his friend's opinion and relied on his judgement.

"He was my anchor," Zdunic says, "as well as my inspiration and my mentor. He was someone I could share my experiences with, someone to rely on, and someone who was helpful in many ways. I would approach him with a problem or a question, and we would hash it out until we had a solution or an answer."

Part of Peter Jacyk's appeal in these situations was his independent state of mind. "He was not a man who wanted to agree with you just to keep your friendship," John Zdunic emphasizes. "A lot of times he would be provocative. He would say things to make you think in a different fashion, just to be sure that you understood your own position."

These qualities, along with Peter's conservative approach to money earned and spent, were demonstrated in a joint venture the two men launched in Woodbridge, Ontario. By the mid-1980s, land prices had begun to climb out of a depression that had been driven for the most part by stratospheric interest rates. A few years earlier, Jacyk had acquired undeveloped land near Woodbridge, on the northern edge of Toronto. His property bordered on a parcel of land owned by John Zdunic and a group of partners, all of them Croatians. Although each developed their properties separately, when it came time to build and market the homes, they formed a joint venture.

"Woodbridge, as it is today, was home for a large number of Italian-Canadians," John Zdunic recalls, "and we came under a lot of pressure from Italian developers who wanted to handle the project. We kept telling them that we wanted to do it ourselves, and we did."

Zdunic, active in the Croatian community in and around Toronto, had far less experience in property development than Peter

Jacyk, who became more than a partner with Zdunic; he became a mentor. "I was so impressed by the things he knew and how easily he shared them with me," Zdunic remembers. "He had vision, he had foresight, and he was persistent." He was also convincing, and Zdunic was soon relying upon Jacyk's wisdom when it came to making major decisions on the design and sales features of the houses they were building.

"Peter wanted to use all-wood casement windows, install energy-efficient furnaces in the homes, and add extra insulation," Zdunic says, noting that this was long before today's heavy emphasis on energy efficiency. "Peter also said that the homes would have insulated steel doors, despite the fact that we were told Italians always insisted on solid wood front doors." Solid wood doors present a problem in the Canadian climate; between the hot, humid summers and bitterly cold winters, solid wood begins to warp, creating a host of problems both practical and aesthetic. It didn't matter; without solid wood doors, the partners were warned, the houses would not appeal to Italian Canadians.

But they did. "We told the people, 'This is the way to go, this is the way to save money on heating costs,'" John Zdunic says, "and we convinced them." An equal billing plan for home heating costs was set up for the first buyers of the homes, based on the projected expenses of similar homes in the area. At the end of the first year, however, the homes built by Jacyk and Zdunic proved so efficient that each owner was awarded a $1,000 credit because the utility had underestimated the homes' energy efficiency and overestimated the heating costs. "Once the word got around about that," John Zdunic smiles, "we sold three homes for every one that other developers in the area sold, and it was all Peter's idea."

Peter Jacyk's influence on Zdunic extended beyond the hugely successful Woodbridge development. Inspired by Peter's charitable activities, the Croatian developer created the John Zdunic Charitable Foundation, which has made substantial contributions to the University of Toronto library fund and various cultural organizations.

The success of the Woodbridge development provided Jacyk with an opportunity to maximize his profits. "My accountant was expecting the high profits," he wrote, "and offered me all kinds of business ideas to eliminate paying a lot of taxes. I decided, contrary to my accountant's suggestions, to pay off my mortgages and accept the huge taxes." When others questioned his move, he replied that he never forgot the biblical lesson of seven fertile years followed by seven disastrous years, and wise people prepared for them. He wanted to bank his earnings, accept the taxes that came with them, and prepare for whatever the future might bring.

By 1990, his seven-year prediction appeared correct. The building industry dropped off sharply, and an estimated 20 percent of builders and developers declared bankruptcy, unable to meet their extended financial obligations.

"My bankers paid me a visit," Peter Jacyk noted, "and said, 'You're doing something right. If you want to expand or buy more property at the current low market prices, we have all kinds of money for you.' It was a complimentary offer, but I was able to control my greed." Then he added: "It was not easy to get into the banks' pockets, but it had become even more challenging to get out of them."

NOTHING IN BUSINESS challenged Peter Jacyk more, however, than his experience with a development near the Denver airport that proved disturbing and exasperating. It involved a series of conflicts with someone whose relationship with Peter dated back to the village of Verkhnie Syniovydne, Ukraine. And it extended several years beyond Peter's death, rising through the Canadian judicial system all the way to the highest court.

Morris Iwasykiw had been a schoolboy playmate of Peter Jacyk in their Ukrainian village. Although they took very different paths, both made their way to Canada following the war and became involved in property development. Unlike Jacyk, Iwasykiw avoided sinking enormous sums of money into construction and property maintenance, preferring to play the role of real estate agent and facilitator; as a result, he fell short of attaining his friend's level of success.

The two men exhibited contrasting styles: Jacyk was cautious, detail-conscious, and conservative; Iwasykiw was risk-taking, impulsive, and prepared to live on the edge, where finances were concerned. Nevertheless, their shared childhood experience provided a bond of sorts, rooted more in history than in business styles, until the day in 1988 when Louis Matukas, a mutual acquaintance of both men, presented an investment opportunity that Peter Jacyk assessed as promising.

Matukas, of Lithuanian birth, had spent several years in the real estate and development market in and around Toronto before launching his own firm, Numat Financial. Among the Toronto-area investors he encountered was Morris Iwasykiw.

"Morris was a fun guy," Louis Matukas says. "I never saw him unhappy. He was a little loud, in many ways. He talked loudly, he dressed loudly, he smoked big cigars and drove a big flashy Cadillac."

At the time, Iwasykiw's company, Jedfro Investments, was actively purchasing and attempting to develop lakeshore land along the western fringe of Toronto, an area dotted with less-than-elegant motels notorious for prostitution and drug dealing. Iwasykiw foresaw the location as ideal for the development of upscale condominiums, a vision that was eventually proven correct. In the mid-1980s, however, it was difficult to find both the visionaries and the financing to make his idea a reality.

During this period, Louis Matukas met Peter Jacyk at a Christmas party and was immediately impressed. "He was reserved and polite, but with a good sense of humour," Matukas says, "a total contrast with Morris Iwasykiw. We talked a little, mostly about business and the kinds of projects we were each working on." This was a man, Louis Matukas decided, with whom he would like to do business some day.

The opportunity arose in early 1989, when Jim Hunter, an acquaintance of Matukas, called him from Edmonton to alert him about an investment in which they could both participate. The deal concerned three hundred acres of land abutting the site of a planned new airport in Denver, Colorado, the largest in the United States and among the three largest in the world. Just a half mile from Interstate 70, the main east-west highway crossing the mid-section of the country, the location would prove irresistible to manufacturing, warehousing, and service companies.

The Edmonton developer was partnered with a Denver lawyer to purchase the Colorado land, and through Matukas they offered Jacyk and Iwasykiw half the deal, awarding Matukas a small portion as a finder's fee. By either holding the property until its value climbed with the completion of the airport, or developing it themselves and leasing or selling buildings to tenants or buyers, the partners stood to make a sizeable profit.

The three hundred acres had been purchased some years earlier by Air Products International, a multi-service organization headquartered in Pennsylvania, marketing a range of products from liquid nitrogen to medical-quality oxygen. Air Products bought the land when it acquired a Denver-area engineering firm developing a technique to recover petroleum from shale deposits; the Denver location would be the site of the subsidiary's head office and operations centre. When the technique proved less efficient than anticipated, Air Products decided to abandon the idea and sell the land. The price was made even more attractive when Air Products offered to take back a mortgage on the property.

"I saw it as a good deal, especially with more than a hundred acres of the parcel already serviced with utilities, curbs, sewers, and so on," Louis says. "When I approached Morris and Peter, they agreed to check it out."

They were a contrasting team. Louis Matukas was essentially a financial person. Peter Jacyk was, in Louis's words, "a developer, a keeper, a man who takes a long view of things." And Morris Iwasykiw was a real estate speculator, someone whose time frame was shorter and who, in Louis's opinion, preferred working with OPM—Other People's Money.

Jacyk, acting in conjunction with his daughter Nadia, approached the purchase with his usual caution and attention to detail. The three men made four trips to Denver, walking the land, searching records, and inspecting it from the air in a helicopter before deciding to proceed. Eventually agreeing that this was a promising investment, they bought in. With the Denver partners holding 50 percent of the investment, the balance was split 30 percent for Jacyk, 15 percent for Iwasykiw, and 5 percent for Matukas. Each became a covenantor in the deal, bringing his own corporation into the venture.

Events unfolded in their own fashion, as many such ventures do. Over the next few years, two small parcels of land were sold to cover costs and generate activity on the otherwise empty land, making it more attractive to prospective buyers. Unfortunately, other developers had foreseen the same opportunity and purchased land on speculation, adding their acreages to the available properties. When the glut became apparent, land prices began to drop, and pressure was put on the group to lower their prices to stay competitive. They refused. "We didn't want to be the cheapest guys on the block," Louis Matukas explains. "We had the best location and we decided to hold the line."

The Denver partners apparently had planned to flip the property within a short period of time and walk away with some quick profits. When this proved unlikely and they realized the deal would take several years to mature, with no guarantee of the kind of profits they had anticipated, they quitclaimed the property, leaving the Canadians in charge of the entire development. This effectively doubled the ownership between them: Prombank USA controlled 60 percent, Iwasykiw held 30 percent, and Matukas owned the remaining 10 percent. It also, of course, doubled the amount owed to Air Products for the balance of the land purchase. With the payment date approaching, Iwasykiw pleaded poverty; he had, he claimed, no cash on hand to cover his portion of the debt. Nor did Matukas. Only Peter had the financial resources to handle the payment, and he felt more than an obligation to save the deal. Walking away in the same manner as the Denver partners would have meant writing off a substantial amount of money already invested, something that did not appeal to Peter Jacyk.

From the outset, Jacyk, Iwasykiw, and Matukas had agreed this would be a joint venture, not a partnership. The distinction was important because, in a joint venture, each would be responsible for a share of the financial obligations and, they anticipated, the future profits.

The Air Products note came due in June 1991, requiring the three men to pay the balance owing. Louis Matukas was dispatched to the Air Products headquarters to negotiate an extension. He returned with an attractive deal: Air Products would extend the due date on the now $5 million balance for three years. The three men would continue making minimum payments to reduce the balance, but by June 1996, the purchase had to be settled or the American company would take back the land.

By June 1996, the Denver airport had been operating for a year, and interest in developing adjoining property for commercial and industrial use was at a peak, but Jacyk, Matukas, and Iwasykiw had not made a major sale to cover the money still owed on the land. Handing the property back to Air Products to settle the now outstanding $4 million owing was out of the question. The long-delayed profits for developing or selling the remaining land would soon become reality, but only if the entire balance was covered immediately.

Peter Jacyk had access to sufficient cash to cover the balance owing, and he offered money to the others as an equity lender, meaning he qualified for interest payments on the loan plus participation. Nadia and Louis Matukas agreed to the terms; Iwasykiw rejected the offer, calling it "ludicrous." Jacyk's response was to suggest that Iwasykiw pay for his share and remain in the joint venture. Iwasykiw refused, leaving Jacyk no alternative except to consider foreclosing on his old friend.

"Morris had access to the money he would need," Louis says, "and Peter told Morris that Morris would have to put up his share out of his own pocket." Iwasykiw apparently balked at the suggestion. "Remember that Morris always wanted to do deals with other people's money," Matukas emphasizes. "That's the style, the trademark of speculators and salesmen like him." It was also, it appears, something of a game to Iwasykiw. Peter Jacyk approached the project as he approached of all of his work—seriously and with careful consideration to details and downsides as well as potential profits. Iwasykiw was, by his actions, more interested in exploiting the ins and outs of business ventures than dealing with matters concerning bricks and mortar.

When Jacyk insisted that Iwasykiw pay for his portion of the deal, Iwasykiw offered to show his bank statements indicating he lacked the necessary cash. Jacyk refused to believe him. "Morris will come around," he assured Matukas. "I've known him since we were little boys in the same village. He's just playing games." The two men had grown up as friends, had witnessed the same horrors and disasters, had ventured to Canada together, and had shared the same drive to succeed. Why couldn't they cooperate on a business venture?

Over several months, Iwasykiw attempted to leverage the money from Jacyk, at times promising to secure the loan with properties he claimed to own. Quick investigation revealed that Iwasykiw had no ownership in the properties, thus providing Jacyk with no assurance that he could ever recover his money should Iwasykiw default—a not unlikely event. "Peter was prepared to cut Morris a lot of slack," Louis Matukas says. "He wanted to give him all the breaks he deserved. So he waited for Morris to do the right thing."

In the midst of back-and-forth exchanges, with a deadline looming that meant all three men would lose their entire investment if they could not reach an agreement, some startling news arrived. "The Ukrainian community in North America is small in some ways," Louis Matukas explains, "and in the middle of Iwasykiw's claim of poverty, word reached Peter that Morris had sold a large parcel of land in the southwestern United States, in California or Arizona, for a cash profit that would cover his share of the Denver deal." According to Louis Matukas, the money from the sale of the U.S. property was moved immediately from Iwasykiw's business account to his wife's bank account, effectively continuing Morris's claim that he was short of cash. Without Iwasykiw's share, the deal would be lost.

Peter Jacyk needed to act and avoid a loss for all three men. His company, Prombank Investments, a non-party to the joint venture, purchased the note from Air Products, preventing the vendor from reclaiming the property and essentially bailing out both Iwasykiw and Matukas. The strategic move benefited all three parties, and when Peter offered the other men an opportunity to buy back in, he and Louis Matukas quickly reached an agreement. Iwasykiw refused to participate, except through vague promises of personal guarantees and mortgages. By this time, Peter Jacyk was in no mood for more of Iwasykiw's antics; either Iwasykiw delivered the amount he owed to stay in the investment or he would lose the estimated $1.4 million he had spent to this point. Iwasykiw refused, and in late 1996, Prombank started foreclosure actions through the Denver courts. Iwasykiw fought the action and lost. Although he had several months to come up with the money and redeem his interest in the venture, he still refused.

It is difficult to criticize Jacyk for his actions. A substantial amount of money was at stake, most of it his, and either he took the lead in meeting the financial obligations or all three would lose. Whatever Iwasykiw's true financial status, Peter Jacyk had little choice: if Iwasykiw indeed had access to sufficient cash to fulfill his obligation (and subsequent events proved he did), he should have used it; if he was in over his head financially, he should have prepared himself for a loss.

Iwasykiw saw things differently. The arrangement, he claimed, had been a partnership, and since no new agreement had been reached, the original contract applied. That was the argument of Iwasykiw and his lawyer when they sued Peter Jacyk and Prombank to recover their $1.4 million loss. Regardless of whether or not he met his financial obligations, Iwasykiw argued, he should not have been prevented from sharing in future profits and should have been paid by Prombank for his lost investment. In 1998, he sued Jacyk, Matukas, and their companies in Ontario, claiming they had breached the joint venture agreement.

The legal process can be painfully slow where civil matters are concerned. Between Iwasykiw's launch of the legal action and the actual trial, both Iwasykiw and Peter Jacyk had passed away—Iwasykiw in 2000 and Jacyk the following year. Both estates continued the litigation process, and in 2005, the trial judge dismissed the action, ruling that Iwasykiw had no legitimate claim and, by failing to make a deal with Peter Jacyk and Prombank, became the author of his own misfortune. The estate of Iwasykiw appealed, and in 2005, the Court of Appeal for Ontario agreed with the trial judge, noting that "when parties act in a way that shows they do not intend to comply with or be bound by the terms of their written agreement, one party cannot later ask to have the agreement enforced for its benefit."[1]

This should have settled the issue, but it did not. Iwasykiw's estate chose to carry its case to the Supreme Court of Canada, arguing that Peter Jacyk and Prombank had breached the terms of their joint venture agreement and thus enjoyed "unjust enrichment." On December 20, 2007, the highest court in the country determined that Jacyk had operated entirely within the law and Morris Iwasykiw and his estate had no claim. In addition to losing its argument, the Iwasykiw estate was ordered to pay court costs estimated at $180,000. In the end, twelve judges heard the case in four different jurisdictions, and all ruled unanimously against Morris Iwasykiw.

Iwasykiw's estate, it appears, was driven to pursue his argument all the way to the Supreme Court at least partly by his legal counsel's belief that he could succeed. Peter Jacyk was determined to defend his position (in the end, it was his estate's action, guided by his daughter Nadia for six years following her father's death) on the basis that he had acted ethically and had expected that others, especially a friend whose association extended back to childhood, would behave accordingly.

Business people at Peter Jacyk's level of success accept legal challenges from time to time. Usually they are based on different interpretations of fixed agreements. Jacyk no doubt would have been appalled to see his schoolyard buddy from so many years and so many worlds ago continue to challenge his business practices and ethics all the way to the Supreme Court. He would have been satisfied and confident, however, that the wisest legal minds agreed that his actions had been ethically, morally, and legally correct.

---

1. Court of Appeal for Ontario (2006) 80 OR (3d), 533.

16

Private Life and Public Stances

*Luck always seems to be against the
man who depends on it.*
UKRAINIAN PROVERB

FOR THE LAST twenty years of his life, Peter Jacyk took pride in his remarkable achievements in business and endured his occasional disappointments. Among the various Ukrainian proverbs with which he was no doubt familiar, he appears to have heeded most the one that declared, "Only cheese in a mousetrap is free." Through all of these peaks and valleys from about 1980 onward however, he enjoyed the steadying influence and company of a remarkable companion.

Jeanette Bayduza grew up, the daughter of Ukrainian parents, in Edmonton, Alberta. An attractive, slim woman, she completed her medical studies at the University of Alberta and fulfilled her residency in pediatrics and allergies at the Hospital for Sick Children in Toronto. With specialist certifications as both a pediatrician and an allergist, she continued in private practice from a clinic in west Toronto until 2012, when she finally retired.

In 1980, while downhill skiing at a resort north of Toronto, Jeanette Bayduza met a tall, curly-haired man with a wide smile. She recognized his name when he introduced himself as Peter Jacyk. "I had heard of him some time before," she recalls. "I knew only that he was a big businessman. He was interesting to talk to, but there was also a mysterious quality about Peter. And a playfulness too." When he offered to drive her somewhere, she asked what kind of car he had. "A Volkswagen," he replied.

"It was a Mercedes," Jeanette Bayduza laughs. "A big black Mercedes!"

Approaching his sixties, Peter Jacyk remained fit and active and in good health, with the exception of the nagging cough that had remained with him since he acquired a lung infection during his teenage years in Ukraine. Working out in a gymnasium, he grumbled, was a waste of time, so he found other ways to maintain his health—playing volleyball at the local YMCA, shovelling snow in winter, and gardening in summer. At age forty-five, he had become an avid downhill skier, leading to his encounter with Jeanette.

The two were compatible from the beginning. He was proud of the fact that Jeanette held two highly regarded university degrees, reflecting his esteem for education. She was his match intellectually, and although she obviously did not share the level of assets he enjoyed, she could hold her own financially while matching his level of intelligence and industriousness.

They became a familiar couple at functions not only in and around Toronto but, over the next two decades, around the world. Peter frequently attended various medical conferences with Jeanette, using the opportunity to encounter and assess other cultures, often finding qualities to admire about them. He especially enjoyed Japan, where he marvelled at the care that handicapped and elderly citizens received, the punctuality of business and social events, and the enthusiasm of schoolchildren. "They don't slouch on their way to school," he commented, "they're happy to be there." When he visited the Hiroshima Peace Memorial Museum, the images he saw of the destruction and carnage created by the atomic bombs dropped on that city and on Nagasaki brought back chilling memories, on a smaller scale, of his own wartime experiences. He and Jeanette also visited China, Singapore, Thailand, Malaysia, Hong Kong, and the Australian resort area of Port Douglas, a location that he especially loved.

Jeanette frequently travelled with him on his trade and business ventures, usually to Europe. In Soviet Russia, aware that the then-Communist government was having him trailed by a police operative, he approached the man and suggested that, as long as they were going to the same places, they might as well introduce themselves and maybe share a drink together. He defied restrictions on travel to St. Petersburg without permission and explored the city, admiring its architectural and cultural appeal and giving credit (and criticism) openly when he felt it was due.

"He believed Ukrainians in Canada were too limited in their outlook, too parochial," says Jeanette Bayduza. "They lacked vision, in Peter's view. Mind you, Peter was always looking for ways to do bigger, more impressive things." Having achieved them himself, he wished others would emulate to some degree his own success, yet he was disappointed at various times by their lack of enthusiasm.

His daughter Nadia suggests that her father wanted Ukrainians in Canada to avoid a ghetto-like mentality, at the same time suggesting they could and should retain their identity within the Canadian mosaic. It was not a matter of either withdrawing from the fabric of Canadian society or losing themselves within it; it was a matter of working to achieve a higher level of status for themselves and their Ukrainian identity within the country. "He did this because he cared for both," she emphasizes. "He cared for his heritage and he cared for Canada, and so much of what he accomplished was the result of this caring attitude."

Jeanette Bayduza recalls that during a visit with an acquaintance in Ukraine, Peter commented that a bathroom repair had not been made since he first noticed it on a previous visit some years earlier. This, he grumbled, was more evidence of the Ukrainian predilection to ignore practical concerns in favour of frivolous matters. Simply put, he wanted to foster improvement among Ukrainians in both Canada and their homeland. Although in some instances he encountered only defensive attitudes and excuses, his attempts were admired and lauded from various quarters. "He was recognized in Ukraine as a hero," Jeanette Bayduza remembers, "and this gave him a boost."

In 1988, Peter and Jeanette travelled to Ukraine with a church group. The trip included a bus tour of the country—an unusual event, because Peter preferred to travel on his own and had an ambivalent attitude toward organized religion. Which is not to say he lacked spirituality. He appears to have had more faith in God as an omnipotent power than in the Church as at least a secular institution. For some years beginning in the late 1960s, he served as president of St. Josaphat's Parish Credit Union on a voluntary basis.

"He didn't believe in the Church very much," Jeanette Bayduza says. "He didn't think churches were as spiritual as they were supposed to be, nor were some of the church leaders. For the masses, he believed churches could teach discipline and morality, and he supported them for that reason."

The Soviets had converted many of Ukraine's churches into museums and storehouses, and when Ukraine regained power as a sovereign nation it spent substantial amounts of money restoring the old churches and building new ones. Although Peter Jacyk had no objection to the restoration of older churches, he was disturbed by the imbalance of funds spent. Far too much money, he contended, was being spent on churches and too little on important needs such as education and infrastructure.

Describing one of his multiple visits to Ukraine in the mid-1990s, he wrote:

> I wanted to do business with the so-called democrats. It took me two years to find out:
> 1. that all democrats are yesterday's communists anyway.
> 2. and that all democrats are politicians and do not know how to do anything.

Ukrainian politicians, in his view, "became politicians by mercilessly blasting communists who managed the country before. They wish to take all the present privileges of communist managers but they do not want to learn how to manage more responsibly than the communists did." Without a healthy economy, politics consisted only of empty talk.

Like many self-made successes, he believed that the same qualities that had propelled him from a Montreal rooming house to become a developer and builder of residential homes and commercial properties could be found, to some degree, in others, despite John Kolasky's admonition that he was exceptional. He wanted Ukrainians to believe in themselves, and to act upon it.

Peter Jacyk proposed practical solutions to the problems that most vexed him about Ukraine. In doing so, he softened his position without giving an inch on his emphasis on the importance of business when tackling serious problems facing humanity:

> When referring to any group of people, not all are bad and not all are good. Some ex-communists are good functionaries. They did good work for the communists, they will also do a good job for non-communists. They know the job and they are realistic in every walk of life. We have to find them, join with them, learn from them and their methods and improve on [their] output and quality, and teach the younger generation to do better. This is easier said than done, but it is the only way—slow but sure.

As passionate as some of his criticisms may have been, they were not evidence of an irate man incensed by the world around him. Peter Jacyk may have been frustrated and disappointed from time to time by the actions of others, especially business associates. But he was also a generally contented man, with a vibrant social life. And, it must be noted, a remarkably engaging sense of humour.

"He loved giving parties," Jeanette Bayduza says, "and he was always a good host, paying attention to guests and sincerely interested in what they had to say. If there was ballroom dancing, he would love to dance. And he was a good dancer too." He also sang well and attended church each Sunday, at least as much for the social benefits he valued as for any deep religious faith he may have followed.

It was at St. Demetrius Church in the Toronto suburb of Etobicoke that John and Vera Seychuk first encountered Peter Jacyk. "We had known Jeanette for some time," John Seychuk recalls, "and after service one day, we went down to the basement room for coffee to find this handsome, slim man speaking to her very gently and warmly. As a matter of fact, I would say he was massaging her with words."

Seychuk, a gregarious man, demanded in mock seriousness to know the name of Jeanette's new friend. "She introduced us," Seychuk says, "and I said to Peter, 'Look, this young lady is fragile, and if you don't treat her well, I'll come after you.' He smiled at me and promised to take care of Jeanette. After that, we became great friends."

Jacyk enjoyed his friendship with the Seychuks, as he did with other friends, who remember him as a man who took as much satisfaction in life and laughter as in his business achievements. He did not choose his friends according to their own success or social standing, but he perhaps felt something of a kinship with John Seychuk. Grandson of a nineteenth-century Ukrainian immigrant who cleared 120 acres of land in Manitoba, Seychuk first worked his way through university to win a degree in engineering, then co-founded a global engineering consulting company. Although Seychuk, unlike Jacyk, was born in Canada, both men were familiar with the challenges faced by immigrants.

"Peter always listened more than he spoke," Vera Seychuk adds. "He never boasted about his achievements and never overstated himself." He was, in her words, "a quiet, understated visionary who never represented himself above his real, tangible success."

To the Seychuks, Peter Jacyk was something of a philosopher whose interests ranged across a wide array of subjects, including astronomy. "Because I was an engineer," John Seychuk says, "he would ask me about astronomy, wanting to know what happened out there in space." "I called him our Peter the Great," Vera Seychuk says with a smile.

Jacyk was also known for his impromptu invitations to social events such as parties and dinner with friends. His friends grew used to a telephone call from Peter inviting them to a party that same day or the next day, an event with several friends sharing meals, drinks, conversation, laughter, and perhaps special entertainment such as a singer or musician.

MEANWHILE, HE WAS building a small but effective team of employees at Prombank. "He had an immigrant's mannerisms," says Joe Fiore, the firm's controller, "in that he was both knowledgeable and humble. I think he never forgot where he came from, his own humble roots. Maybe that's why he took so much care in listening to other people. He paid attention to things you had to say, to your opinion."

By the time Fiore arrived, Peter Jacyk's daughter Nadia was involved in most of the major decision-making aspects of the business. The father-daughter combination may have seemed a formidable team when Fiore wished to make his own voice heard, but he soon grew comfortable with the knowledge that he could make his point in discussions with father and daughter. "If Nadia and I disagreed on some matter," he says, "neither of us would hesitate to go to Peter with it, make our case and hear his decision." Never, Fiore says, did he feel that Peter showed favouritism to Nadia. "Sometimes he agreed with me, sometimes with her, but he always listened and gave his reasons, and who could argue with that?"

On many occasions when Joe Fiore found himself working late, Peter Jacyk would stop by his office for an informal discussion, often about politics or some other topic, and the two men would exchange ideas in a casual atmosphere, often agreeing, sometimes disagreeing. During one of these discussions on a Friday afternoon, Peter Jacyk disagreed with the controller rather more forcefully than usual. The following day Fiore received a telephone call at home from his boss, who apologized deeply.

"It hadn't really bothered me," Joe Fiore says with a smile, "because he had always been so open with his praise about my work that I didn't feel threatened." His apology was, in Joe Fiore's opinion, the act of a gentleman.

When alone at home, Peter relaxed with an extensive library of books and opera recordings, most of the books covering history of various epochs and locations. "He especially enjoyed Peter Newman's *The Canadian Establishment* and Newman's book on the Hudson's Bay Company," Jeanette says.

The tension created by the pressures of business from time to time revealed itself in a normal manner. "Sometimes little things would make him boil over," Jeanette Bayduza explains, "but I always saw it as the result of too much stress." This was, after all, a complex man who needed someone to understand him—a role Jeanette played well, according to those who knew them both.

She played another role as well. "I think he used me as a kind of shield against women," Jeanette laughs. "When you are an attractive unattached man and you have millions, well..." With Jeanette at his side, Peter managed to deflect any woman who seemed interested only in Peter's money.

In a speech marking the donation of the microfilm collection to the Thomas Fisher Rare Book Library at the University of Toronto Robarts Library in March 1992, Peter Jacyk referred to the widely held belief that behind every successful man is a woman assisting and encouraging him in his endeavours. In his case, he admitted, there were two. One was his daughter Nadia and the other was Dr. Jeanette Bayduza. Jeanette played a consultant's role, he suggested, advising him on the projects to support and those to decline. He joked that while she was very good at this function, the best part was that she performed it without charging a consultation fee.

He was similarly effusive on various other occasions. At the awarding of an honorary doctorate of laws from the University of Alberta in 1995, he commented: "Every manager is only as good as the people surrounding him. In my case, my daughter and business associate Nadia deserves half the credit people apply to me, including my support of higher education. My respect for the University of Alberta comes to a great degree from my dear friend Dr. Jeanette Bayduza, a graduate of this university, who praises it highly for its exchange programs and its international assistance programs."

In public comments such as these, Peter Jacyk revealed his deep respect and affection for the two women who had so steadfastly offered their wisdom and support, and who provided a much-needed other dimension to his life of hard work and dedication to reaching his goals. During a newspaper interview in the 1980s, the reporter referred to an industry banquet occurring that evening. "Will we see you there tonight?" the interviewer asked Jacyk.

"I don't go to banquets," Peter responded, perhaps with a smile. "I work."

17

Looking Back
with Pride

*A philanthropist is a person who loves
his homeland not only from the
bottom of his heart but also from his pocket.*

YEVHEN CHYKALENKO

ENTERING HIS SEVENTIES, Peter Jacyk could look back on a life
of remarkable achievement. The boy who had shared the
family's one pair of boots, in a land and time where they were to
survive on a hand-to-mouth basis, had accrued success undreamed
of in the Ukraine of the 1930s. He had not only surpassed most
other WWII refugees from Ukraine in his business successes; he
had outpaced many native-born Canadians, whose careers had
begun with advantages in language, culture, social position, education, and a dozen other parameters unavailable to the young
Jacyk, who was busy cleaning butcher shop machinery from dusk
to dawn in Montreal.

He appeared to have found a balance that eludes many business
people—especially those whose duties involve dealing with a wide

range of customers and suppliers, many of whom place demands on their time and patience. The balance was achieved between his business instincts to maximize profit and his humanity, which enabled him to appreciate the other person's position if and when a conflict arose.

"He was very popular with his tenants," Yurko Drab points out, "and that's not always the case with someone in his position." Yurko Drab is an example of Jacyk's good instincts when it came to assessing people. Drab arrived in Canada in 1988, an eighteen-year-old Polish-born Ukrainian whose first job in his new country was to assist a relative in home construction. When the work dried up after just six months, he was introduced to Peter Jacyk, who offered him a job finishing Peter's new Mississauga home.

"I didn't have a car, of course," Yurko Drab explains, "and public transit didn't take me all the way to Peter's house. So he arranged to meet me each morning at the nearest subway stop and drive me to his home. Some days the subway would be fifteen or twenty minutes late, but he would always be there."

Impressed with the young man's ambition, Peter Jacyk offered him a job performing building maintenance for Prombank when work on the new Jacyk home was completed, and after three years, he appointed Yurko Drab to the position of property manager. It was a major step for a young man who, barely four years earlier, had been an unskilled labourer on a construction site. "He had a way of looking ahead, beyond other people," Yurko Drab says, "and he appreciated hard work."

In his management position, Yurko Drab frequently proposed ideas that were different from those of Jacyk's. "We didn't always agree," he says, "but you could approach him. He would listen to you and make up his mind that way."

Peter Jacyk remained flexible with tenants as well. Yurko Drab recalls approaching a long-term industrial equipment tenant with news that the tenant's rent was about to be raised. This is never good news, and normally a tenant's angry response reflects it. But not in this case. "The tenant said he didn't mind paying a little more rent each month," Yurko Drab says, "because he remembered when he had been having a difficult time in the past and Mr. Jacyk kept his rent low to help him out. He appreciated Mr. Jacyk's assistance and never forgot it. Other tenants felt the same way."

Despite maintaining his hands-on management at Prombank, Peter Jacyk continued his involvement in a range of activities that might have taxed the energies of much younger men. In the eyes of others, he could do the work of ten men without displaying any sign of tension or stress. "After the age of sixty, he actually grew more mellow," Nadia Jacyk says, "and achieved even more than in the decades before." He continued to travel to Ukraine on special occasions and to his cottage, where he relaxed by performing maintenance chores, growing re-energized in the quiet calm and fresh air of the country. He managed to have his life in order without feeling frenzied.

Unlike many of his peers, Jacyk did not find it necessary to increase his workload during economic downturns. By this point in his life, he had witnessed enough of them to realize they were always temporary, and most efforts under these conditions amounted to little more than make-work projects.

Other pursuits beyond Prombank kept him busy. He helped organize annual Ukrainian youth track and field meets in the U.S. and Canada and remained active as a member of the Mississauga Board of Trade, the Canadian Federation of Independent Business, the Ukrainian Canadian Professional and Business Club, and the Canada-USSR Business Council.

Events in Ukraine in the early '90s, tracing the collapse of the Soviet Union, were not always as fruitful as Peter Jacyk hoped. He still took comfort in the fact that his beloved native land was out from under the direct grip of Russia. His country and his company had followed two parallel but very different tracks toward success, and the result was a philosophical approach to life and business that Jacyk articulated in his unpublished writings.

His views on the role of money in life and society are especially enlightening. Poor people, he believed, were motivated to overcome their sense of inferiority and rise to a higher status of society, but money and its accumulation should not be considered an end in itself. Unfortunately, for many people it served as a yardstick with which to measure others—a foolish concept, in his opinion:

> Money is only superficial... Money hardly ever helped to prove someone is smart—often the contrary. We all know people who won or inherited millions but did not know how to invest [and] lost it all. Money has its own strict rules and regulations. One has to know these rules... and possess self-discipline. One must force oneself to follow these rules... otherwise they could easily lose everything. The best examples are Hollywood actors and artists. Many of them make big money and very often end up in bankruptcy, not being able to afford their taxes.
>
> We all tend to live selfishly, but at the same time live comfortably. There are almost no limits to our comfort. People emigrate to Canada searching for a better, more comfortable life for themselves and their loved ones. To achieve even the least comfort, they have to have consciously or subconsciously a control for money.

In one revealing passage of his unpublished memoirs, Peter Jacyk grappled with this ambition, connecting it with the wisdom of his mother and a wide range of historical imperatives. He begins by suggesting that his dedication to Ukraine and its causes was a response to demands from others:

Because of my company and its status I became more visible, more than average. I first made a donation toward the publication of an encyclopedia. Then I was slowly dragged into its fundraising committee... [and] I began to realize that I was being recognized on a higher level...

My mother was very much for learning. In [our] library I found Jewish books from the 12th Century that stated, "If you convert a Synagogue into a reading house, the Synagogue will gain value. If you do the opposite, the Synagogue will diminish."...

It was after 800 years that... Jewish thinkers gained a lot in the world on their philosophical values of education. I was convinced that this was the right way to spend my extra time and money. At that time in Ukraine, there existed a higher level of education but under Russian destructive rule. Everything non-Russian was grossly suppressed, and all the education in Ukraine was directed toward the benefit of one imperial party... controlled by the Russians.

HE FREQUENTLY DREW comparisons between Russian society and the freedom and constructive attitude he found in Canada. If nothing else, the comparisons provided him with the opportunity to praise his adopted country, which had provided opportunities in a fashion and to an extent that he believed could never be obtained anywhere else.

"He would often come home from a trip abroad and tell me, 'Canada is the best country in the world to live in,'" says Nadia Jacyk. "As much as he loved and cared about Ukraine and its people, he was always extremely thankful and supportive of Canada. He acknowledged the opportunity it had given him, and he didn't mind paying taxes to enjoy the freedom of living there."

Canada, he observed, was more open, free, and tolerant of other cultures than most other nations. Much of its strength, he believed, grew out of the assimilation of the various nationalities who chose it for themselves and for their descendants. No other country built its success as a prosperous, peaceful nation more successfully than Canada, he felt, and the secret was Canada's recognition and support of its immigrants.

Immigrants to Canada could, to a degree unmatched anywhere else in the world, contribute to their newly adopted country while retaining many aspects of the culture in which they had been born. This made it unique. "In comparison, Russia is only for Russians who are of red colour," he said. "America from Day One is only American, and they're coloured blue." Canada, however, is "a mosaic of many colours, and it has beauty."

OF ALL THE achievements in his life, perhaps no single event generated more pride in Peter Jacyk than the honorary doctorate of laws bestowed upon him by the University of Alberta in June 1995 during its spring convocation.

His selection by the university more than surprised him. "It overwhelmed him," says Nadia Jacyk. "As tough as he could appear on the outside, he had a sentimentality, and some things, such as the honour of being granted a doctorate by a major university, would choke him up, as this did." He never forgot, she explains, where he came from. Here was a man who began life as a poor peasant boy in a corner of the world where his heritage was constantly being attacked and denied, receiving a doctorate of law in a different country from his own. He had built properties covering hundreds of thousands of square feet and given millions of dollars to advance higher education, but this single event became, in many ways, the crowning of his life.

Dr. Frank Sysyn's introduction at the ceremony lauded Peter Jacyk's contribution to Ukrainian culture and identity. "Long before the rebirth of an independent Ukraine awakened the

academic community, government and the media to the importance of Ukrainian studies," Dr. Sysyn noted, "Mr. Jacyk laid the
foundation for understanding his native land."[1]

Peter Jacyk's response, and his address to the convocation gathering, impressed not only the graduating students and guests at
the event but University of Alberta president Dr. Roderick Fraser,
who, some years later, recalled it as "one of the best convocation
speeches" he heard during his ten-year service with the university.[2] The rest of those present, including almost a thousand new
graduates and two thousand guests, obviously agreed, for the
twelve-minute speech by the newly minted doctor of laws was
interrupted eight times by applause.

After briefly reviewing his experiences as a youth in Ukraine
and Germany, and his early life in Canada, Jacyk addressed his
favourite topic of higher education, following it with the recommendation that students learn to "know yourself first. Be realistic.
Demand more of yourself before you demand from others." Then
he added:

> Despite the disadvantages with which I began my life in Canada,
> many people have told me that I am successful. By now, I believe
> them.
>
> Surely you graduates know how lucky you are. You live in a
> country with great opportunities. You are obtaining a diploma
> from an institution with a fine world-wide reputation. With your
> education and knowledge, with your friends and families, you
> definitely have the foundation to accomplish a great deal in life.
> Some of you will be educators, and I hope you will find some of

1. Olenka Dobezanska, "University of Alberta Honours Patron of Education," Ukrainian Weekly (July 23, 1995), 9.

2. Anna Biscoe, "University of Alberta and CIUS Honour the Memory of Peter Jacyk,"
Ukrainian Weekly (May 15, 2005), 20.

what I have said of value in teaching your students. Others will enter careers that they could not even imagine today. With an education and a dedication to hard work, you are well-equipped to seize the many opportunities that Canada offers.

Peter Jacyk could not fail, on such an occasion, to speak once again of Ukraine and its people in an admiring manner that puts all of his expressed concerns and criticisms in proper perspective. At this time and in this place, he wanted to praise and encourage his people, along with the province and university so closely identified with them, and he did:

> I have been especially gratified by the development of Ukrainian studies at the University of Alberta. Ukrainians played a major role in the building and cultivating of Alberta, and the Province has recognized this contribution by promoting bilingual schools and establishing the excellent Canadian Institute of Ukrainian Studies. I am pleased that I have been able to contribute to this effort.

Then, after noting that governments at all levels were cutting funds and grants to the education sector and imploring private citizens to fill the gap ("we, the citizens who value education, must step in and contribute our share and make up for the shortages"), he expressed his gratitude:

> Thank you for this opportunity. Speaking to you on this occasion is one of the greatest pleasures of my life. May you all have good luck in your endeavours. God bless you.

18

The Practicality of Life

Only a life lived for others is a life worthwhile.
ALBERT EINSTEIN

UKRAINIANS EVERYWHERE celebrated the collapse of the Soviet Union in 1991 and the lifting of restrictions imposed on Ukraine by that country for so many years. The new freedom and independence promised new opportunities for the nation and its people, and in 1996, with much hope and enthusiasm, Ukraine adpoted a constitution declaring itself an independent republic.

In that same year, Peter Jacyk celebrated his seventy-fifth birthday. Both events marked significant milestones, one personal and one political. While Jacyk may have expressed some concern over the new republic's failure to achieve all of its objectives in the first few years of indepenedence, he shared the same hopes for the future as its citizens.

He may even have taken some pride in Ukraine's accomplishments. Almost from the beginning of his business career, Jacyk

262

had dedicated a good deal of his energy and assets toward building Ukraine's identity and the awareness of its history. It would have been immensely gratifying to look back on his seventy-five years of life, measuring all the goals he had realized and all the distance he had travelled.

It's unlikely that he spent much, if any, time patting himself on the back, however. Peter Jacyk was not the kind of man to practise self-congratulation. Nor did he need to; others began doing it for him.

The honorary degree from the University of Alberta in 1995 appeared to launch a new wave of recognition and honours for him. The following year, Ukrainian president Leonid Kuchma granted Peter Jacyk the Presidential Prize of Ukraine for his patronage of Ukrainian culture, education, and scholarship, which was followed a few years later by the country's highest distinction. Ukrainian studies programs continued to flourish at the University of Toronto and University of Alberta, as well as Harvard and Columbia Universities.

Both his mind and his determination remained as strong as ever, but the seventy-five-year mark triggered a decline in his physical strength and condition. Jeanette Bayduza remembers the day when, while working in the garden, he found himself uncharacteristically short of breath. He had, he admitted, been feeling somewhat frail recently. "He realized this was serious," Jeanette explains. Overcoming a dislike and distrust of doctors (despite his closeness to Jeanette), he agreed to a physical checkup. The verdict was instantaneous: he needed a quintuple bypass operation and a new heart valve to treat advanced coronary artery disease.

The operation, by all accounts, was successful, but it drained Peter of energy and left him a changed, substantially older man. Among other things, it drew his attention to his own mortality and limited his horizons. "You know," he said to Walter Jacyk after recovering from the bypass surgery, "I'll be happy if I get just five years' more life out of this."

A year or two following his open-heart surgery, Peter and Walter got together to watch a television documentary, delivered in Ukrainian, honouring Peter Jacyk's life and achievements. "The producers, in my opinion, provided an excellent picture of Peter's accomplishments," Walter Jacyk says. The program, he recalls, covered Peter's early struggles to achieve success and his acceptance of the need to take risks when necessary. It also detailed his financial support for the translation of the *History of Ukraine-Rus'*, the encyclopedia, and other steps he had taken to aid Ukraine and its people.

"When the program ended," Walter Jacyk recalls, "I turned to Peter and there were tears in his eyes. It was shocking. I had never seen him so moved before. He said, 'Walter, if the time came for me to leave, I'm ready to go now, after seeing this.' Then he added, 'Don't get me wrong, I would like to stay around, because I have so much to do.' He truly appreciated the fact that people were giving him some wide recognition for what he had achieved."

Peter Jacyk's comment that he would be happy to enjoy another five years of life following the heart surgery proved prescient.

Throughout his life, he had suffered from the often debilitating cough, attributed to a condition known as bronchiectasis. It had kept him out of military service as a young man and remained, more an irritant than a concern, through his mature years. Now, as he suffered the normal process of aging, aggravated by the physical demands of the heart surgery, the cough became a source of some worry.

He ate well but carefully. "He never used a scale, yet he never gained more than five pounds as an adult," his daughter Nadia noted. "He just trusted his belt size—if he had to let out his belt a notch, he ate less until the belt fit again." He never indulged in alcohol beyond a sip of his favourite Scotch at night, and he remained physically active, though he had abandoned skiing in his early seventies.

BY 2000, his years of effort and substantial contributions on behalf of Ukraine had garnered the level of recognition and appreciation they deserved, though not nearly as widely in the diaspora as in Ukraine itself. This was underlined in June of that year with an invitation for Peter to address the graduating class of generals at a ceremony taking place at the National Defence Academy in Kyiv.

"He was unsure what to say to this group," Nadia recalls. "He had no trouble addressing business people, but these were senior military officials and he had no military background. 'What could I say to them?' he asked me, and in the end he decided just to be himself and tell his life story."

The reception that Peter Jacyk received in Kyiv, according to Jeanette Bayduza and Nadia, who travelled with him, was almost comparable to that afforded a visiting head of state. Jacyk was seen as a VIP of the first order in his native land, and the five hundred or so people listened with respect to a remarkable story delivered in Ukrainian and peppered with wise and stimulating observations.

"There is nothing perfect in this world, and much can usually be improved upon," he said early in his delivery, adding: "One must constantly focus on self-improvement and self-discipline. I practise this all my life, because I believe that every small thing done is more important than a big thing planned."

He followed this with a brief but revealing history of his life, framing it as a dramatic tale filled with challenges and achievements. From his childhood and the death of his father through the horror and destruction of the war to his arrival in Canada and his first steps as an independent businessman, Peter Jacyk set the stage for his business success. Along the way, he sprinkled asides that pulled his Ukrainian audience into the picture. Noting the inability of his eighteen partners in Accurate Builders to agree on any decision of substance, he labelled it "non-constructive group psychosis" and suggested that it was also apparent in the Verkhovna Rada, the parliament of Ukraine.

Life had taught him, Peter said, that it was best to be himself. He was born a Ukrainian and would die a Ukrainian, and throughout his life he had been careful to maintain a high level of values and integrity lest he lower the values of his birth nation. He was proud of his origins and of the historical legacy of Ukraine. Unlike their neighbours, he noted, Ukrainians worked and gained financial independence and did not "organize themselves in groups and... rob the ready-made," adding: "Our Ukrainian instinct for self-preservation and perseverance has preserved us. [It has] allowed us to stand as a valuable nation with a well-developed government on our own soil, and has given us political accomplishments [and] a government with highly developed people at the helm."

When he moved on to the second-rate status historically accorded the Ukrainian language over centuries by Russia, he delivered phrases that would not have been out of place in an oration from a populist-based politician in the midst of a tight election campaign. Citing his support for the translation of the Hrushevsky *History* into English, he quoted an observer's opinion: "That which the destructive and hostile power may destroy in Ukraine, we will rebuild, and in the English language, which will be distributed throughout the world, thereby [proving] that we are not the younger brother to anyone!"

Ukraine, he suggested, was like a large tree whose roots are planted in and draw nourishment from the Ukrainian soil but whose branches spread throughout the world. Some branches, he acknowledged, would die from time to time, but as long as the roots remained strong, the branches would regrow. By renewing true pride in their origins, Ukrainians could reach the same level as any other respected country anywhere on the globe, and no one would prevent them from feeling good about themselves, their country, and the world.

It was an inspiring discourse, building on his personal achievements, linking them to the qualities of an entire nation, and extending the premise toward the future. Then, rising to an appropriate climax, he closed with these words:

> Times are changing. Today, it is not... confiscation but... honest work and productivity that brings strength and prosperity to individuals, people, countries, and the world. The current changes in the world situation are creating opportunities for constructive values.
>
> The Ukrainian nation has all the abilities and character traits needed to quickly climb to its proper place in the world. Leaders of government need to work out a level-headed method of [improving] the national production. And more important: let every citizen in independent Ukraine work on developing self-respect and pride in his heritage.
>
> It depends on each of you what place on the world's stage we will take tomorrow.

An impressive message from a man who professed that he was unsure what to say to his audience when his invitation arrived.

IN 2001, PETER JACYK began to focus on his memoirs, preparing about one hundred pages of recollections detailing his early life in Ukraine, the horrors of WWII, his life in Germany, and his arrival in Canada.

He explained that he was "attempting to express in my writings the practicality of life. [It is] practical approach and experience... that can make a difference in one's life, as well as hard work, honesty and dedication."

Shortly after expressing these thoughts, he fell ill. It appeared to be a case of influenza, and both Nadia and Jeanette suggested he visit a hospital, but he refused for three days. Neither of them was aware of how much his condition was deteriorating. When he finally agreed to seek medical attention, "he insisted on walking down the stairs and into Jeanette's car on his own despite his weakness," Nadia remembers. "He was that strong, in his own mind at least."

At Toronto General Hospital, he waited in the emergency ward for seven hours while various tests were conducted and an ICU bed was finally prepared for him. The results of the tests were grave; he was even weaker than he, Nadia, or Jeanette had feared. He had contracted pneumonia, and his body was unable to overcome the impact. He passed away within twelve hours of being admitted. It was All Saints Day, November 1, 2001.

"I remember he had been in the office that week," Joe Fiore says, "and he looked a little frail, but we never suspected he was so ill. We said goodbye as usual. When I returned to work on Monday, I was amazed to hear that he had been admitted to hospital."

"I was totally shocked and surprised," John Zdunic says. "Nadia called me the next day and said, 'Peter passed away yesterday,' and I said, 'What?' I couldn't believe it. I valued his presence and his wisdom for so long, I could not believe he was gone."

Nadia Jacyk was struck by the hundreds of people who attended the visitation to pay their respects to her father, including workers and colleagues from many years in the past.

On November 6, 2001, St. Mary's Dormition Ukrainian Catholic Church in Mississauga overflowed with mourners who consoled each other and spoke in reverent tones of the life of Peter Jacyk. At the visitation, the Ukrainian Prometei Men's Choir sang several Ukrainian hymns. For the service itself, the funeral mass was celebrated by the bishop and two priests. A number of mourners travelled some distance to be present and express their sorrow.

Among the speakers who praised Jacyk's generosity and support were Mark von Hagen, from Columbia University, and Zenon Kohut, from the University of Alberta.

In May 2000, Peter Jacyk had been awarded Ukraine's highest honour, the Order of Yaroslav the Wise, by Ukrainian president Leonid Kuchma in recognition of his service to the country of his birth. Peter had not managed to travel to Ukraine to accept the medal before his death. At his funeral service, Ukrainian ambassador His Excellency Dr. Yuri Scherbak read condolences from President Kuchma before placing the medal on Peter's casket. In lieu of flowers, those wishing to express their sorrow at his passing were requested to make donations to the Petro Jacyk Education Foundation for the Ukrainian-language contest.

Tributes to Peter Jacyk were universal in their admiration for the man and his achievements. One newspaper described him as "a man of vision, a philanthropist and a great example to his community," adding: "Ukraine and its community has been orphaned by the sudden death of a great leader, philanthropist, realist and patriot."[1] Dr. Marko R. Stech, managing director of CIUS Press and project manager of the Hrushevsky Translation Project, wrote an extensive and moving homage to Peter Jacyk in the *Ukrainian Weekly.* Among his comments:

> The Ukrainian community of North America [has] lost one of its notable personalities—an energetic and authoritative individual who worked constructively for the good of the community and did not fear to stand in defence of the honour of Ukrainians, even in trying and controversial situations...
>
> He had an intuitive sense of what could work and, fittingly, the guiding principles of his strategy were based on his professional experience. Mr. Jacyk was primarily a "builder" and in

---

1. *The New Pathway* (November 8, 2001), 7.

his philanthropic activities—just as in his business work in the construction industry—he strived to erect a solid "edifice" of Ukrainian studies in the West.

From his professional experience, Mr. Jacyk clearly understood that no structure could exist without a stable, steadfast foundation. This also held true for the "intangible edifice" of Ukrainian studies... Mr. Jacyk clearly understood that as long as the world studied the history of the Ukrainian people written by representatives of those nations that regarded Ukraine as a "younger brother" or as its own rebellious colony... it could be expected that the world would neither accept the national aspirations of Ukrainians nor objectively judge their efforts to realize them.[2]

Marco Levytsky, writing in the *Ukrainian News*, noted that Peter "believed that in the face of suppression of Ukrainian culture and scholarship in the Soviet Union, Ukrainian studies had to be nurtured in the West so Ukraine's voice could be heard." In Levytsky's view, Peter Jacyk's major contribution was to give the Ukrainian community an opportunity for its story to be studied elsewhere. "And this was terribly important up to the collapse of the Soviet Union because the feeling was [that] everything was being destroyed in the USSR and that the Ukrainian nation or people would disappear."

Professor James Mace made similar remarks following Peter Jacyk's death, writing: "He knew if the people of this benighted land or those abroad came to understand the full tragedy of the past, there would be a beginning of something new and as impetuously indefatigable as this Ukrainian who refused to be poor, started from nothing, made his fortune, and began to give something back to his people."

2. Dr. Marko R. Stech, "Peter Jacyk, 1919–2001, Builder of Ukrainian Studies," *Ukrainian Weekly* (February 17, 2002), 6.

YEARS AFTER HIS DEATH, Peter Jacyk's personality and presence are still being felt in programs to promote and preserve Ukrainian language and culture, in the continued growth and success of Prombank, and in the memories of those who knew him best.

At the inauguration of the University of Toronto Petro Jacyk Program for the Study of Ukraine in the year following her father's passing, Nadia Jacyk recalled his generosity. "He leaves behind a vast and impressive legacy," she noted. "Following in his footsteps will be, if not an impossible task, certainly not an easy one. Nevertheless, if I am but a mere 'chip off the old block,' I consider myself to be privileged and extremely fortunate, and will endeavour to continue his beliefs, his goals, and his passions."

Some time later, in a private moment of reflection, she smiled and said, "Whenever I have to make a difficult decision in business or in my personal life, I still stop and ask myself, 'What would Peter do?'"

Appendix

PETER JACYK'S ENORMOUS energy and financial contributions to academic activities highlighting Ukraine benefited numerous universally renowned universities and created a mosaic of programs stretching from Brazil to the U.K. Although major programs and their creation and direction have been addressed in the main text, it is enlightening to review them as a group. Only then can the scope of his commitment to the vision he held of Ukraine establishing its position in the world, both pre- and post-Soviet, be fully appreciated.

UNIVERSITY PROGRAMS

Petro Jacyk Centre for Ukrainian Historical Research/Canadian Institute of Ukrainian Studies, University of Alberta

Established in 1989 on a $3 million endowment from Peter Jacyk and the Province of Alberta, the centre promotes research and publications in the field of Ukrainian history. It also sponsors Ukrainian translations of Western works on Ukrainian history and an English-language monograph series; publishes archival and documentary materials; supports archival projects in Ukraine, Russia, and Poland; and organizes various conferences, panels, and seminars.

Petro Jacyk Endowment Fund at Harvard University

The Harvard Ukrainian Research Institute (HURI), dating back to 1973, has benefited substantially from Peter Jacyk's support over the years. The Petro Jacyk Education Foundation has sponsored two permanent programs within HURI: the Petro Jacyk Bibliographer for the Ukrainian Collection at Widener Library, which enables the development and maintenance of the institute's library, incorporating one of the West's largest collections of Ukrainian publications, and the Petro Jacyk Distinguished Fellowship program, providing gifted Ukrainian scholars, scientists, artists, and politicians with the opportunity to spend a year at Harvard conducting research and establishing contacts with other specialists in their fields.

Petro Jacyk Visiting Professor of Ukrainian Studies Program (Harriman Institute) at Columbia University

Established in 1995 on a $500,000 grant to foster the teaching of specialized knowledge of Ukraine to graduate students preparing for professional careers in government, diplomacy, business, and journalism.

Petro Jacyk Ukrainian Studies Unit, School of Slavonic and East European Studies, University of London

The Petro Jacyk Education Foundation provided seed money in 1991 to establish the lectureship in Ukrainian Studies, which evolved into a program funded by the University of London. In 1995, the lectureship received the prestigious British Telecom Award in recognition of its "development of a British presence in Eastern Europe."

Petro Jacyk Program for the Study of Ukraine at the Centre for European, Russian, and Eurasian Studies, University of Toronto

Established in 2001, the Petro Jacyk Program for the Study of Ukraine actively encourages scholars at the University of Toronto and other North American institutions to develop joint projects and facilitates the study of contemporary Ukraine through workshops, conferences, lectures, and seminars.

Petro Jacyk Graduate Fellowship in Ukrainian Studies, University of Toronto

Maintaining a graduate student exchange with Kyiv-Mohyla Academy in Ukraine, this program brings visiting scholars from Ukraine to U of T for a one-month period and invites Ukraine's statesmen and cultural figures to speak in its guest lecture series.

Ukrainian Studies at the University of North London (now London Metropolitan University)

A 1993 grant permitted the university to expand its Ukrainian studies postgraduate and research programs to the undergraduate level as part of its contemporary European studies program.

Petro Jacyk Program for the Study of Modern Ukrainian History and Society

Established in 2008 with capital funding of $1 million (from the Petro Jacyk Education Foundation and matching funds from the Province of Alberta), the program is a cooperative venture between the University of Alberta, the Ivan Franko Lviv National University, and the Ukrainian Catholic University in Lviv, Ukraine. Responsible for the academic journal *Ukraina Moderna*, as well as organizing international symposia on topics in modern Ukrainian history, the program fosters international collaboration in scholarship, research, and education, primarily between Ukraine and Canada.

LIBRARY PROJECTS

Petro Jacyk Central and East European Resource Centre,
University of Toronto Robarts Library

One of the largest research libraries in North America, this facility includes two thousand references in twenty languages, special collections as well as current publications, and electronic telecommunications links to central and eastern Europe, and conducts seminars.

Petro Jacyk Microfilm Collection of Ukrainian Serials,
University of Toronto Robarts Library

This is the richest holding of pre-1918 Ukrainian serials in North America. Included are four hundred microfilm reels of newspapers and journals published in western Ukraine during the Austro-Hungarian Empire, plus Ukrainian periodicals from around 1850 to 1920, among the oldest publications to use the western Ukrainian dialect. Also included are official publications of Galicia/Halychyna political and cultural organizations and National Liberation Movement publications from WWI.

Stefanyk Scientific Library Microfilm Laboratory in Lviv

Funded by the Petro Jacyk Education Foundation in 1994, the installation included a computer system and quality microfilm laboratory to provide materials for the University of Toronto Robarts Library and other resource centres around the world.

PUBLISHING AND EDUCATIONAL PROJECTS

Hrushevsky Translation Project

Mykhailo Hrushevsky's ten-volume *History of Ukraine-Rus'* in twelve books, a fundamental historical and scholarly work, is being translated into English. The appearance of the English translation permits a wider community to examine Hrushevsky's achievement and serves as a basis for understanding the Ukrainian historical process.

Entsyklopediia ukrainoznavstva
(Encyclopedia of Ukraine)
Peter Jacyk's financial support for this project, published by the Shevchenko Scientific Society, was instrumental to its success.

Ukraine: A Historical Atlas
Sponsored by Peter Jacyk in 1985, this publication employs thirty-five maps to trace the historical shaping of Ukraine.

Petro Jacyk Foundation Awards in Ukrainian History
This awards program, launched in 1995, provides stipends for distinguished works in Ukrainian historical studies.

Publications of Western Literature on Psychiatry in Ukraine
A grant from the foundation assisted this initiative to provide specialized publications for psychiatrists in the former Soviet Union.

Ukrainian Physicians in Cancer Research
Grants from the foundation in 1991 and 1993 enabled the Organization for International Cancer Control to organize a training program for prominent Ukrainian oncologists to study in the West.

Ukrainian Schools and Orphanages in Brazil
Among the first Ukrainian groups to receive financial assistance from Peter Jacyk were Brazilian schools and orphanages with Ukrainian links, which have received funding since the early 1970s. This included significant aid in the construction of a Cultural and Religious Centre for Brazilian-Ukrainian Youth (Poltava) in Curitiba, Paraná, in 1982.

Thousand-Year Anniversary of Christianity in Ukraine
Published in Portuguese in 1987, with full funding by Peter Jacyk.

Ontario Heritage Foundation
A 1992 grant from the Petro Jacyk Education Foundation financed the full restoration of the Ontario Heritage Centre's boardroom.

Other Education Activities
The foundation has funded scholarships, TOEFL exams, and travel grants for Ukrainian students and scholars and published guidebooks providing information on grants and educational opportunities in the West.

OTHER PROJECTS

Seminary of St. Josaphat, Brazil
Full funding to complete the altar, 1995.

St. Olga Ukrainian Orphanage, Prudentópolis, Paraná, Brazil, 1988
Significant assistance in constructing the building, as well as annual donations to the needs of the Eparchy and orphanage for a twenty-year period.

Bloor West Village Ukrainian Festival, Toronto
The PJEF is an annual sponsor of this popular festival promoting Ukrainian heritage and culture.

Petro Jacyk International Ukrainian Language Competition, Ukraine
From 2000 to 2006, the PJEF provided major funding and assisted its partners in Ukraine to establish and develop a national competition, in which several hundred prizes were awarded.

Acknowledgements

BASED ON PETER (Petro) Jacyk's unpublished memoirs and written correspondence, Nadia Jacyk's objective was to have her father's story told in a meaningful and accurate manner. She did more than make it possible for me to relate the tale; she made it pleasurable, and I owe her my deep gratitude.

Professor Frank Sysyn's memories of Peter Jacyk, and his unexcelled knowledge of Ukrainian culture and history, helped shape the book. Dr. Jeanette Bayduza was both charming and immensely helpful in bringing to life many aspects of Mr. Jacyk's personality.

Others were equally generous with their time and assistance, and I appreciate the kindnesses they showed me. They include Yurko Drab, Rose and Andrew Dutko, Joe Fiore, Bogdan Halkiw, Walter Jacyk, Zenon Kohut, Andrij Makuch, Louis Matukas, Uliana Pasicznyk, John and Vera Seychuk, Peter Solomon, Mark von Hagen, Valya Workewych, and John Zdunic.

Amid the sometimes challenging process of bringing this book to fruition, several people contributed in more ways than I can name and with more dedication than I can measure. Susan Rana and Shirarose Wilensky played their exceptionally professional roles, ultimately assisted by Barbara Pulling, who, if this were a football game, picked the ball up and carried it over the goal line. None of these achievements would have mattered without Chris Labonté's (to complete the analogy) coaching, cheering, and refereeing.

Finally, the usual thanks to my agent, the indefatigable Hilary McMahon of Westwood Creative Artists, and to my wife, Judy, both of whom provide desperately necessary support and encouragement for every project I undertake.

JOHN LAWRENCE REYNOLDS
January 2, 2013

Index